Public Medical Insurance Reforms in China

Xinxin Ma

Public Medical Insurance Reforms in China

Springer

Xinxin Ma
Faculty of Economics
Hosei University
Tokyo, Japan

ISBN 978-981-16-7789-2 ISBN 978-981-16-7790-8 (eBook)
https://doi.org/10.1007/978-981-16-7790-8

This Springer imprint is published by the registered company Springer Nature Singapore Pte Ltd.
The registered company address is: 152 Beach Road, #21-01/04 Gateway East, Singapore 189721, Singapore

To my family

Acknowledgments

The research was conducted with support from several research grants offered to the author as the project leader, which are as follows: Grant-in-Aid for Scientific Research (B) from the Japan Society for the Promotion of Science (JSPS) (Grand number: 20H01520 from 2020–2022, *Economics Analysis on Social Security Policies in China: Empirical Studies Based on Survey Data*); Grant-in-Aid for Scientific Research (C) from the JSPS (Grant number: 16K03611 from 2016–2018, *The Impact of Minimum Wage on the Wage Gaps between Local Urban Residents and Migrants in China*; and 25380297 from 2013–2015 *The Research on the Wage Gaps between Public and Private Sectors in China*). It was also supported by several research grants offered to the author as a project member: Grant-in-Aid for International Joint Research Program from the JSPS (*Pension Reform in the PRC: Searching for a New Framework Based on Japanese Experiences* from 2017–2019); Grant from the Joint Usage and Research Center, Institute of Economic Research, Hitotsubashi University in 2015 (*Informal Sector and Income Inequality in Urban China*), and 2016 (*The Determinants of Elderly Labor Participation: A Comparison between China and Japan*).

I am grateful to the colleagues and staffs at the Faculty of Economics, Hosei University, for giving me such an excellent research environment and support. I am thankful to Professor Noriyuki Takayama (Research Institute for Policies on Pension & Aging) and Professor Takashi Oshio (Hitotsubashi University) for their encouragement and suggestions. I would like to thank Yanlan Li and Sho Komatsu for their effort as research assistants.

The contents of this book are developed studies based on the research work conducted in Kyoto University from 2012 to 2015. I am grateful to the colleagues and staffs at the Graduate School of Pharmaceutical Sciences, Kyoto University, Tetsuya Suzuki (Kyoto University Press), and Shigekazu Tagakagi (Kyoto University Press) for their support and encouragement for the research.

I would like to thank the editors and staff at Springer Nature for their interest in my research work and editing the manuscript.

Finally, I am truly grateful to my family for their warm wishes and strong support throughout my research work.

Tokyo, Japan
September 2021

Xinxin Ma

Contents

About the Author

Dr. Xinxin Ma is a professor at the Faculty of Economics, Hosei University, and she has served as the editor of the *Japanese Journal of Comparative Economics*, *Asian Studies*, and the *Journal of Chinese Economics*. Her current research project focuses on social security policy reform and its impacts on the labor market, population aging and labor force participation of women and the elderly, and income inequality in China and Japan. Her articles have appeared in peer-reviewed journals such as *China Economic Review*, *China & World Economy*, *Journal of Asian Economics*, *Journal of Economics and Business*, and *Journal of Happiness Studies*. Her recent books are *Female Employment and Gender Gap in China* (Springer Nature 2021), *Employment, Retirement and Lifestyle in Aging East Asia* (Palgrave Macmillan 2021), and *Economic Transition and Labor Market Reform in China* (Palgrave Macmillan 2018).

Abbreviations

CHARLS	China Health and Retirement Longitudinal Survey
CHIP	Chinese Household Income Project Survey
CHNS	China Health and Nutrition Survey
CMS	Cooperative Medical Scheme
COE	Collectively owned enterprise
FDI	Foreign direct investment
FOE	Foreign-owned enterprise
GDP	Gross domestic product
LTC	Long-term care
LTCI	Long-Term Care Insurance
NBS	National Bureau of Statistics
NRCMS	New Rural Cooperative Medical Scheme
NRSPI	New Rural Social Pension Insurance Scheme
OOP	Out-of-pocket
POE	Privately-owned enterprise
PRC	People's Republic of China
SIMI	Serious Illness Medical Insurance
SOE	State-owned enterprise
SWB	Subjective well-being
UEBMI	Urban Employee Basic Medical Insurance
URBMI	Urban Residents Basic Medical Insurance
URRBMI	Urban and Rural Residents Basic Medical Insurance
WHO	World Health Organization

List of Figures

List of Tables

Chapter 1
Introduction

Abstract This chapter introduces the background and aim of this book and summarizes the main contents of each chapter and significance of this book.

Keywords Public medical insurance reform · Urban and rural residents · China

1.1 Aim of This Book

The economic policies and systems have transformed since 1949 when the People's Republic of China was established. Economic historians usually divide the Chinese economy into the planned economy period (1949–1977) and the market-oriented economy reform period (post-1978) (also called as "transition period"). In the planned economy period, based on the socialism ideology, Chinese government emphasized equality as an important socialist ideology; in urban areas, the labor insurance was implemented in the 1950s, the public medical insurance covered the entire employees in government office, state-owned enterprises (SOEs), and collectively owned enterprises (COEs), and in rural areas, the Cooperative Medical Scheme (CMS) was implemented in the 1950s, which covered the entire rural residents and was managed by people's commune. In other words, in the planned economy period, the universal medical insurance was established by the Chinese government in the 1950s. In this period, the income inequality was smaller, while the inequality in healthcare service was larger between urban and rural residents (Ma, 2015). After 1978, Chinese government started the market-oriented reform. With the progress of economy system transition, particularly with the state-owned enterprise reform (SOE reform), the public medical insurance system was reformed. Simultaneously, various problems, particularly, the widening of income inequality, have become more serious (Li et al., 2013, 2017; Sicular et al., 2020). Various social policies are being discussed as measures against income inequality, and the income redistribution policy was implemented as one of the important measures. Based on the experience of developed countries, the social security policy plays the most important role in income redistribution.

This book focuses on the public medical insurance reform under the market-oriented reform period in China. It introduces the background and change process

X. Ma, *Public Medical Insurance Reforms in China*,
https://doi.org/10.1007/978-981-16-7790-8_1

of the public medical insurance system reform from institutional research approach. It also investigates the mechanism of joining the public medical insurances and the impacts of public medical insurance reform on household and individuals' behaviors (e.g., utilization of healthcare service, medical care expenses, household portfolio, and subjective well-being) based on empirical study approach. It is expected that these results may provide rich evidence for future reforms on public medical insurances in China.

1.2 Main Contents of This Book

This book consists of two parts—Part I Institutional Transformations of Public Medical Insurances in China (Chaps. 2–4), and Part II Impacts of Public Medical Insurance Reform in China: Evidence Based on Empirical Studies (Chaps. 5–10). The main contents of each chapter are as follows.

Chapter 2 introduces two types of medical insurance schemes implemented in rural China that covered the rural residents during the planned economy and market-oriented reform periods. The CMS was implemented in the 1960s and managed by people' commune; it was funded by people's commune and rural residents. The New Rural Cooperative Medical Scheme (NRCMS) was implemented in 2003 and gradually carried out to all rural areas, which was managed by provincial level government and funded by central and local governments, collective village, and rural residents.

Chapter 3 introduces the transition of the public medical insurances in urban China. During the planned economy period, the public medical system consisted of a labor insurance medical system and a publicly funded medical system, which covered the entire employees in government office or organization, SOEs, and COEs. The public medical systems changed with the SOE reform since the 1990s. The public medical insurances for urban residents under market-oriented reform period mainly include the Urban Employee Basic Medical Insurance (UEBMI) that covers urban employees, publicly funded medical system that covers civil servants, and the Urban Residents Basic Medical Insurance (URBMI) that covers the urban residents who have not been covered by the UEBMI and publicly funded medical system. Moreover, the government announced a Long-Term Care Insurance (LTCI) based on the UEBMI in 2016. This chapter summarizes the regulation contents, establishment, and management of fund and benefits of the UEBMI and URBMI and introduces the pilot reforms of the LTCI.

Using official data and survey data, Chap. 4 reveals the problems of public medical insurance in China. It mainly focuses on four issues: disparities between urban and rural areas, regional disparities between provinces, inequality in enrollment of public medical insurance aside from income inequality, and inequality in insurance enrollment by employment sector (state-owned sector vs. non-state-owned sector), which are related to inequality in medical care.

Using the data from Chinese Household Income Project Survey (CHIP) of 2007, Chap. 5 conducts an empirical analysis to verify the determinants of participation in medical insurances in urban China. Several major conclusions emerge. Both the adverse selection and liquidity constraints hypotheses were supported. The probability of participation in medical insurance was higher in the middle- and high-income groups than in the low-income group; there were some low-income groups who were not covered by either the public medical insurance or the private medical insurance system in 2007, which suggests that there maintained a problem of disparities in the enrollment of public medical insurance caused by income inequality. In addition, the participation in medical insurance differs by state- and non-state-owned sectors.

Using the longitudinal data from the China Health and Retirement Longitudinal Study (CHARLS) of 2011, Chap. 6 tests three hypotheses and verifies the determinants of participation in public medical insurance systems in rural and urban areas. The main findings are as follows. First, we found differences in the probability of participation in public medical insurance between rural and urban residents. It was caused because the establishment and implementation of public medical insurance programs differ by rural and urban areas. Second, the liquidity constraints hypothesis was rejected, whereas the adverse selection hypothesis was supported. Third, education, gender, and drinking behavior also affected participation probabilities; however, the effects of these factors were different for the rural and urban residents.

Chapter 7 conducts an empirical analysis using a long-term longitudinal data from the China Health and Nutrition Survey (CHNS) of 2000–2011 and econometric methods (the random effects probit regression model and the difference-in-differences method) to estimate the impact of the NRCMS on the utilization of healthcare services. The study mainly found that, first, predisposing factors, enabling factors, health care needs factors, and lifestyle factors affect the utilization of healthcare services. Second, results of the difference-in-differences method analysis indicate that NRCMS did not affect the utilization of healthcare services (e.g., outpatient and inpatient) of patients. However, it might increase the possibility of getting a health examination. Third, the utilization of healthcare services (both outpatient and inpatient) between the NRCMS enrollment and non-enrollment groups in both the working age (15–59 years) and the elderly groups (60 years and over) did not differ. However, NRCMS positively affected disease prevention behavior in the working age group. Fourth, from a long-term perspective, the NRCMS did not affect the utilization of healthcare services (outpatient or inpatient). Further, its positive effect on health examination dissipated.

Using a longitudinal data from the CHNS 2000, 2004, and 2006, Chap. 8 conducts an empirical analysis to explore how the public medical insurance affect the out-of-pocket (OOP) expense on medical care and the probability of catastrophic medical expenses (CME). The results revealed that the impact of public medical insurances on OOP expense and the probability of CME are not statistically significant for both urban and rural residents. The other factors, such as age, education, health status, and lifestyle, affect the OOP expense and the probability of CME, and the effects of these factors are greater for rural residents than for urban residents.

Using three-wave longitudinal data from the CHARLS of 2011, 2013 and 2015, Chap. 9 estimates the influence of public medical insurances on financial portfolio choice. Three new findings emerge. First, public medical insurance positively affects the probability of holding risky financial assets, but when addressing the heterogeneity problem, the effect of public medical insurances on the probability of holding and share of risky financial assets are not significant, which suggests that the unobservable individual heterogeneity might affect risky financial market participation. Second, the influence of public medical insurance differs by risky financial asset type. It is greater for higher-risk (stocks) than for lower-risk (bonds) financial assets. Third, the influences of public medical insurance differ by age and urban/rural resident group, the positive effects are higher for older and urban resident group than middle-aged and rural resident group.

Using three waves longitudinal data from the CHARLS of 2011, 2013 and 2015, Chap. 10 investigates the correlation between NRCMS and subjective well-being (SWB) among middle-aged and older adults in rural China. The dynamic fixed effects model and lagged variable model was used to address the endogeneity problems. The results suggest that the impact of NRCMS on SWB is not significant, while public pension positively affects life satisfaction in rural China, and the positive effects of public pension on SWB differ by gender, age, migrant, income, and regional groups.

1.3 Significance of This Book

The social and academic significances of this book can be summarized in the following four points.

First, regarding the previous studies on the public medical insurance in China under the market-oriented reform period, there are many studies (institutional researches) focusing on the transition of the system from the viewpoint of social policy history (Feng, 2021; Gao, 2019; Guo & Zhang, 2021; Han, 2014; Liao, 2019, etc.). However, the quantitative analyses (empirical studies) that use individual or household survey data are not enough compared to the researches for developed countries.

This book uses two approaches—institutional research approach and empirical study approach—to study the public medical insurance reform and its influences, focusing on the systems/policies transformation and its economic effects, and provides the academic evidence, such as the mechanism of participation in medical insurance based on economic theories and hypotheses (e.g., the liquidity constraints and adverse selection hypotheses), which can provide the evidence to understand the enrollment disparities of public medical insurance aside with the income inequality problem in China. It also investigates the impact of public medical insurance reform on household and individuals' behavior, such as its effects on utilization of healthcare service, OOP expenses on medical care, financial portfolio choice and SWB based on empirical studies, particularly the empirical studies on the issues, such as the impact of public medical insurances on financial portfolio choice and SWB in China, are scare. These results may provide rich evidence to reveal the influences of public medical insurance reform from multi-perspectives.

Second, this book conducts the empirical studies based on the economics theories and econometric analysis methods using many kinds of long-term Chinese nationally representative survey data, including cross-section survey data—CHIP and Chinese national longitudinal surveys data—CHNS and CHARLS.

Empirical studies on the impact of public medical insurances are mainly conducted for the U. S. Most of these studies utilize RAND[1] data and conduct empirical studies on institutional evaluation using the analytical methods of social experiments. However, the actual RAND medical insurance experiment is restricted in recent years. One reason is that in other developed countries, such as Japan, the United Kingdom, France and Scandinavia, all citizens are legally required to join the public medical insurance system, which means that they are compulsory, and "universal medical insurance" has already been realized. Therefore, it is difficult to evaluate causality effects of the policies. However, in China, the government has performed the public medical insurance reform since the 1990s, but the timing of introduction differs depending on the region. In addition, participation in the NRCMS for rural residents and URBMI for urban residents is voluntary. Therefore, the reform of the public medical insurance system in China under the market-oriented reform period can be thought as a kind of social experiment (quasi-natural experiment). The empirical studies for China in this book by using the quasi-natural experiment method can be a complement to empirical research on the issue targeting the U. S. and other developed countries.

Third, from a global perspective, since 1978, after the market-oriented reform and implementation of opening up polices, the foreign direct investment (FDI) and international trade (e.g., imports and exports) have increased sharply. China, which has 1.4 billion people (about one-fifth of the world's population), is attracting attention as a huge market. China has become the "factory of the world," and in 2010, China became the second largest GDP in the world. Therefore, social and economic issues, such as inequality in China, are thought to have a major impact on the world economy. As a measure against inequality, the Chinese government has reformed the public medical insurances since 1990, and a set of new systems were established, which aims to cover both urban and rural residents. It can be considered that the public medical insurance reform in China will lead to the stability of the world economy and human development worldwide. Thus, the research on public medical insurance reform in China is an important issue not only for China but also for the world development.

In China, economic development and system transition are progressing simultaneously. Therefore, the experience gained from the public medical insurance reform in China can be a reference case for other developing countries (for example, developing countries in Africa) to build an appropriate public medical insurance. It is also considered to be an important reference material when reforming the public medical insurance system for transition economies, such as Russia and Eastern Europe. In that sense, the studies in this book on the reform of the public medical insurance in China can provide evidence for the medical insurance reform in the future for both developing countries and transition economies.

Finally, this book also aims to provide academic evidence for policymakers. Based on the principle of "evidence-based policymaking," [2] the book conducts an empirical study based on quasi-natural experiment method, which is usually used for policy evaluations. In addition, this book can generate interests for various groups, such as scholars with econometric analysis backgrounds, policymakers, and readers who are interested in Chinese economy.

Notes

1. The RAND experiment is a randomized controlled trial using medical insurance in the U. S. In the U.S., to curb medical costs, managed care was enacted based on the Health Maintenance Organization Act published in 1973. In 1971, the United States Department of Health and Human Services funded the RAND Corporation (a famous non-profit organization for military and defense research in the United States) to assess the effectiveness of the policy, established an insurance company called RAND Medical Insurance Experiment, and started to conduct a social experiment (RAND Medical Insurance Experiment). In the RAND medical insurance experiment, from 1971 to 1982, six cities were selected to strike a balance between urban and rural areas, of which 2,750 households and 7,700 insured persons were selected. Randomly selected medical insurance was assigned to each household. Over a three- to five-year period, changes in the health status of each insured person and family, frequency of medical institution visits, and medical expenses were tracked. In this social experiment, it was found that the negative effects of OOP medical expenses (at least for non-poor people) on health status was not significant, and the expenditures for medical care did not increase.
2. Evidence-based policymaking is an approach that helps people make well-informed decisions about policies, programs, and projects. It puts the best available evidence from research at the heart of policy development and implementation (Davies, 2004; Davies et al., 2000).

References

Davies, H. T. O. (2004). *Is evidence-based government possible?* Jerry Lee Lecture, presented at the 4th Annual Campbell Collaboration Colloquium.

Davies, H. T. O., Nutley, S. M., & Smith, P. C. (2000). *What works? Evidence-based policy and practice in public services.* P&E.

Feng, P. (2021). From 1921 to 2021: A glimpse of China's medical insurance and commercial health insurance for a century. *Shanghai Insurance, 7*, 16–122. (in Chinese).

Gao, X. (2019). 70 years of rural cooperative medical care: Review, problems and prospects based on the perspective of social change. *Fujian Forum: Humanities and Social Sciences, 8*, 164–175. (in Chinese).

Guo, X., & Zhang, R. (2021). Memorabilia of 100 years of medical insurance. *China Health Insurance, 7*, 16–21. (in Chinese).

Han, F. (2014). The historical evolution of medical insurance system in China. *China Medical Insurance, 6*, 20–24. (in Chinese).

Liao, Z. (2019). 70 years of reform of China's medical insurance system. *Social Security, 11*, 28–31. (in Chinese).

Li, S., Sato, H., & Sicular, T. (2013). *The changes in China's income inequality-research on Chinese Residents' income distribution IV*. People's Press. (in Chinese).

Li, S., Yue, X., Sicular, T., & Sato, H. (2017). *The latest changes in China's income distribution pattern: Research on Chinese Residents' income distribution V*. China Financial and Economic Press. (in Chinese).

Ma, X. (2015). *Public medical insurance reform in China.* Kyoto University Press. (in Japanese).

Sicular, T., Li, S., Yue, X., & Sato, H. (2020). *Changing trends in China's inequality: Evidence, analysis, and prospects.* Oxford University Press.

Part I
Institutional Transformations of Public Medical Insurances in China

Chapter 2
Medical Insurance Reform in Rural China

Abstract This chapter introduces two types of medical insurance schemes implemented in rural China covering rural residents with rural *hukou* during the planned economy and market-oriented reform periods. The Cooperative Medical Scheme was implemented in the 1960s and managed by people's commune, which was funded by people's commune and rural residents. The New Rural Cooperative Medical Scheme was implemented in pilot rural regions in 2003 and gradually carried out in all rural areas, which was managed by the provincial-level government, and funded by central and local governments, collective villages, and rural residents.

Keywords Cooperative medical scheme · New rural cooperative medical scheme · Rural residents · China

2.1 Introduction

This chapter describes the transition of the rural cooperative medical system (CMS) for residents with rural household registration (*hukou*)[1] implemented during the planned economy period[1] and introduces the main contents of the New Rural Cooperative Medical Scheme (NRCMS) enforced by the Chinese government since 2003.

Regarding medical insurance in rural areas, during the planned economy period, the Cooperative Medical Scheme (CMS) which was a mutual aid medical insurance and the public medical aid system, were implemented (Xu, 1997a, b; Gao, 2019; Song, 2006, 2009; Yang, 2019; Zou et al., 2018). Since the 1950s, the medical aid system which covers individuals called as "*Wubaohu*"[2] in rural areas and individuals called as "*Sanwu*"[3] in urban areas has been implemented. The number of recipients was small because eligible qualifications were required, and the examination was strict. Most rural residents were eligible for the CMS.

In the early phase of the market-oriented reform period, the enrollment rate of RCMS decreased dramatically with the dismantling of people's commune, and most rural residents had to pay higher out-of-pocket (OOP) expenses on medical care, thus, falling into poverty during illness became a severe problem in rural areas. To address this problem, the NRCMS has been established and implemented by the

X. Ma, *Public Medical Insurance Reforms in China*,
https://doi.org/10.1007/978-981-16-7790-8_2

Table 2.1 Medical insurances in rural China during the market-oriented reform period

Type	Insurance name	Implemented period
Public medical insurance	NRCMS	2003
Private medical insurance	Commercial insurance	1980s
Public medical assistance	Medical aid system	1950s

Source Created by the author

Chinese government since 2003. The medical aid system has also been implemented for poverty and non-dependents individuals. Since the 1980s, commercial insurance as private medical insurance has expanded into rural areas. Only certified low-income individuals can join the medical aid system and only high-income individuals can join the commercial insurance, and most rural residents are eligible for the NRCMS (Table 2.1).

The CMS and NRCMS were implemented as basic medical systems in rural areas. In the following section, we will introduce the detailed contents of these two medical insurance systems in rural areas. For the details of policies and events related to public medical insurance reform in rural areas, please refer to Appendix Table 2.4.

2.2 Medical Insurance Scheme Under the Planned Economy Period

2.2.1 Development History of Cooperative Medical Scheme

Before the establishment of the People's Republic of China (PRC), the medical care system in rural areas began with a mutual aid system. The establishment and implementation of the CMS during the planned economy period were closely related to the establishment and development of the people's commune, which is a rural terminal management organization of the government (Xu, 1997a, b; Gao, 2019; Song, 2006, 2009; Yang, 2019; Zou et al., 2018).

Immediately after the PRC was established, the land was distributed to farmers due to land reform. Most farmers in rural areas owned the land, and they farmed on a household basis. However, they faced the problem of labor shortage in the busy agricultural season and insufficiency of agricultural equipment. To address this problem, the central government promoted the establishment of a collective agricultural production group. There were three types: (b) mutual aid group of agricultural production cooperatives (the group that cooperates in agricultural production), (b) elementary-level agricultural production cooperatives (the number of participants is more than (a)), and (c) high-level agricultural production cooperatives (the number of participants is more than (b)).

Along with the establishment of agricultural production cooperatives, rural residents voluntarily established medical mutual aid associations and cooperative medical centers in some rural regions. The first cooperative medical center was established in 1953 in *Mishan* village, Gaoping town in Shanxi province, and three private pharmacies and ten physicians jointly established a medical center, which was officially established on May 1, 1955, with the support of the local government (Xu, 1997a, b; Han, 2014; Zou et al., 2018). The first medical mutual aid association was established in 1950 in Changsheng town, Henan province. These cooperative medical centers and medical mutual aid associations are the predecessors of the CMS. At the National People's Congress in 1956, the establishment of agricultural production cooperatives was enforced in all rural areas, and the agricultural production cooperatives (predecessor of the people's commune) were obliged to address occupational accidents and illnesses of rural residents. In 1956, the number of privately owned federation clinics and township medical centers increased significantly from 803 in 1950 to 51,000 (Editorial Department of "Contemporary China" Series, 1986), and the number of aid mutual medical centers established by agricultural production cooperatives increased to 10,000 (Xu, 1997a, b). In 1959, a medical scheme as mutual aid for rural residents was established, which was called the "cooperative medical scheme (CMS)" managed by the people's commune. The CMS was first named in the "*Report on the Rural Hygiene Work Conference*" in 1960, and it was positioned as a medical security system in rural areas (Xu, 1997a, b; Gao, 2019; Zou et al., 2018).

In 1965, Zedong Mao (chairman of the RPC) instructed that "the key points of medical projects should be in rural areas," and the establishment of the CMS was promoted by the local government. In 1968, Zedong Mao visited rural areas, praised the CMS being operated in Hubei Province, and promoted its model to all rural areas (Xu, 1997a, b; Zou et al., 2018; Gao, 2019). In addition, urban medical labors were dispatched to rural areas. Due to political-led promotion, the CMS was promoted throughout the rural areas during the Cultural Revolution period (1966—1976), with an enrollment rate of 10% in 1958, 32% in 1960, and 46% in 1962. It increased to 80% by the end of the 1960s, and approximately 90% in the 1970s (Song, 2006, 2009).

2.2.2 *Operation of the Cooperative Medical Scheme*

In order to promote the "heavy industry priority development policy," the government developed a social security system in urban areas, the medical care systems for both civil servants and employees in urban areas were funded by the government. However, the CMS was funded by rural residents themselves and the community (i.e., people's commune).

Both rural residents and people's communes paid a premium to fund the CMS. Participants of the CMS were exempted from all or part of the outpatient fee, health examination fee, surgery, and other treatment fees when they paid the premium of the CMS (0.5–1 yuan per person). With the spread of the CMS, some farmers with second jobs as physicians called "barefoot physician" (*chijiao yishen*) were trained and engaged in the treatment of mild illnesses in rural areas (Han, 2014). The salaries of medical care technicians, including barefoot physicians were paid by the people's commune. The CMS was not managed by the government; it was managed and operated in various types, which can be roughly divided into the following four types:

(i) Village-led type

The village committee and villagers shared the costs of creating a cooperative medical center managed by a village committee. The coverage target of the CMS was limited to the residents of the village, and the village set the content and standard of medical care. This is the main type of the CMS.

(ii) Village operation and town management

The village committee creates a cooperative medical center, the cost was shared by the village and the villagers, the content and standard of medical care were determined by negotiation between the town and the village, and the cost was the cooperation of the town sanitation center or the town government. It was managed by the medical management committee, and the excess expenses of medical care were paid by the village committee.

(iii) Village and town cooperatives

The town and village jointly created a cooperative medical center, and the cost was subsidized by the town government in addition to the investment of the village committee and the villagers. Expenses were managed uniformly by the town government, but the settlement was divided into the town government and the village committee; the ratio of expenses was decided by the negotiation between the town government and the village committee, and the content and standard of medical care were decided by the town government.

(iv) Town government-led type

The town government creates a cooperative medical center, and the expenses for medical care are paid in three parts: (a) the town government, (b) the village committee, and (c) the villagers, and the expenses are managed uniformly by the town government.

In Fig. 2.1, the part surrounded by the dotted line shows the contributors of the CMS. The three main contributors were (a) the rural residents, (b) the village committee, and (c) the town government. In China, the administrative department is divided into five levels: central government, provincial government, county/county-level city government, town-level government, and village (people's commune). Based on this, medical care facilities are divided into four types: provinces,

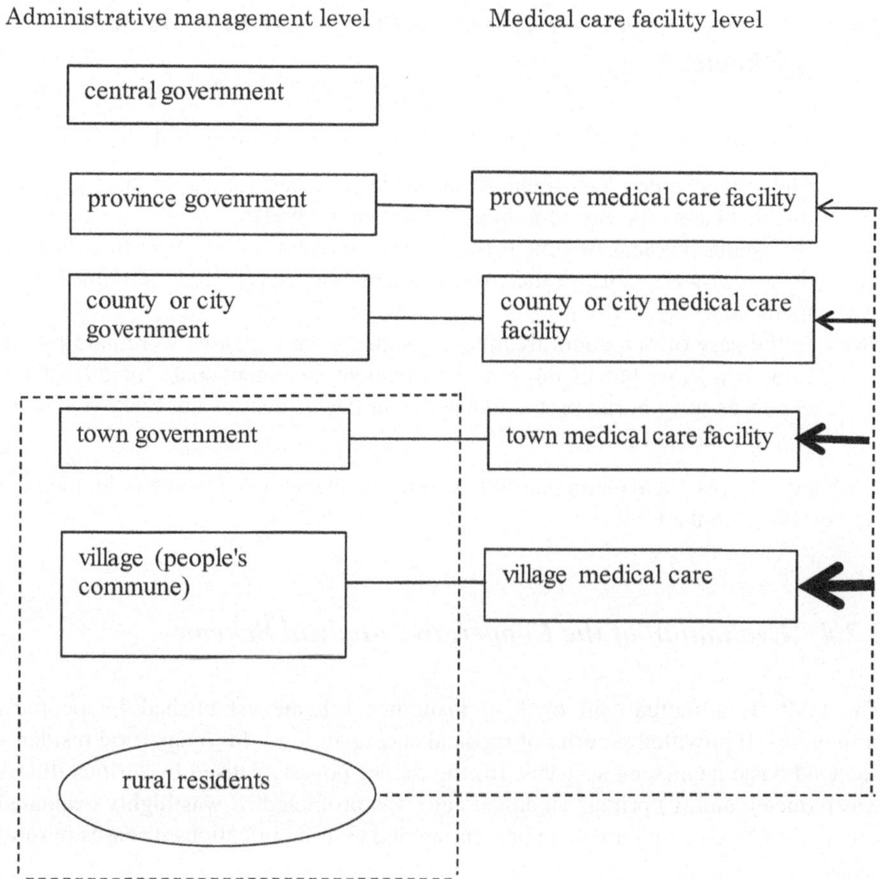

Fig. 2.1 Management level and medical care facility level of the CMS in China. *Source* Created by the author. *Note* The thickness of the arrow shows the image of the number of patients

county/county-level cities, towns, and villages. The level of medical technology is highest in the provincial medical care facilities and lowest in the village cooperative medical care center. Regarding the types of medical care facilities used by rural residents, rural residents could visit medical facilities at each level for medical care, but they could not receive higher-ranked healthcare services without recommendation letters from physicians in lower-ranked medical care facilities. In fact, it was difficult for rural residents to receive healthcare services in urban areas. Therefore, moderate illnesses were to be treated in villages (cooperative medical centers) and town medical care facilities, and only patients with severe illness were introduced and treated at city/province medical care facilities.

2.2.3 Medical Expense Payment in the Cooperative Medical Scheme

There were three main types of medical expense payment methods in the CMS.

(i) The management department of the CMS paid part (or all) of drug fees and medical care expenses (combined medicine method).
(ii) Receiving medical treatment (injections, treatments, etc.) was free, but the drug fees were paid by the rural residents themselves (not combined drug method).
(iii) In the case of outpatient treatment, medical care expenses were paid by the rural residents, but in the case of inpatient treatment, part (or all) of the expenses were borne by the management department of the CMS (inpatient benefits method).

Of these, (ii) Medical incompatibility was the main method of payment for medical care expenses in the CMS.

2.2.4 Evaluation of the Cooperative Medical Scheme

The CMS is a mutual aid medical insurance scheme established by people's communes. It provided security of medical care as follows: (a) many rural residents received basic healthcare services, (b) the risk of poverty caused by serious illness was reduced, and (c) primary medical care was promoted. It was highly evaluated because it played a major role in preventing and treating infectious diseases in rural areas.

From the 1950s to the 1980s, with the development of the CMS, the number of medical care facilities and medical care labors increased significantly in rural areas. For example, in 1978, there were 94,395 village sanitary offices, 55,108 town and village medical facilities, and 47.775 million rural medical care labors (total of doctors and nurses). The percentage of villages that established medical care centers in 1985 was 87.4%. The increase in medical care facilities and labors in rural areas has contributed to the increased usage of primary healthcare services in rural areas, which has dramatically improved the health status of rural residents. According to statistical data from the National Bureau of Statistics of China, life expectancy in rural areas increased from under 35 years old (males 34.85 years, females 34.63 years) to 68.55 years old (males 66.84 years, females 70.47 years) in 1990.

The CMS has been endorsed by rural residents and governments in China and has been highly evaluated worldwide. In the 1980–1981 report by the Women and Children's Foundation of the United Nations, it has been stated that "The barefoot physician in the CMS is a model of improving medical care in developing countries to address the problem of high OOP expense for primary medical care in rural areas." The World Bank and World Health Organization (WHO) has noted that "China has achieved great success in controlling infectious diseases and reducing mortality. The results are significantly higher than those in many other developing countries," and has praised it saying "the cooperative medical scheme has attracted the attention, and it is the only model of a successful medical care revolution in developing countries that can address the problem of high OOP expenditure for primary medical care".

2.3 The New Rural Cooperative Medical Scheme

2.3.1 Background of the Establishment of the NRCMS

Although the CMS has been implemented in almost all rural areas and has contributed to improving the health status of rural residents, with the progressive reform in rural areas during the market-oriented reform period, the CMS has changed significantly. In the early 1980s, the government implemented a "Household Contract Responsibility System" in rural areas. Households have become the basic unit of agricultural production, and the number of cooperatives, such as people's communes, decreased and finally dismantled (Liao, 2019; Song, 2006). For example, the enrollment rate of the CMS decreased from 63.8% in 1980 to 5.4% in 1985 and 4.8% in 1989 (Fig. 2.2).

At the same time, the government implemented reforms in the healthcare services market. During the planned economy period, the government managed the prices of drugs and healthcare services (wage levels of doctors and nurses, prices of drug production materials, prices of drugs, prices of treatments in medical care facilities, etc.). However, with the progressive market-oriented reform, the principle of

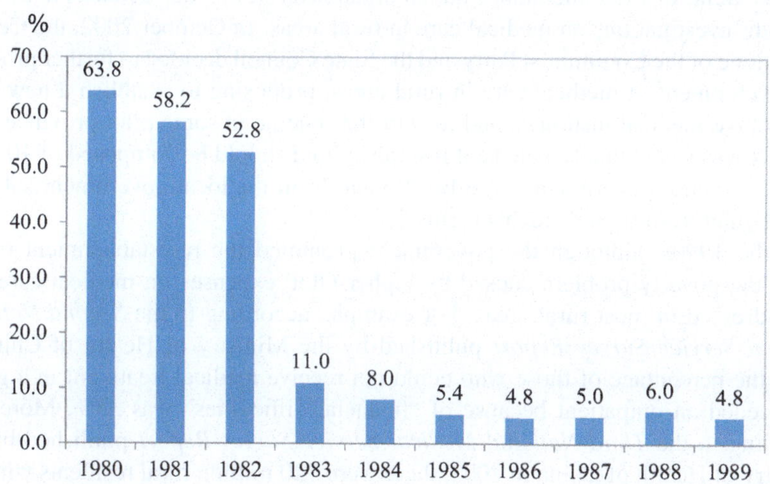

Fig. 2.2 The enrollment rate of the CMS (1980–1989). *Source* Created by the author based on data from *International Pharmaceutical Hygiene Guide*.Vol. 6, 2002

a competitive market was introduced to the healthcare service and pharmaceutical industry sectors. These medical care facilities changed from non-profit organizations to profit organizations, and some pharmaceutical manufacturing firms and drug logistics companies changed from state-owned enterprises to privately owned enterprises. These medical care-related organizations, in which the market competitive principle was introduced, pursue high profits based on market mechanisms. As a result, medical care expenses have increased. In the 1990s the function of the CMS disappeared in rural areas, while medical care expenses increased dramatically. The majority of households with patients fell into poverty in rural areas, and the poverty and inequality problems became more serious in China.

To address these problems, the Chinese government has promoted the rebuilding of medical insurance in rural areas since the 1990s (see Table 2.2). For example, in March 1990, the Ministry of Health of China, the State Planning Commission, and the Hygiene Movement Commission of the Central Government jointly published the *Planning Goal of Everyone Enjoys Medical Insurance in 2000 in Rural Areas*, which stipulated that the coverage rate of the CMS will be increased to 50%—60% by 2000. In 1991, the State Council emphasized the restoration and implementation of the CMS in the *National 8th Five-Year Plan National Economic Development 10-Year Plan*. In December 1992, the State Council promulgated the *Rural Residents' Payments and Labor Management Ordinance*, stating that the local government should support the fund of the CMS. In January 1997, the State Council stated that "We will implement a cooperative medical system in most rural areas as possible by 2000 and develop a rural cooperative medical insurance" in *Decision on Medical Reform and Development*. In May 1997, the State Council approved the *Several Opinions on the Development and Improvement of Rural Cooperative Medical Care*, which promoted the implementation of rural cooperative medical insurance to a certain extent. In 1999, the State Council organized relevant departments to conduct in-depth investigations on medical care in rural areas. In October 2002, the Central Committee of the Communist Party and the State Council decided to further promote the development of medical care in rural areas, proposing to establish a new rural cooperative medical insurance and to start the scheme in some pilot provinces and cities. It was stated that the medical insurance fund should be composed of 10 yuan from the central government subsidy, 10 yuan from the local government subsidy, and 10 yuan from rural residents themselves.

In the 1990s, although the government promoted the re-establishment of the CMS, the poverty problem caused by higher OOP expenses on medical care was not addressed in most rural areas. For example, according to the *Second National Medical Service Survey Report* published by the Ministry of Health of China in 1998, the percentage of those who could not receive medical treatment in a group that needed an outpatient because of "financial difficulties" was 35%. Moreover, according to the *Third National Medical Service Survey Report* published by the Ministry of Health of China in 2003, there were 720 million rural residents who did not participate in any medical insurances in 2003, the proportion of non-medical insurance to total rural residents was 79.1%. With the growth of income inequality between rural and urban areas, inequality in medical care between these two groups

Table 2.2 Medical insurance policy reform from 1990–2003 in rural areas

Year	Government	Name	Main contents
March 1990	Ministry of Health of China, State Planning Commission, and Hygiene Movement Commission of the Central Government	Planning Goal of Everyone Enjoys Medical Insurance in 2000 in Rural Areas	The coverage rate of the cooperative medical scheme was raised to 50–60% by 2000
January 1991	State Council	Notification of Some Opinions on Reform and Strengthening of Rural Medical Care	Promote the cooperative medical scheme and provide social insurance to cover all citizens so they can receive healthcare services
September 1992	Ministry of Health, Ministry of Finance	Notification of Some Opinions on Strengthening Rural Hygiene Projects	In principle, voluntarily join and establish cooperative medical insurance, as well as raise medical insurance funds from state-owned enterprises/group enterprises, and social organizations
December 1992	State Council	Rural Resident's Payment and Labor Management Ordinance	Guarantee local government to support the fund for the rural cooperative medical scheme
November 1993	State Council	Decisions on Some Issues in Establishment of a Socialist Market Economy System	Develop and improve the rural cooperative medical scheme
January 1997	State Council	Decision on Medical Reform and Development	Implement a cooperative medical scheme in as many rural areas as possible by 2000 and develop a rural cooperative medical scheme

(continued)

has also expanded. If the inequality between rural and urban areas continues to widen, it may lead to social instability. Therefore, establishing public medical insurance in rural areas has become an urgent issue for the Chinese government.

Then, on January 10, 2003, the Ministry of Health, the Ministry of Finance, and the Ministry of Agriculture promulgated the *Opinions on the Establishment of a New Rural Cooperative Medical Scheme*. Since 2003, each province, autonomous region,

Table 2.2 (continued)

Year	Government	Name	Main contents
May 1997	State Council	Notification of Some Opinions Regarding the Development and Maintenance of the Rural Cooperation Medical Scheme	Funding is established by individual contributions, village committees, and government subsidies. Cooperative medical insurance premiums voluntarily paid by rural residents are considered to be private consumption in rural areas
May 2001	State Council, State Planning Commission, Ministry of Finance	Guidance on Rural Medical Reform and Development	In principle, the local government will strengthen the management of the rural cooperative medical scheme, rural residents will voluntarily join it, and the situation in each region would be considered. The fund should be mainly funded by rural residents and the government will support it. The medical insurance scheme for serious illnesses should be established by unifying counties (cities) in some areas
January 2003	Ministry of Health, Ministry of Finance, and the Ministry of Agriculture	Opinions on the Establishment of a New Rural Cooperative Medical Scheme	Since 2003, each province, autonomous region, and municipality level government selected at least two or three counties/county-level cities to implement the model of the NRCMS, and the successful cases have been promoted in all rural areas

Source Created by the author

and municipality level government has selected at least two or three counties/county-level cities to implement the NRCMS model, and successful cases have been gradually promoted in all rural areas.

2.3.2 Eligible Participants of the NRCMS

The eligible participants of the NRCMS were rural residents with rural *hukou* (including local rural residents and rural–urban migrants). Participation in the NRCMS is voluntary, but in 2014, the enrollment rate reached 98.7% (NBS, 2014). A "New Rural Cooperative Medical Certificate" will be issued to rural *hukou* residents who have joined the NRCMS. Insurance contracts are renewed annually.

2.3.3 Three Major Principles of the NRCMS

"*Opinions on the Establishment of a New Rural Cooperative Medical Scheme*" stipulates that the following three principles must be obeyed when constructing the NRCMS.

First, it involves voluntary and multi-route funding. Specifically, rural residents should voluntarily join the NRCMS on a household basis and pay a premium for the NRCMS by the specified date. The town government and village committee should provide financial subsidies, and the central and local governments should provide a certain amount of subsidies to support the fund.

Second, the benefit should be determined based on the amount of the fund and should be appropriately guaranteed. The legislation adheres to the principle of balance of insurance fund and benefit, guarantees the sustainable operation of the system, and ensures that rural residents can receive primary healthcare services.

Third, trials should be conducted in some regions and gradually spread them throughout rural areas. Specifically, it is stated that when constructing the NRCMS, it should perform the new system in the selected pilot areas, summarize the experience, disseminate successful cases, and develop it comfortably. Moreover, with the economic growth and the rise of income levels, the insured level of the NRCMS and its function to respond to risks should be improved.

2.3.4 Management of the NRCMS

According to "*Opinions on the Establishment of a New Rural Cooperative Medical Scheme*," the main departments that manage the NRCMS are counties or county-level city governments (see Fig. 2.3).

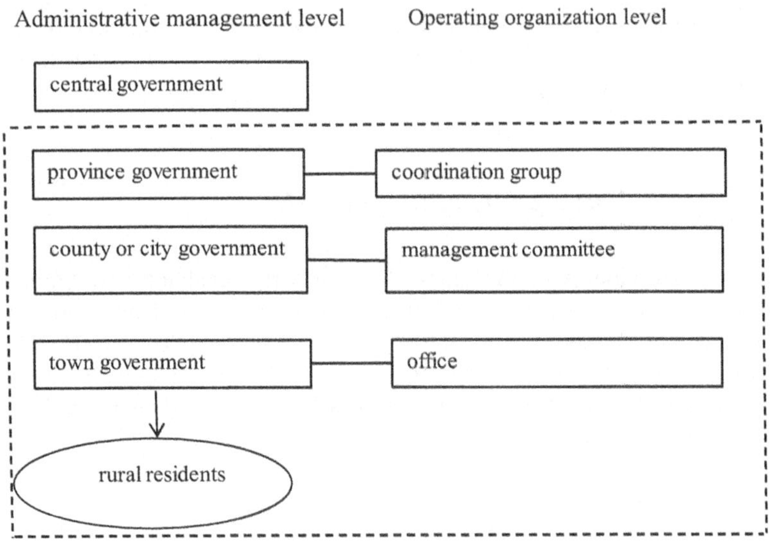

Fig. 2.3 Management and operating organization level of the NRCMS in China. *Source* Created by the author

The NRCMS generally has a social pooling managed by each county-level city government. In less-developed regions, social pooling funds are established at the town and village level governments in the first stage.

The NRCMS was established based on the principle of simplicity and efficiency. The provincial-level government should build a coordination group composed of various departments such as financial, agricultural, welfare, accounting audit, and poverty alleviation departments.

The local government of county/county-level cities will establish a management committee of the NRCMS, including the related departments and representatives of participants, and entrust the operation and management of the NRCMS. A handling organization was set up under the committee to carry out specific operations. The county-level government will assign staff to these operations and management agencies, and the administrative expenses will be borne by the financial budget of the county-level government and not be charged by the NRCMS fund. If necessary, it is possible to establish an office in the town- or village-level government.

2.3.5 Fund of the NRCMS

There are three types of financing for the NRCMS: (a) individual medical insurance contribution, (b) village subsidy, and (c) government subsidy.

First, the annual contribution of rural resident individuals should not be below 10 yuan, and it is possible to raise the premium appropriately in well-developed regions.

The county-level city government will decide whether employees with rural *hukou* who are working in township and village enterprises can join the NRCMS.

Second, well-developed villages should support NRCNS funds. The contribution standard is set by the county-level city government, and the contributed funds are allocated to rural residents in the region. It also encourages the participation of privately owned enterprises and individual donations to support NRCMS funding.

The total amount of subsidies from each level of government (e.g., central or local government) to a participant of the NRCMS should not be less than 10 yuan per capita each year, and the specific subsidy standards and the ratio of the local government's financial sharing are determined by the provincial government. It is stated that "in well-developed regions (i.e., the eastern region), it is desirable to increase government subsidy at each level government." It is also stated that "since 2003, the central government will provide a subsidy of per capita 10 yuan to a participant of the NRCMS in the central and western regions as a special social transfer expenditure in government budget each year". Since 2003, the government has gradually raised subsidies for the NRCMS (see Table 2.3). It should be noted that subsidies differ by region.

Table 2.3 Annual subsidies from the central and local governments in the NRCMS Unit: Yuan/yearly

Year	Central government		Local government		Total	Individual
	West	Central	West	Central		
2003	10	10	10	10	20	10
2004	10	10	10	10	20	10
2005	10	10	10	10	20	10
2006	20	20	20	20	40	10
2007	20	20	20	20	40	10
2008	40	40	40	40	80	20
2009	40	40	40	40	80	20
2010	60	60	60	60	120	30
2011	124	108	76	92	200	50
2012	156	132	84	108	240	60
2013	188	156	92	124	280	70
2014	220	180	100	140	320	90
2015	268	216	112	164	380	120
2016	300	240	120	180	420	150
2017	324	258	126	192	450	180
2018	356	282	134	208	490	220

Source Created by the author based on data from Zhao (2019) (p.6), and regulations published by the Chinese government each year.

Note Total amount is the sum of subsidies of central and local governments.

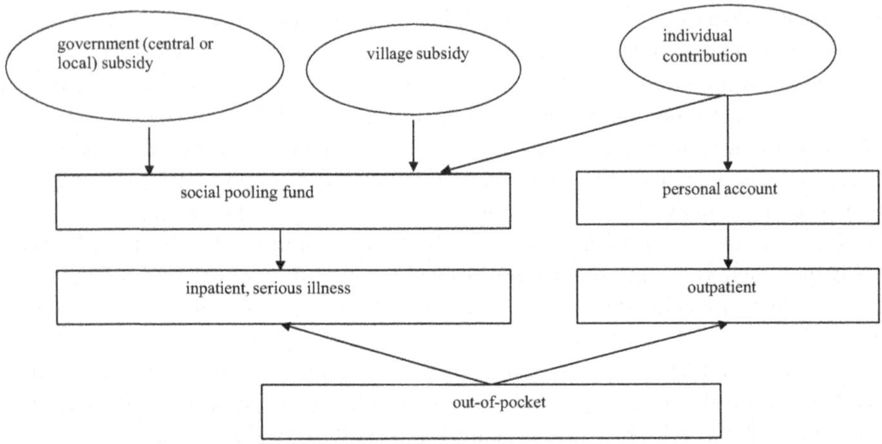

Fig. 2.4 Fund and payment of medical care expenses in the NRCMS. *Source* Created by the author based on the regulations of the NRCMS

2.3.6 Fund Management of the NRCMS

In "*Opinions on the Establishment of a New Rural Cooperative Medical Scheme*," it is stated that "the fund for the new rural cooperative medical scheme is provided by three routes: (a) rural resident individuals' insurance contribution, (b) collective rural committees support, and (c) government (central or local governments) subsidy. It is a public fund including the individuals' contributions collected, and it must be used as a special fund, deposited in a special account, and not diverted" (see Fig. 2.4).

The NRCMS fund is managed by the management committee of the NRCMS and its handling organizations. The handling organizations establish a dedicated account for the NRCMS fund at a state-owned commercial bank approved by the management committee, guarantee the safety of the fund, and conduct examinations on time.

The insurance contributions of participants and the subsidies of collective rural committees are collected annually by the town government or the consignment organization of the handling organizations. The collected contributions are deposited in a dedicated account for the NRCMS fund. Subsidies from local and central governments will also be transferred to a dedicated account of the NRCMS.

2.3.7 Payment of Medical Care Expenses in the NRCMS

The NRCMS fund is stipulated to mainly subsidize high medical care expenses and inpatient treatment expenses for participants. It is stated that "the government at the county/county-level city should prepare a list of basic medicines for calculating medical care expenditures in the region," and "the county/county-level city government should decide the basic medicines list according to the total amount of funds in the region. The benefit level in NRCMS should be determined based on the medical care situation in the region."

The details of the benefits are as follows: (a) in the case of inpatients, the fees for medicines, beds, surgery, health examinations, medical care, long-term care, blood transfusions, inpatient, and childbirth will be paid; (b) for chronic diseases such as severe diabetes and mental illness, some treatment expenses will be paid in the case of outpatient visits, and (c) medical care expenses incurred in general outpatient clinics will be paid. As a general rule, medical care expenses of inpatient treatment are prioritized over outpatient visits, and the benefits vary depending on the region. Only part of the medical care expenses in the case of inpatients is paid, and all outpatient expenses are paid by the patients themselves in most regions.

Part of the expenses for the medical care of specified diseases, drugs, and examinations specified in the benefit provisions will be paid, but there is a minimum and maximum limit. If the minimum limit of medical care expense is not reached, it will be borne by patients; if the medical care expenses exceed the minimum limit and are less than the maximum limit, a part of medical care expenses is paid by the NRCMS; it will be borne by patients; if the medical care expenses exceed the maximum limit, the exceeding part will be paid by patients.

There are two main types of medical care expense payments for inpatients: exemption methods and reimbursement payment methods.

(i) In the case of the exemption method, after a participant visits the medical care facility designated in the NRCMS, the medical care facility should calculate the total amount of medical care expenses, and the participant should only pay the expenses based on the ratio of OOP expenses. The other parts of medical care expenses excluding OOP expenses will be paid by the NRCMS fund.
(ii) In the case of the reimbursement method, after a participant visits the designated medical care facility designated in the NRCMS, the patient should pay the full amount of the medical care expenses, and the medical care facility will provide a "cooperative medical expenses subsidy application form" to the patient. The patient will submit it to the management organization of the NRCMS for the reimbursement of medical care expenses.

The expenses for outpatients will be paid by the personal account first; when the amount of expenses is more than the level of the personal account, a part of the expenses will be paid by the social pooling fund. In the case of inpatients, part of the medical expenses will be paid by the social pool fund of the NRCMS. However, in both inpatient and outpatient settings, part of medical care expenses should be paid by participants (see Fig. 2.4). The proportion of OOP expenses differs by region. In fact, in less-developed regions, this proportion is usually higher than that in well-developed regions. We provide detailed information on this issue in Chap. 4.

2.3.8 New Regulations After 2003

After the NRCMS was implemented in 2003, on January 10, 2006, the Ministry of Health, the National Development and Reform Commission, the Ministry of Civil Affairs, the Ministry of Finance, the Ministry of Agriculture, the Food and Drug Administration, and the Chinese Medicine Bureau Jointly promulgated the "*Notice Concerning Prompt Promotion of Trial of New Rural Cooperative Medical Scheme.*" The following content is stated:

First, the number of trial counties will be raised to about 40% of the total number of counties nationwide in 2006, expanded to 60% in 2007, spread nationwide in 2008, and extended to cover all rural residents in 2010.

Second, it may be promoted faster in the eastern region, where the level of economic development is higher than in other regions. In well-developed regions, a wide variety of rural medical insurance schemes can be implemented.

Third, after 2006, the central government will raise the annual subsidy per capita from 10 to 20 yuan for participants of the NRCMS in the central and western regions. Correspondingly, the subsidy per capita of local government will increase from 10 to 20 yuan, and it will be raised by 5 yuan in 2006 and 2007 for local governments with less fiscal revenue. Subsidies of local governments are mainly borne by province-level governments. The individual contributions of the NRCMS will be maintained at 10 yuan per person.

Moreover, in the *12th Five-Year Plan* published in 2012, the following seven goals were set:

(i) To increase the number of participants covered by basic medical insurance (implementation of universal medical insurance).
(ii) To increase the level of basic medical insurance (to increase the amounts of subsidies and benefits).
(iii) To reform the medical care payment system (to establish faster and more appropriate medical care payments, to strengthen the management and supervision of medical insurance institutions and medical care facilities, etc.).
(iv) To improve the medical care payment level (expense support for those who have difficulty of paying medical expenses).
(v) To establish a medical insurance system for serious illnesses (medical insurance will cover serious and intractable illnesses).
(vi) To improve the functions of medical insurance management (reimbursement at the place of consultation, insurance coverage at the destination, balance of medical insurance funds and benefits, and unification of urban and rural resident medical insurance).
(vii) To promote the development of commercial insurance (private medical insurance)

The government has gradually increased subsidies for the NRCMS since 2003. For example, in 2015, the annual subsidy standards per person of the central and local governments were raised to 380 yuan (central) and 120 yuan (local) (see Table 2.3).

On January 1, 2016, the State Council announced "*Opinions of the State Council on Integrating the Basic Medical Insurance System for Urban and Rural Residents,*" and stated that "to implement the requirements of the Central Committee of Party and the State Council on deepening the reform of the medical insurance, we will follow the policy of full coverage, basic protection, multi-level, and sustainability, strengthen overall coordination and top-level design, follow the principle of promoting the policies step-by-step, start with improved policies, promote the integration of the Urban Residents Basic Medical Insurance (URBMI) and the NRCMS, gradually establish a unified Urban and Rural Residents Basic Medical Insurance (URRBMI) nationwide, promote fairer guarantees, provide more standardized management services, and promote the effective usage of healthcare service, as well as the sustainable development of the universal medical insurance system. By the end of 2018, most provinces should intergrate medical insurance management systems for urban and rural "residents."

In 2016, the Chinese government proposed the establishment of a linking mechanism for basic medical insurance, serious illness medical insurance (SIMI), and medical aid to form a joint guarantee, and to increase the subsidies for poverty-stricken individuals with a poverty certification.

In January 2017, the State Council issued the "*Thirteenth Five-Year Plan for Deepening the Reform of the Medical and Health System*" which aimed to put forward the principles for the reforms of medical insurance, medical treatment, and medicine. The medical insurance system reform is mainly focused on improving the level of financing and security, integrating the basic medical insurance system for urban and rural residents, expanding the coverage, and improving the SIMI and medical aid system.

In 2019, 77.82 million participants in the NRCMS obtained government subsidies. The central government supported 24.5 billion yuan for medical assistance. Four billion yuan in special subsidies were used to support funds for poverty individuals in less-developed regions. As of the end of 2019, the enrollment rate of the NRCMS in the low-income group reached 99.9%, and the comprehensive medical insurance policy for poverty alleviation benefited 200 million poor people and helped 4.18 million people who were impoverished due to illnesses to get out of poverty[1]. It was reported that the vulnerability to poverty was significantly lower for participants in the NRCMS than for non-participants, suggesting that the NRCMS has a positive effect on poverty reduction during illness.

Moreover, on June 30, 2020, the National Medical Security Administration, the Ministry of Finance, and the State Administration of Taxation issued the "*Notice on Doing a Good Job in Basic Medical Security for Urban and Rural Residents in 2020,*" the main contents of which are as follows.

First, it is stipulated that in 2020, the per capita annual financial subsidy standard of the URRBMI for urban and rural residents will increase by 30 yuan, reaching no less than 550 yuan, and the annual individual insurance contribution will be simultaneously increased by 30 yuan, reaching 280 yuan. At the same time, based on the fund of the URRBMI and the operations of the SIMI, the funds of the SIMI should be improved. It is expected that the steady increase in the amount of funds and the gradual optimization of the fund structure may promote the realization of stable and sustainable funds for medical insurance and provide a solid foundation for consolidating the level of healthcare services."

Second, it states that in 2020, the treatment guarantee mechanism will be improved from three aspects to enhance citizens' sense of gain, happiness, and security as follows:

(i) Fully realizing the system integration of NRCMS and URCMS, the share of inpatient expenses paid by medical insurance will reach 70%, and medical care expenses for outpatients with hypertension and diabetes will be paid by medical insurance.
(ii) It will consolidate the benefit level of serious illness, decrease the deductible line, unify it to half of the per capita disposable income, and increase the proportion of medical care expenses paid by medical insurance to 60%, as well as encourage well-developed regions to pay much more than 60%.
(iii) It will provide special subsidies for those in the extreme poverty group, the recipients of medical aid system, and the rural poverty group who have poverty certification and have participated in the URRBMI to ensure that poor people are fully insured.

Third, it will promote four requirements for handling services as follows:

(i) It will promote enrollment in medical insurance, increase insurance contributions, and implement a universal medical insurance plan. Under the unified organization of local governments, it will consolidate work responsibilities, strengthen the coordination of insurance contributions collection and payment, strengthen the management and cooperation between medical insurance and tax departments, improve the efficiency and service levels of medical insurance, and ensure the achievement of the annual quantitative goals of medical insurance funds.
(ii) It will promote integrated handling operations. The basic medical insurance, SIMI, and medical aid within the city/region will be operated by the "one-office service, one-window operation, and one-single system settlement." It will enforce national medical insurance management and administrative services and improve the coordinated management mechanism in regions.
(iii) It will promote the establishment of a unified national medical insurance management system, integrate the urban and rural management system, establish a unified service hotline, and vigorously promote the sinking of services.
(iv) It will accelerate the promotion of unified national standardization and informatization.

2.4 Conclusions

In rural China, the CMS based on people's commune was established and implemented during the planned economy period. With the implementation of the CMS, most rural residents received primary medical care services and were prevented from developing infectious diseases (Xu, 1997a, b). International organizations such as the World Bank, the United Nations, and WHO highly evaluated the CMS in rural China (Ma, 2015). During the market-oriented reform period, the government reformed the economic system in rural areas, implemented the "Household Contract Responsibility System" and changed the agricultural production unit from collectives to a household unit. Along with this, the people's commune was dismantled, and the CMS collapsed in the late 1980s. The problem of falling into poverty caused by high OOP expenses on medical care has become more serious in rural areas.

In 1990, the government promoted the re-establishment of rural medical insurance, but medical insurance was not implemented in rural China. In 2003, the government implemented the NRCMS and promoted it nationwide. In 2016, to reduce the inequality between rural and urban residents, the government implemented the URRBMI to integrate the URCMS and NRCMS, and raised subsidies for public medical insurance. In 2020, the government raised subsidies greatly and promoted reforms in medical insurance management and healthcare services.

However, since the NRCMS or URRMS is operated and managed by the regional government (especially the government at the county/county-level city), the operations and management systems, and the ratio of OOP expenses are different depending on the region, there is a regional disparity in medical insurance. Currently, although the medical insurance fund is funded annually by government subsidy, village subsidy, and individual insurance contribution, the reimbursement level of medical care expenses is low. Even if they join the NRCMS or URRMS, most of the medical care expenses are paid by rural residents themselves, and there remains the problem of falling into poverty when illness for the low-income group. Further reform of public medical insurance for rural residents is required.

Notes

1. The household registration system (*hukou*) is a population management system implemented by the Chinese government for citizens of the PRC who settled in mainland China, with households as the unit. *Hukou* shows the legality of a person's life in a certain place. Since the 1950s, the formulation and implementation of the population management policy in China have been based on this system. Based on the *hukou* system, the population is divided into two groups: rural residents and urban residents based on the birth region and family member relations. Although rural *hukou* residents can obtain land use rights in rural areas, they cannot enjoy social insurance (i.e., public pension, publicly funded medical care system). By the 1980s, mobility from rural areas to urban areas

was prohibited for rural residents without the permission of the government. The *hukou* system has been deregulated gradually since the 1980s.

2. "*Wubaohu*" in rural areas are elders for whom the local government guarantees food, clothing, housing, medical care, and burial expenses.
3. "*Sanwu*" in urban areas are those who have lost the ability to work, have no source of income, and have no legal relatives to support them.
4. Based on the *2019 Medical Security Development Statistics Bulletin*. Accessed on May 28, 2021. http://www.gov.cn/guoqing/2020-03/30/content_5507506.htm.

Appendix

See Table 2.4.

Table 2.4 Government policies and events on public medical insurance systems in rural areas from 1949 to 2021

Year	Policy or event	Main content
May 1, 1951	Mishan county, Gaoping Town, in Shanxi Province	Primarily in rural areas, 3 private pharmacies and 10 private doctors voluntarily established the cooperative clinic
November 1959	The National Rural Health Work Conference was held in Jishan County in Shanxi Province	The government formally affirmed the cooperative medical system and unified the name into the CMS, which was later referred to as the "old rural cooperative medical system."
June 26, 1965	Mao Zedong gave instructions to "put the focus of medical and health work in the countryside."	The CMS is further promoted in all rural areas
December 15, 1979	The Ministry of Health, Agriculture, Finance, the State Administration of Medicine, and the National Supply and Marketing Cooperative jointly issued the "*Rural Cooperative Medical Regulations (Trial Draft)*."	The implementation of the CMS was officially established in the system
October 19, 2002	The Central Committee of the Communist Party of China and the State Council issued the "*Decision on Further Strengthening Rural Medical Care Work*."	It specifies policies and measures to rebuild the CMS in rural areas

(continued)

Table 2.4 (continued)

Year	Policy or event	Main content
January 16, 2003	The General Office of the State Council forwarded the Ministry of Health and other three departments' "*Notices of Opinions on Establishment of a New Rural Cooperative Medical System.*"	Proposed the establishment of a new rural cooperative medical system (NRCMS) and started to implement the NRCMS
November 18, 2003	The Ministry of Civil Affairs and other ministries jointly issued the "*Opinions on the Implementation of Rural Medical Aid.*"	The government began to establish a social medical aid system in rural areas
January 3, 2004	The General Office of the State Council forwarded to the Ministry of Health and other departments' "*Notice of Guiding Opinions on the Pilot Work of Rural Cooperative Medical Care.*"	Promote the pilot work of the NRCMS
October 28, 2010	The 17th meeting of the Standing Committee of the 11th National People's Congress passed the "*Social Insurance Law of the People's Republic of China*"	The UEBMI, NRCMS, and URBMI have been upgraded to legal systems, causing the social insurance system— including medical insurance—to move from an experimental stage to a finalized, stable, and sustainable development stage
August 24, 2012	Six ministries and commissions, including the National Development and Reform Commission, jointly issued the "*Guiding Opinions on Carrying out Serious Illness Medical Insurance for Urban and Rural Residents.*"	Begin to establish a serious illness medical insurance system for urban and rural residents
March 5, 2013	State Council Government Work Report	It was officially announced that "The universal basic medical insurance system has been established initially, with more than 1.3 billion people participating in various medical insurances, and universal medical insurance system has basically been established."
May 1, 2014	The "*Interim Measures for Social Assistance*" came into effect	It stipulates that the government shall establish a medical aid system to ensure that the government should provide the basic medical care services to participants of medical aid system and poverty people

(continued)

Table 2.4 (continued)

Year	Policy or event	Main content
April 21, 2015	The General Office of the State Council forwarded to the Ministry of Civil Affairs and other departments' "*Notice on the Opinions on Comprehensively Carrying Out the Medical Assistance Work for Major and Serious Illness*"	Promote the medical aid system to realize the overall planning of urban and rural areas, and comprehensively provide serious illness medical aid
January 3, 2016	The State Council issued the "*Opinions on Implementation on Integrating the Basic Medical Insurance System for Urban and Rural Residents.*"	Promote the integration of the URBMI and the NRCMS
June 20, 2017	The General Office of the State Council issued the "*Guiding Opinions on Further Deepening the Reform of Payment Methods in Basic Medical Insurance*"	It is proposed to comprehensively establish and continuously improve a medical insurance payment system that conforms to the national conditions of healthcare services
May 13, 2018	The State Council's institutional reform plan was announced	The National Medical Security Bureau, as an agency directly under the State Council, was established
February 25, 2020	The government issued the "*Opinions of the Central Committee of the Communist Party of China and the State Council on Deepening the Reform of the Medical Security System.*"	Clarify the blueprint for the development of medical insurance by 2025 and 2030, and put forward the overall reform framework. This is the first top-level design specially formulated by the Party Central Committee and the State Council, for the reform of the medical security system, since the foundation of the PRC
February 19, 2021	The State Council promulgated the first administrative regulation of the National Medical Security System "*Regulations on the Supervision and Administration of the Use of Medical Insurance Funds.*"	This law became the basis for the legalization of the medical insurance system. It came into effect on May 1, 2021

Source Created by the author based on government regulations, Han (2014), Zhao (2019), Liao (2019), Weng and Sun (2020), Feng (2021), and Guo and Zhang (2021)
Note CMS: cooperative medical scheme; NRCMS: new rural cooperative medical scheme; URBMI: urban resident basic medical insurance; UEBMI: urban employee basic medical insurance; PRC: People's Republic of China

References

Editorial Department of "Contemporary China" Series. (1986). *Contemporary China's medical service*. China Social Sciences Press. (in Chinese).

Feng, P. (2021). From 1921 to 2021: A glimpse of China's medical insurance and commercial health insurance for a century. *Shanghai Insurance, 7*, 16–122. (in Chinese).

Gao, X. (2019). 70 years of rural cooperative medical care: Review, problems and prospects based on the perspective of social change. *Fujian Forum: Humanities and Social Sciences, 8*, 164–175. (in Chinese).

Guo, X., & Zhang, R. (2021). Memorabilia of 100 years of medical insurance. *China Health Insurance, 7*, 16–21. (in Chinese).

Han, F. (2014). The historical evolution of medical insurance system in China. *China Medical Insurance, 6*, 20–24. (in Chinese).

Liao, Z. (2019). 70 years of reform of China's medical insurance system. *Social Security, 11*, 28–31. (in Chinese).

Ma, X. (2015). *Public medical insurance in China*. Kyoto: Kyoto University Press (in Japanese).

Song, X. (2006). *Reform: Enterprise, labor and social security*. Social Science Literature Press. (in Chinese).

Song, X. (2009). Retrospect and prospect of China's medical insurance system in the 60 Years since the founding of the People's Republic of China. *Chinese Journal of Health Policy, 2*(19), 6–14. (in Chinese).

Weng, N., & Sun, M. (2020). Changes of China's rural basic medical security system. *Environment and Society, 4*(1), 53–55. (in Chinese).

Xu, J. (1997a). History review and think on China medical policies. *China Health Economics, 16*(176), 7–8 (in Chinese).

Xu, J. (1997b). History review and think on China medical policies. *China Health Economics, 16*(177), 8–9 (in Chinese).

Yang, Y. (2019). The sick can be treated, and the elderly can be provided for: The retrospect and prospects of the 70-year reform of the rural medical and old-age security system in China. *Social Development Research, 6*(1), 185–203. (in Chinese).

Zhao, L. (2019). Healthcare reform and the development of China's rural healthcare: A decade's experience, development predicament and promotion of good governance. *China Rural Economy, 9*, 1–22. (in Chinese).

Zou, C., Tian, Y., Xu, B., Sun, C., Yuan, B., Zhao, H., & Song, J. (2018). Historical evolution of the development of Chinese medical insurance system (1949–1978): Discussion on the history healthcare policy. *Medicine and Philosophy, 39*(6), 81–86. (in Chinese).

Chapter 3
Medical Insurance Reform in Urban China

Abstract This chapter discusses the transformation of medical insurance in urban China. During the planned economy period, the public medical system consisted of a labor insurance medical system and a publicly funded medical system, which covered all employees in state-owned enterprises and government offices. The public medical system has changed with state-owned enterprise reform since the 1990s. Currently, public medical insurance mainly includes the Urban Employee Basic Medical Insurance that covers urban employees and the Urban Residents Basic Medical Insurance that covers unemployed urban residents. This chapter introduces the contents, such as funds and benefits, of these medical insurance types.

Keywords Labor insurance medical system · Urban employee basic medical insurance · Urban residents basic medical insurance · Urban residents · China

3.1 Introduction

This chapter discusses the transformation of the medical insurance system in urban China.

Currently, the medical insurance system implemented in urban China has mainly three types: public medical insurance, private medical insurance, and other medical insurance types. Among them, public medical insurance covers the majority of urban residents. It is composed of the Urban Employee Basic Medical Insurance (UEBMI), which covers urban employees, and the Urban Residents Basic Medical Insurance (URBMI), which covers unemployed urban residents. In the following section, we introduce the details of public medical systems in urban China under the planned economy period and their transformations under a market-oriented reform period. For the details of policies and events related to public medical insurance reform in urban areas, please refer to Appendix Table 3.3.

X. Ma, *Public Medical Insurance Reforms in China*,
https://doi.org/10.1007/978-981-16-7790-8_3

3.2 Medical Insurance Types Under the Planned Economy Period in Urban China

During the planned economy period, public medical systems comprised of a labor insurance medical system and a publicly funded medical system (Table 3.1).

3.2.1 Labor Insurance Medical System

The predecessor of the labor insurance was the "*Temporary Labor Law*," which was enforced in the central Soviet jurisdiction in 1930. The law stipulates that, when a long-term employee becomes sick, the employer will pay part of the medical care expenses. After the establishment of the People's Republic of China (PRC) in 1949, the government promulgated the "*China Labor Insurance*" act in February 1951. In 1953, part of the system was amended and then promulgated as the "*Labor Insurance*" act (Song, 2006, 2009; Zou et al., 2018).

Employees and mandatory retirees in state-owned enterprises (SOEs) and collectively owned enterprises (COEs) in urban areas are the eligible participants. The employers should pay 50% of medical care expenses of the dependent family members of their employees. In 1953, the number of participants was 11 million, which increased to 137 million in the early 1990s.

In 1951, the premium of labor insurance was 3% of the total wage bills of employees in a corporate, but this was raised to 4.5–5.5% in 1957. Insurance premiums per industry sector vary. For example, the insurance premium in the heavy, forestry, railway, and transportation industries was 7% of the total wage bill, but only 5% in light, spinning, postal communication, and trade industries. As the government's fiscal revenue was improved, the contribution rate on insurance in heavy industry and forestry was reduced to 5.5% of the total wage bill; 5% in light, spinning, railroad, postal communication, agriculture, and construction industries; and 4.5% in the trade industry. A corporate should pay insurance contribution, but, at that time, a corporate activities, such as production, employment, and wage levels,

Table 3.1 Medical insurance types under the planned economy period in urban China

Types of insurance	Eligible target
Labor insurance medical system	Employees, retirees, and dependent family members of employees in state-owned enterprises and collectively owned enterprises
Publicly funded medical system	Employees, retirees, and dependent family members of employees in government offices and government-related organizations (*Shiye Danwei*)

Source Created by the author

were all managed by the government. Thus, a corporate paid insurance contribution to the government as part of the government's revenue.

Regarding the labor insurance management, the China National Trade Union (*Gonghui*) was the management organization, and the local government's labor administration department was the supervisory organization. However, after the Cultural Revolution movement (during 1966–1976), the management function of the National Trade Union was paralyzed, and the labor insurance system changed from "publicly funded insurance" to "corporate insurance" managed by each corporate. In 1969, the Ministry of Finance merged the corporate incentive and insurance funds into the "corporate employee welfare fund." A total of 5.5% of employees' total wages were collected as employee welfare funds. Medical insurance was funded by employee welfare funds and non-operating expenditures, and insufficient funds were filled by corporate profits.

Regarding the benefits of labor insurance, a participant will receive medical treatment at a corporate medical care facility or a designated medical care facility, and the majority of the medical care expenses were paid by the corporate. The dependent family members of the participants (e.g., spouse, children under 16 years old, and unemployed parents) could receive the healthcare service from the medical care facility of the corporate, and the corporate should pay about 50% of the medical care expenses of the dependents of their employees who joined the labor insurance. However, employees should pay for their medical examination, meal, transportation, and out-of-pocket (OOP) drug fees (i.e., nutritional supplements).

3.2.2 *Publicly Funded Medical System*

In June 1952, the State Council promulgated "*Instructions on the Implementation of Publicly Funded Medical Care Prevention for Government Officials of People's Governments, Parties, Organizations and Their Related Organizations.*", which was the first legislation on publicly funded medical system in the People's Republic of China.

Eligible participants were civil servants, retirees, military individuals with second-class B or higher levels of revolutionary disability who retired and even worked in government offices and government-related organizations and students in universities. The number of participants in the publicly funded medical system was only 4 million in 1952. However, it increased to 7.4 million in 1957 and to 14.25 million in 1980.

All expenses related to the publicly funded medical system were supported by the government's financial budget; that is, the publicly funded medical system was "government insurance." The funding of medical expenses from the public was established by the central government. The flat-rate standard was 18 yuan annually until 1961. However, it increased to 70 yuan in 1979 and 150 yuan in 1993 (206 yuan in the municipality under direct control).

The organization that managed the publicly funded medical system was the publicly funded medical management committee, which also managed the publicly funded medical office. The medical office also managed the publicly funded medical fund.

The publicly funded medical management committee was supposed to pay medical expenses upon request of a work unit (*Danwei*) [1]. When a participant received healthcare services at a designated medical facility and when he received healthcare services at a local medical care facility, the insurance would regularly pay the full amount of their medical care expenses. Hence, the OOP expense of the medical care was "zero." When medical care expenses exceed the standard fixed amount of the fund, the government pays the excess amount. The benefits included the medical care expenses of inpatient, health examination, drug, treatment, and surgery. Meanwhile, medical care expenses for artificial abortion surgery, organ transplantation (only part of the medical care expenses), injuries or disabilities due to labor accidents, serious illness emergency and injury treatment, and nutritional medicine were also paid by the fund.

For the payment of medical care expenses of the dependent family members of the participants, the Ministry of Finance, Ministry of Health, and State Council jointly promulgated "*Medical Problems for Children of Employees in Government Organizations*" in September 1955. Two types of system were used.

(i) The first type was a collective medical fund system. The government organizations collected the contributions from the dependent family members of the participants, and they managed and used it as a unified collective medical fund. The excess amount was paid by the government. According to the system, dependent family members of the participants could receive healthcare services in designated medical care facilities.
(ii) The second type was to establish the medical fund for dependent family members of participants as "national welfare fund".

Both the labor insurance and the publicly funded medical system were close to the "free medical insurance." From the institution establishment perspective, "universal medical insurance" was realized in urban China under the planned economy period, and public medical care system covered all urban residents, including employed and unemployed. Public medical care systems have contributed to improving the utilization of healthcare services for employees and their dependent family members in urban areas. However, because participants that are both employees and civil servants were not obliged to pay insurance contributions, and the OOP expenses on medical care were almost "zero," overconsumption of medicines and medical care treatment became a problem. Further, when a medical care facility requests for the medical care expenses, these expenses would be paid by corporates or government organizations. Oversupply of healthcare services became a problem also. As a result, medical care expenses increased dramatically, and the government's fiscal burden of public medical care systems became serious. To address these problems, a government-led reform of public medical care systems was implemented in the 1990s.

3.3 Medical Insurance Reform in Urban China

3.3.1 *Urban Employee Basic Medical Insurance (UEBMI)*

In 1984, the Ministry of Health and the Ministry of Finance issued the "*Notification on Further Strengthening the Management of Publicly Funded Medical Care.*" This notification stated that the following.

The reform of the publicly funded medical care system is imperative. Various reform methods are available to ensure better healthcare services and no over-consumption. For experiments, in terms of specific management measures, it can be considered to be appropriately linked to employer, employee and medical care facility.

Some provinces and cities attempted to increase the OOP expenses on medical care in some medical care facilities, and many firms implemented the medical insurance reform since then. Systems with a fixed amount of medical care expenses for outpatients or a certain share of medical care expenses paid by employees for outpatients and inpatients were established, but they varied by region. The OOP ratio was approximately 10%–20% of the total medical care expenses. After 1989, this method was gradually promoted over the entire urban area.

The social pooling fund of serious illnesses medical insurance (SIMI) was first established in cities such as Dandong, Siping, Huangshi, and Zhuzhou, and it gradually spread to other regions. In 1992, the Ministry of Labor issued the "*Opinions on the Trial Implementation of Social Coordination of Medical Expenses for Serious Illnesses of Employees,*" requiring all cities to implement this (Ministry of Labor and Social Security, 2002; Song, 2009).

In 1993, based on the "*Central Committee of the Chinese Communist Party's Decision on Issues Related to the Establishment of the Socialist Market Economic System,*" resolved at the Third Plenary Meeting of the 14th Central Committee of the Chinese Communist Party, the National System Reform Committee and the Labor Department, Ministry of Health, and Ministry of Finance have promulgated "*Draft on Employees' Medical Care System Reform.*" The reform stated that "A new medical insurance system will be established including both a social pooling fund and a personal account, with the goal of building a medical insurance for all employees in urban areas." At the end of 1993, more than 80% of corporates implemented this medical insurance reform (Song, 2009).

In 1994, the State Commission for Economic Restructuring and other four departments issued the "*Opinions on the Pilot Reform of the Medical System for Employees.*" They also decided to conduct pilot projects in the cities of Zhenjiang and Jiujiang in Jiangsu and Jiangxi Provinces, respectively, to establish a medical insurance system that is a combination system of social pooling fund and personal account.

In 1996, based on the reform experiences of the "Liangjiang (Zhenjiang and Jiujiang) Pilot Project," the State Council published the "*Opinions on the Expansion of the Pilot Reform of the Employee Medical Insurance System,*" and more than 50 cities were selected as pilot areas. In accordance with the reform goals and basic principles determined by the relevant documents of the State Council, many cities have explored methods to ensure the insurance financial balance between benefits and funds. During this period, many models, such as the "Liangjiang model," "Beijing model," "Hainan model," and "Zhenjiang model," were considered. After comparing the results of these models, the State Council promulgated the "*State Council Decision on the Construction of the Urban Employees Basic Medical Insurance Scheme*" on December 14, 1998, and started the medical insurance reform in urban areas.

The UEBMI applies to all corporates (e.g., state-owned, collectively owned, foreign-owned, privately owned enterprises) and non-corporate sectors (e.g., government office, government-related organizations, social organizations, and non-profit organizations) in urban areas. Whether employees in township and village enterprises, self-employed, and employees in small firms in urban areas can join the UEBMI is determined by each province-level government.

The UEBMI is operated at the social pool government level. The social pool level can be at the district or city level, and the three municipalities, namely, Beijing, Tianjin, and Shanghai, can establish a unified social pooling fund. All companies and organizations should pay for the contributions of social medical insurance. Meanwhile, the local government managed the social medical insurance fund.

The UEBMI insurance fund has two types: a social pooling fund and a personal account. An employer will pay the insurance contributions for their employees, which is 6% of total wage bill, and an employee will pay 2% of wage bills as an individual contribution. All of the employee's contribution (i.e., 2% of salary income) is accumulated in the personal account. The medical insurance contributions paid by employers and employees are divided into two parts: one is portion of 70% of the employer's contribution, which is 4.2% of the total wage bill (=70 × 6%), is accumulated in the social pooling fund; the other is portion of 30% of the employer's contribution, which is 1.8% of the total wage bill (=30 × 6%), is accumulated in personal accounts (Fig. 3.1).

The social pooling fund and personal accounts are established independently after determining the benefits. The minimum limit of medical care expenses paid by social pooling funds is set to approximately 10% of the annual average wage of the relevant local employee, and the maximum limit is set to around four times of that. Medical care expenses below the minimum limit will be paid from personal accounts. When the expense is higher than the amount of personal accounts, it will become OOP expenses (Fig. 3.2). The majority of medical care expenses above the minimum limit and below the maximum limit will be paid by social pooling funds. However, part of the expenses will be paid by OOP expenses. Medical care expenses that exceed the maximum limit can be covered by private medical insurance (e.g., commercial insurance) or other medical insurance (e.g., firm subsidy medical insurance, and SIMI).

The minimum and maximum limits of benefits and the proportion of OOP expenses are determined based on the principle of the balance between benefits and funds. The ratio of OOP expenses varies by region; the majority of the proportions range from 20 to 30%.

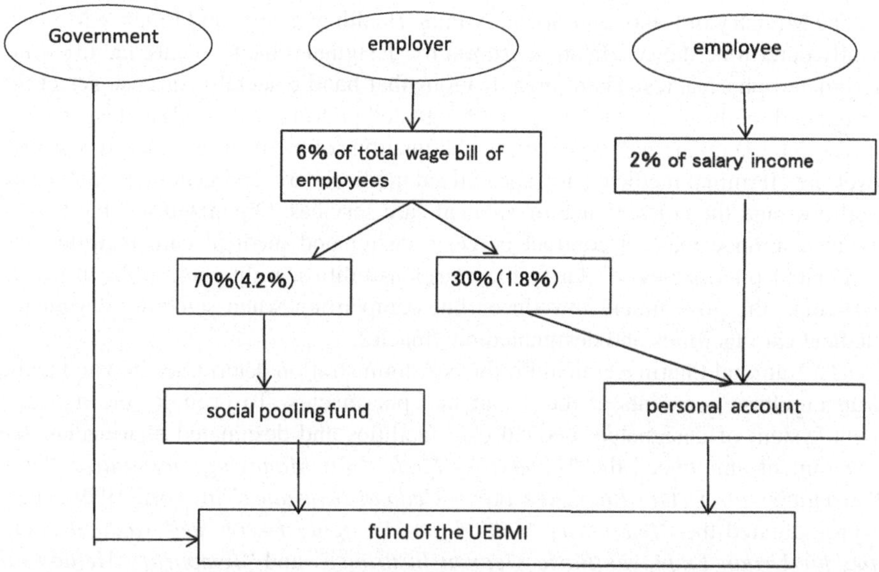

Fig. 3.1 Fund of the UEBMI. *Source* Created by the author based on the regulations of the UEBMI

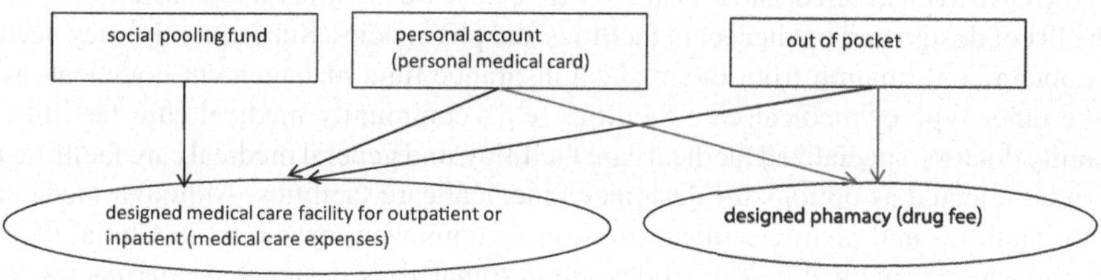

Fig. 3.2 Benefit and payment of the UEBMI. *Source* Created by the author based on the regulation of the UEBMI

Regarding the management of medical care facilities, the Labor and Social Security Ministry, Health Ministry, and Finance Ministry jointly set the basic levels of healthcare services, method of reimbursement of medical care expenses, management of drug inventory, and determination of regulations to manage medical care facilities. Labor security administration organizations in each province and municipality will establish implementation standards and methods for the relevant areas in collaboration with the relevant departments based on the regulations of the central government.

The UEBMI stipulates that a management system that has designated medical facilities and pharmacies will be implemented. When a participant receives a healthcare service at a medical care facility other than the designated facility, the medical care expenses will not be paid by the social pooling fund. Designated medical care facilities and pharmacies were selected using the following process.

The Ministry of Labor and Social Affairs, Health Ministry, and Finance Ministry jointly determine the certification criteria for designated medical care facilities and designated pharmacies. Then, organizations that handle social insurance select the designated medical care facilities and designated pharmacies based on the principle of recognizing medicines, considering the functions of medical care facilities at each level (i.e., terminal medical care, specialized medical care, and general medical care facilities) and the convenience of medical care services. Organizations that handle social insurance make a contract between designated medical care facilities and designated pharmacies to clarify their responsibilities, rights, and obligations. In particular, the government introduces fair competition when selecting designated medical care facilities and designated pharmacies.

The National Pharmaceutical Products Administration determines how to handle drug purchase accidents at the designated pharmacies. To promote the management system of designated medical care facilities and designated pharmacies, the government announced the "*Temporary Method for Managing Designated Retail Pharmacies for Urban Employee Basic Medical Insurance*" in April 1999. Then, it promulgated the "*Temporary Method for Managing Designated Medical Facilities for Urban Employee Basic Medical Insurance*" and "*Temporary Method for Managing the Range of Drug Usage* for *Urban Employee Basic Medical Insurance*" in May 1999. According to these regulations, the insured corporates or organizations of the UEBMI will select and register 3–5 medical care facilities and pharmacies from the list of designated medical care facilities and pharmacies. Subsequently, they need to obtain confirmation from the medical insurance fund management organization. The other type of medical care facilities (e.g., community medical care facilities, family doctors, specialized medical care facilities, and general medical care facilities) can be selected as options for designated medical care facilities. Although medical care facilities and pharmaceutical division systems were promoted in China, most pharmacies in medical care facilities are designated as designated pharmacies. A participant in the UEBMI can select the most desirable medical care facility from the list of designated medical care facilities and receive healthcare service, obtain a doctor's prescription, and select a designated pharmacy to buy drugs. Specifically, the implementation of the designated medical care facility system can intensify competition for patient acquisition in regions with a large number of medical care facilities. This system is expected to help improve the efficiency of healthcare services to a certain extent.

Moreover, some special provisions have been implemented as follows:

(i) Medical treatment for retirees will not change, and medical care expenses will be paid by special funds. If the fund is insufficient, the government will provide subsidies.
(ii) The medical treatment of the revolutionary disability military of the second-class B and above will not change, and medical care expenses will be paid by special funds. Organizations that handle social insurance manages the fund. If the fund is insufficient, the government will provide subsidies.

(iii) Retired employees who joined the UEBMI will not pay the insurance premium, and the proportion of OOP expenses will be considered.
(iv) Firms in specific industry sectors can establish corporate supplementary medical insurance. The premium of corporate supplementary medical insurance will be 4% or less of the total wage bills and can be paid as an employee welfare fund. If the employee welfare fund is insufficient, it will be supported by the financial department of the government.
(v) Insurance premiums for laid-off employees at SOEs will be calculated based on 60% of the average wage of employees in the previous year in a region, and these employees will be paid by the reemployment service center of the government.

3.3.2 Urban Resident Basic Medical Insurance (URBMI)

Employees in urban areas are covered by the UEBMI implemented in 1998. However, unemployed urban residents were not covered by public medical insurance. To achieve the goal of building a medical insurance system that covers all urban residents, the State Council announced the "*The State Council's Guidance Opinion on the Development of Trial Site Trials for Basic Medical Insurance for Urban Residents*" on July 10, 2007. It is stated that the trial will be started by selecting some well-developed cities from some provinces, autonomous regions, and municipalities. This trial will be expanded in 2008, and the number of pilot cities will reach more than 80% in 2009. Further, it will be implemented nationwide in 2010 to achieve the goal of gradually covering all unemployed individuals in urban areas.

The trial's principle is to start the trial at a low level, set the level of funds and security based on the economic development level and government fiscal capacity, and focus on covering expenses on serious illness treatments. Enrollment insurance is optional, and the central and local governments will fulfill their respective responsibilities. The central government will establish basic principles and policies, whereas the local government will formulate concrete operation methods, implement the insurance scheme, and manage the insured.

The URBMI applies to elementary, junior high, and senior high school students (including vocational schools), children, and other unemployed individuals who have urban *hukou* and do not join the UEMBI or other public medical insurances.

The URBMI states that "each region set the insurance standards in consideration of the economic development level of the relevant region, the basic medical care needs, and the burden capacity of both the residents and local government." The URBMI fund consists of individual contribution and government subsidy. First, the local government subsidizes more than 40 yuan per capita yearly for each participant. Meanwhile, the central government subsidizes 20 yuan per capita for the central and western regions (less-developed regions) yearly since 2007. The government will subsidize more than 10 yuan per capita yearly for students/children with severe disabilities or those joining the minimum living subsidy scheme. Moreover, it will provide 60 yuan per capita yearly for individuals who are covered by the minimum living subsidy scheme, severely disabled individuals who have lost their working ability, and poor elderly aged 60 and over. The central government subsidizes 30 yuan per capita yearly for urban residents in central and western regions. Individual insurance contributions vary depending on the education attainment levels of students (i.e., elementary school, junior high school, senior high school, and college), employment status, and region. Insurance premiums paid by individuals are generally flat rate, and the amount is less than 200 yuan yearly. Therefore, it is considered that to compare with high-income group, the proportion of insurance premiums to the total income is higher for low-income group, and, thus, there maintains the problem of regressive insurance premium payments.

As the URBMI for urban residents focuses on inpatients and treatment of serious illnesses, the benefit level must be based on the balance between funds and benefits. The benefit level, ratio of OOP expenses, and maximum benefit level vary by region. Specifically, the benefit level will be considerably lower for the URBMI than for the UEBMI. Therefore, part of medical care expenses regulated by the URBMI will be paid by the insurance. However, part of expenses that cannot be paid by the URBMI can be paid by other types of insurance, such as supplementary medical insurance, commercial insurance, medical aid, and private charity donations.

The medical service management of the URBMI has indicated that the labor security organization of the city joined with the development and reform committee, government finance organization, and government health organization to conduct URBMI trials. The following are stipulated to strengthen the organizational management.

First, a joint meeting system between the ministries and agencies of the State Council of the URBMI was set. Under the guidance of the State Council, during joint ministry meetings, related operations and guidance in the trial city are coordinated, related policies are set, implementation status of the policies is supervised, and implementation status of the pilot city is supervised. This meeting will evaluate and supervise trial activities and report and provide recommendations to the State Council on critical issues.

Second, the provincial-level government will select some cities as trial cities while considering situations in relevant regions, report them to the joint ministry meeting, and receive examination and certification. After reporting and recording the trial implementation plan of the pilot city, the local government in the province, autonomous region, and municipalities will approve and implement the plan.

Finally, the labor security organization will set and implement policies in collaboration with the development and reform committee, finance ministry, civil welfare ministry, education ministry, drug supervision and management bureau, and Chinese medicine management organizations.

3.3.3 *Unifying the Medical Insurance of Urban and Rural Residents*

In April 2009, the "*Opinions of the Central Committee of the Communist Party of China and the State Council on Deepening the Reform of the Medical and Health System*" (hereinafter referred to as the "Opinion") was announced. The Opinion officially promises that China will achieve the following.

The basic medical insurance fully covers urban and rural residents in 2011, and preliminary establish an essential drug system, improve the primary medical care, establish universal basic medical care services, enforce the reform of public hospitals, improve the accessibility of basic healthcare services, and reduce the fiscal burden of public medical care expenditure. By 2020, we will establish the basic medical care system covering the whole urban and rural residents. The following is also stated in the Opinion:

(i) We will establish a basic medical insurance system covering urban and rural residents: the UEBMI, UREMI, NRCMS and medical aid system, respectively cover urban employee, unemployed urban resident, rural resident, and the poverty urban and rural resident.

(ii) According to the principles of "wide coverage, basic protection, and sustainability", we will start with key protection for serious illnesses, and gradually extend to outpatient clinics for minor illnesses, and continuously improve the level of protection.

(iii) We will establish a national, a multi-channel funds with clear responsibilities of government, corporate, families, and individuals, and reasonable sharing of responsibilities, realize mutual assistance in society. With economic and social development, we will gradually increase the level of benefit to narrow the inequality in social security, and ultimately unify different social insurances.

(iv) We will improve the UEBMI, expedite the coverage of insurance, and focus on the problems of employees and retirees in state-owned bankrupt enterprises, and enterprises with poor performance as well as employees in non-SOEs, and non-regular workers.

(v) In 2009, the basic medical insurance for urban residents will be implemented in the whole urban areas, which focuses on the basic medical insurance for the elderly, the disabled and children; the New Rural Cooperative Medical Scheme will be fully implemented, the level of government subsidies will be gradually increased, and the individual contribution will be increased to improve insurance level.

(vi) To improve the medical aid system for both urban and rural residents, we will provide subsidies for individual who did not participate in insurance and build a solid medical insurance minimum line.

(vii) We will explore the establishment of a basic medical insurance management system which integrates the insurance for urban and rural residents.

3.3.4 Long-Term Care Insurance (LTCI) Reform

(1) **Policy on the LTCI in 2016**

To address the population aging and long-term care (LTC) problem, since 2013, the new government of Jinping Xi has promoted the development of the elderly service industry and the establishment of an LTC system (Wang, 2018). Referring to LTC systems in developed countries[2] and regarding the actual situation in China, the government published in 2013 "*Some Opinion on Accelerating the Development of Elderly Service Industry*" in an attempt to establish a medium- to long-term policy of elderly LTC. Among these opinions, it was emphasized that service infrastructure related to home-based care should be improved and cooperation networks of health, medical care, welfare, and LTC should be strengthened. Further, a home-based care network will be established in all urban areas by 2020 and in more than 90% of townships and villages and more than 60% of rural areas. The "*12th Five-Year Plan*" stated that a home-based care network will be established in more than 80% of townships and villages and more than 50% of rural areas, and community-based care service bases will be established.

In June 2016, the Ministry of Human Resources and Social Security of China promulgated the "*Guidance Opinion on the Development of the Long-term Care Insurance System Pilot Project*" and designated 15 cities, including Beijing, Shanghai, and Qingdao, as pilot areas for the LTC insurance (LTCI) project. The Chinese government has promoted an experiment to establish an LTCI in the current period. The following are the four basic policies:

(i) Coverage

The LTCI aims to secure the disabled for a long time. It focuses on the expenses of severely disabled individuals for basic living nursing and medical nursing. The pilot areas can determine the insurance target and specific guarantee content according to the affordability of the fund and gradually adjust the insured coverage and level with the economic development.

(ii) Eligible participants

In the trial phase, the LTCI mainly covered the participants of the UEBMI. According to their own actual conditions, the pilot areas can explore and improve the insurance system, comprehensively balance factors such as fundraising and insurance needs, reasonably determine insurance coverage, and gradually expand the coverage.

(iii) Fund

In the trial phase, funds will be established through many channels, such as optimizing the social pooling fund structure of the UEBMI, transferring part of the social pooling fund of the UEBMI, and adjusting the UEBMI premium. Then, establishment of a multi-channel fund for the LTCI with mutual assistance and shared responsibility will be explored gradually. The fund standard will be determined reasonably based on, for example, the local economic development level, nursing demand, nursing service expenses, and coverage and level of insurance, in accordance with the principle of balance between funds and benefits. The standard also establishes a dynamic funding mechanism with economic development and security levels.

(iv) Benefit

The LTCI fund will be mainly used to proportionally pay expenses to nursing service institutions and nurses when participants receive nursing services. Various insurance policies should be formulated based on nursing levels and nursing service delivery methods, and the fund should pay 70% of the expenses for LTC that meet the regulations. The specific conditions for insurance benefits and the OOP expense ratio are determined by the pilot cities.

(2) **Policy on the LTCI in 2020**

In September 2020, the National Medical Insurance Administration and Ministry of Finance issued the "*Guidance on Expanding the Pilot Program of Long-Term Care Insurance*" and announced new pilot areas. By 2020, the number of pilot areas has increased to 49. The following are the three basic policies:

(i) Coverage and eligible participants

The pilot phase started with the participants of the UEBMI, focusing on securing the basic nursing needs of the severely disabled and prioritizing the eligible disabled elderly and severely disabled. Where conditions permit, the pilot areas can explore further, along with the comprehensive consideration of various factors (e.g., level of economic development, fund capacity, and insurance needs) and gradually expand the coverage and adjust the LTCI coverage.

(ii) Fund

These areas will explore the establishment of a multi-channel fund mechanism, such as mutual assistance and shared responsibility. The central government determines the funding requirements for basic nursing services and reasonably determines the total annual funding in a pilot area. Fund is mainly established by employers and employees. In principle, insurance premium should be shared by the employer and employees in equal proportion. The employer's contribution is based on the total wage bills of employees, which can be deduced from the contributions of the UEBMI at the initial stage without increasing the employer's burden. An employee's contribution is based on their salary income, which can be paid by the personal account of the UEBMI for the employee. Meanwhile, exploring other fund channels to provide appropriate subsidies to the contributions of retired employees with special difficulties by the local government is also possible. Thus, a dynamic funding adjustment mechanism compatible with economic and social development and security levels is established.

(iii) Benefits

The LTCI fund should be mainly used to proportionally pay expenses to nursing service institutions and nurses when participants receive nursing services. Participants who were disabled for more than six months, received treatment by a medical care facility or a rehabilitation facility, and have taken an application and passed the evaluation can receive the benefits of the LTCI based on regulations. Various insurance policies should be formulated according to the nursing level and nursing service delivery methods, and home-based care and community-based care should be encouraged. The fund should pay 70% of the expenses for LTC that meet the regulations. Specific conditions to receive the benefits and the proportion of OOP expenses will be determined by the assigned pilot area. The LTCI will be kinked with other policies, such as subsidy policy for the older people and poor disabled persons, as well as subsidy policy for the severely disabled elderly.

(3) **Institutional fragmentation of the LTCI in China**

Because the pilot areas can determine the establishment of funds, coverage, insured care content, and payment standards, the LTCI differs per region (Lu & Wu, 2015; Zhao, 2015; Sun & Xie, 2016; Yang et al., 2016; Dong et al., 2019; Sheng et al., 2020; Li & Ming, 2020). We present a case in Qingdao City of Shandong Province, and compare the LTCI in 15 pilot areas.

- Model case of the LTCI in Qingdao City

Qingdao City in Shandong Province, has become an aging society since 1987, which was 13 years earlier than China nationwide. At the end of 2011, the number of people aged 60 and over in Qingdao reached 1.327 million, which was 17.3% of the total population of the city, exceeding the national average of 13.3%. Expenses on nursing facilities such as nursing homes and medical care facilities for the elderly in Qingdao City was high, and monthly expenses for rent, food, and nursing were generally over 3,000 yuan. However, the average benefit level of Qingdao pension was 1,767 yuan, which was less than that of the LTCI. To address the LTC problem, in July 2012, the government of Qingdao City began trials regarding the LTCI system, which is similar to the Japanese LTCI system. In June 2012, the government announced a "*Qingdao City Long-term Medical Care Insurance Management Opinion*" and started a trial on the LTCI. Initially, eligible LTCI participants were limited to those who participated in public medical insurance in urban areas. The main contents of the LTCI are summarized as follows.

(i) Eligible participant

Eligible participants were members of the UEBMI, URBMI, and New Rural Cooperative Medical Scheme (NRCMS). This system is similar to the LTCI in Korea and Germany wherein the insured are all age groups who have participated in public medical insurance, and the LTCI is established based on public medical insurance.

(ii) Fund

The fund is established by pay-as-you-go, which consists of three parts:

- 20% of the fund from the UEBMI (approximately 1.96 billion yuan)
- 0.5% of the average monthly amount of personal account reserves of UEBMI participants (approximately 600 million yuan per year)

- 10% of the total annual premium of the URBMI (determined according to the operating situation, approximately 300 million yuan per year)

Since 2015, the Qingdao City Human Resources and Social Security Bureau has signed a consignment contract with the Qingdao branch of a Chinese longevity insurance company and the Qingdao branch of People's Health Insurance Co., Ltd. as an insurer of long-term insurance. The expertise of these insurance companies is utilized to manage the LTCI.

(iii) Benefits

Regarding the benefits of the LTCI, the designated medical care facility in Qingdao City will certify the applicant for LTC based on the activities of daily living and the doctor's diagnosis. After being qualified for LTC, the insured individual will select a kind of LTC such as LTC at a designated nursing facility (institutional care), special LTC at a designated medical care facility, home-based care, and home-visiting nursing.

The benefit is 50 yuan per day for home care, 65 yuan per day for designated nursing facility care, and 170 yuan per day for specialized nursing at designated medical care facilities. For home-visit nursing, service providers are annually paid 1,600 yuan per year for a twice-a-week visit or 800 yuan for once a week. The insurance payment ratio is 90% of the total nursing expenses on all types of LTC for the UEBMI participants, 80% of the total nursing expenses on LTC services excluding home nursing for Type I adults in the URBMI, and 40% of the total nursing expenses for Type II adults in the URBMI.[3]

In January 2015, the "*Qingdao City Long-term Medical Protection Insurance Management Measures*" was announced as an improved policy stating that the LTCI will be expanded to all rural residents.

In 2016, Qingdao City was identified as a national pilot city for the LTCI. In 2018, the Qingdao city government published the "*Interim Measures for Long-term Care Insurance of Qingdao City*" and innovatively implemented a new LTCI that integrates medical nursing and life nursing among urban employees.

By the 2020, the government of Qingdao City has paid a total of 2.8 billion yuan in LTCI funds, benefiting more than 60,000 individuals with severe disability and dementia and their families. More than 850 nursing service institutions have been established and utilized. A nursing service platform based on privately owned institutions has been gradually established. In 2020, the government of Qingdao City paid 498 million yuan in LTCI funds. As the main force of nursing services, nurses and caregivers provided 1.03 million home-visit nursing services and accumulated 2.35 million hours of nursing services in 2020. Among the 70,000 elderly people with multiple disabilities, approximately 23,000 elderly people with the UEBMI participated in the LTCI, which achieved a full insurance coverage. The total number participants in the LTCI was approximately 48,000, and 6,400 disabled insured enjoyed the benefits in 2020.

Moreover, in April 2021, the government of Qingdao City published a new "*Qingdao City Long-term Care Insurance Measures*" to improve the reform of the

LTCI. It was stated that "adhere to the basic principles of comprehensive coverage, integrate insurances of urban and rural areas, basic security, and easily access to nursing services. The two types of insurance systems of the employees and residents will be uniformly designed, the system structure, the treatment items, and the handling of nursing services will be unified, and the level of urban and rural treatment will be maintained at a certain level. We will effort to address the problem of the lack of nursing service in rural areas." According to the 2021 LTCI policy, the fund structure has been reformed, and the benefits, especially for rural residents, have been increased.

(iv) Fund

First, the fund structure of the LTCI for employees is optimized. 0.3% of the UEBMI fund transfer to the fund of the LTCI. The individual contribution transfer of current employees and retirees are unified at 0.2% of personal accounts. The government financial subsidy is 30 yuan per person yearly.

Second, the source of funds of LTCI for residents who have not joined in the UEBMI is clarified. With the aim of not increasing the government and individual burden, the social pooling fund of resident medical insurance (i.e., URBMI, URRBMI) will be transferred at the standard of 30 yuan per person yearly, of which 20 yuan will be used as financial subsidy and the other 10 yuan will be used as individual contribution, and individuals do not need to pay additional contributions for the LTCI.

(v) Benefits

Qingdao City Long-*term Care Insurance Measures* states that "We will emphasize practicality and focus on ensuring the urgently nursing needs of people with disabilities and dementia as follows:

- Focus on the protection of severely disabled and demented persons. Anyone who has been assessed for the level of nursing needs and has reached the III, IV, and V levels of disability or severe dementia can receive the LTCI benefits in accordance with the regulations.
- Increase the living nursing benefits of insured residents, similar to urban insured employees, provides both medical nursing and living nursing, thus realizing system fairness.
- Maintain a moderate level of protection. Regardless of medical care service expense or nursing service expense, the specific reimbursement ratio for individuals is uniformly set as to 90% for employees, 80% for Type I resident, and 75% for Type II resident (the Type II resident' reimbursement ratio is 5% higher than the prior policy). For individuals, the medical care service benefits are reimbursed in proportion to the actual medical care service expenses incurred by the participant; the nursing service benefits are linked to the evaluation level of nursing needs of participants. When assessed to have III, IV, and V level disabilities, insured ones can enjoy up to 3, 5, and 7 hours of home-visit nursing service per week, respectively, and up to 660, 1,050, and 1,500 yuan per month; meanwhile, the insured

ones can enjoy 2, 3, and 5 hours of home-visit nursing service per week and up to 450, 660, and 1,050 yuan per month, respectively. The actual expenses differed according to the actual nursing service time provided by the nursing labors.

- In response to the multi-level and diversified nursing service needs of different groups of people, the City Medical Insurance Bureau has designed three types of nursing service forms: home-based care, institutional care, and daily care.[4]
- We will actively explore the protective mechanism for the delay in disability and dementia. Additionally, we have established a "Delayment of Disability and Dementia Protection Fund" to extend preventive interventions for people with mild to moderate disability and dementia.
- **Comparison of the LTCI in 15 pilot areas**

The main contents of the LTCI in 15 pilot areas are summarized in seven parts: (a) coverage (eligible participant), (b) fund, (c) benefit object, (d) enjoy service, (e) enjoy nursing type, and (f) benefit scope (Table 3.2).

It is clear that LTCI differs by pilot city, and the LTCI systems in China are fragmented (Yang et al., 2016; Dai & Yu, 2021). The main reason is that central and local governments implement fiscal and administrative decentralization. Due to the different levels of economic growth and social development in various regions, the central government no longer manages all local affairs, allowing local governments to pilot some policies first; if a policy succeeds, then it is promoted nationwide.

In the case of the LTCI in 15 pilot cities, 60% of the pilot cities covered urban employees and urban residents, while fewer rural residents were covered. Most of the pilot cities benefited from severely disabled elderly people, and most of the elderly with moderate and mild disabilities and dementia were not included. The LTCI funds were established by multiple channels: the medical insurance fund, individual contributions, government subsidies, and welfare lotteries. Employers do not pay LTCI contributions, and the government's financial support is small. The level of nursing treatment in most pilot cities was lower than the average. Half of the pilot cities only provided daily nursing services. Nearly 70% of pilot cities provide community-based care and institutional care, and home-based care is insufficient. Moreover, nearly half of the pilot cities paid nursing service expenses in a narrow range of nursing services.

3.4 Conclusions

In urban China, the labor insurance medical system and publicly funded medical system were implemented during the planned economy period. People with urban *hukou* were mostly covered by public medical insurance, thereby achieving the policy goal of universal medical insurance in urban areas. However, labor insurance medical systems and publicly funded medical systems were close to free medical care. Thus, problems such as over-supply of healthcare services were severe, and medical care expenditure increased drastically.

Table 3.2 Comparison of LTCI in 15 pilot cities

	Coverage			Fund			Benefit object			Benefit level			Service			Care type			Benefit content		
Pilot city	All	U	E	One	Two	More	I	II	III	H	M	L	I	II	III	I	II	III	I	II	III
Qiqihaer			○		○		○					○	○				○		○		
Changchun		○		○			○			○				○		○					○
Chengde			○			○	○				○		○				○		○		
Qingdao	○				○			○		○				○				○		○	
Shanghai	○					○	○			○					○		○		○		
Nantong	○					○	○			○			○				○				○
Suzhou	○				○		○					○			○		○				○
Ningbo			○	○			○					○	○				○		○		
Guangzhou			○	○				○		○					○		○				○
Anqing			○		○		○					○	○					○			○
Shangyao			○			○	○					○	○					○			○
Jinmen	○					○	○			○					○		○				○
Chongqing			○		○		○				○				○	○			○		
Chengdu			○		○		○				○				○			○		○	

(continued)

Table 3.2 (continued)

	Coverage			Fund			Benefit object			Benefit level			Service			Care type			Benefit content		
Pilot city	All	U	E	One	Two	More	I	II	III	H	M	L	I	II	III	I	II	III	I	II	III
Shiherzi		○				○	○			○			○					○	○		

Source Creation by author referring to Dai and Yu (2021) (pp. 59–60, Table 1) and published LTCI regulations by each city government

Note

(1) Coverage: All participants in public medical insurance; U: participants in the UEBMI or the URBMI; E: participants in the UEBMI

(2) Fund: One: social pooling fund of medical care insurance; Two: social pooling and personal account; More: social pooling fund, personal account, government subsidy, and other

(3) Benefit object: I: severely disabled; II: moderately and severely disabled; III: mildly disabled

(4) Benefit level: H: payment rate by LTCI is higher than 70%; M: payment rate is equal to 70%; L: payment rate is lower than 70%

(5) Enjoy service: I: daily life nursing; II: basic medical nursing and rehabilitation nursing; III: including both I and II

(6) Care type: I: institutional care; II institutional care and community-based care service center; III: home-based care, institutional care, and community-based care service center

(7) Benefit content: I: payment for LTC expenses; II: payment for expenses including equipment usage, related consumables, and nursing service; III: all expenses for treatment, medicines, equipment usage, consumables, beds, nursing services, etc.

To address these problems, the government implemented a reform on public medical insurance during the market-oriented reform period. Specifically, the UEBMI was implemented on December 14, 1998, and the URBMI was promoted on July 10, 2007. Currently, all employees, as well as retirees and unemployed individuals, with urban *hukou* are covered by the public medical insurances, and the universal medical insurance is maintained for urban residents in China. However, large differences are observed between the UEBMI and the URBMI in terms of funding, contents of healthcare services, and payment of medical care expenses. Public medical insurance in urban China has encountered a number of problems, such as inequality in employment sectors. Chap. 4 of this book will provide a detailed discussion of the issues in public medical insurance.

It should be noted that, since 2016, the government has enforced the establishment of LTCI in pilot areas. The number of pilot areas (i.e., cities in provinces) increased to 49 by 2021. However, the institutional design differs per pilot area, and a large institutional fragmentation in LTCI exists (Sun & Xie, 2016). Therefore, integrating these LTCIs and establishing a unified LTCI by considering the balance between benefits and funds has become an important issue for the Chinese government. In particular, to reduce new medical care inequality—the LTC inequality between urban and rural areas—the establishment of a unified LTCI covering both urban and rural residents should be discussed.

Notes

1. The work unit refers to the workplace, including government organizations and corporates (e.g., state-owned, privately owned, foreign-owned enterprises) in China.
2. For a review survey of LTC systems in different countries (e.g., Japan, Germany, Korea, and France), please refer to Chen et al. (2020).
3. Participants in the URBMI are classified into three types, namely, Type I adults, Type II adults, and university students, depending on the amount of insurance premiums paid. The annual premium in 2017 was 370 yuan for Type I adults, 175 yuan for Type II adults, and 110 yuan for university students.
4. Home-based care refers to nursing services provided by designated nursing facilities during the home life of disabled persons; institutional care is a medical care facility (e.g., hospital, nursing facility, and elderly care institution); and daily care is a day care service provided by designated nursing facilities for the disabled and demented persons within the facility. The insured persons can choose the appropriate types of nursing service themselves. Regarding the relative shortage of resources in nursing institutions, the government encourages insured persons to use home-based care and daily nursing services. Additionally, to meet the needs of diversified care services for disabled persons, "Assistive Device Rental" service security items have been added to the new policy, and specific measures are being formulated.

Appendix

See Table 3.3.

Table 3.3 Government policies and events on public medical insurance systems in urban areas from 1949 to 2021

Year	Policy or event	Main content
February 26, 1951	The State Council promulgated "*The People's Republic of China' Labor Insurance Regulations*"	The labor insurance system has been implemented in case of illness, non-work-related injury and disability policy, called "Labor Insurance Medical Care."
June 27, 1952	The State Council promulgated the "*Instructions of the Government Affairs Council of the Central People's Government on the Implementation of Publicly Funded Medical Prevention System for State Staff in People's Governments, Parties, Organizations, and Affiliated institutions.*"	Decided to implement a publicly funded medical system for civil servants
August 30, 1952	The Ministry of Health issued the "*Measures for the Implementation of Public-funded Medical Security for Civil Servants.*"	Officially began to implement the publicly funded medical system
Jane 9, 1953	The State Council promulgated the "*Decision on Several Amendments to the Labor Insurance Regulations of the People's Republic of China.*"	Expand the scope of labor insurance, though its targets were still limited to employees in state-owned enterprises and collectively owned enterprises
March 4, 1989	The State Council issued the "*Key Points of the Economic System Reform of the National Economic Reform Commission in 1989.*"	It was proposed to conduct pilot reforms of the medical insurance system in Dandong City in Liaoning province, Sipping City in Jilin Province, Huangshi in City Hubei Province, and Zhuzhou City in Hunan province, while conducting comprehensive reform pilots of the social security system in Shenzhen City and Hainan Province. This is the Chinese government's first medical insurance system trial
September 7, 1992	The Ministry of Labor issued the "*Notice on the Trial Implementation of Social Pooling of Medical Expenses for Serious Illnesses.*"	Began to explore the establishment of a pooling fund system to ensure the employees' medical treatment of serious illnesses

(continued)

Table 3.3 (continued)

Year	Policy or event	Main content
November 14, 1993	The Third Plenary Session of the 14th Central Committee of the Communist Party of China passed the "*Decisions on Several Issues of the Socialist Market Economic System.*"	It was proposed that we will establish a multi-level social security system. The contributions of pension and medical insurance for urban employees will be shared by the employers and the employees, and the combination of social pooling and personal accounts will be implemented
April 14, 1994	The National Economic Reform Commission, the Ministry of Finance, Health, and Labor jointly issued the "*Opinions on the Pilot Reform of the Employee Medical Insurance System.*"	Propose a pilot project to establish a social medical insurance that combines social pooling and personal accounts, and explore the establishment of the UEBMI
1995	Zhenjiang City and Jiujiang City officially began the pilot work of reforming the employee medical insurance system	Began to explore the establishment of the UEBMI
March 5, 1996	The General Office of the State Council issued the "*Opinions on the Expansion of the Pilot Reform of the Employee Medical Security System*"	On the basis of summarizing the experiences of "*Liangjiang*" pilot project, the scope of the pilot medical insurance reform was expanded to more than 40 cities in more than 20 provinces
December 14, 1998	The State Council issued the "*Decision on Establishing an Urban Employee Basic Medical Insurance System.*"	The establishment of the UEBMI marks the end of the publicly funded and labor insurance medical system that has been implemented for more than 40 years. The public medical system began to transform from government and enterprise medical security to social medical insurance
May 26, 2003	The Ministry of Labor and Social Security issued the "*Guiding Opinions on the Participation of Basic Medical Insurance for Urban Flexible Workers.*"	Flexible workers were included in the scope of medical insurance, with expanded coverage
July 10, 2007	The State Council issued the "*Guiding Opinions on the Pilot Program of Urban Resident Basic Medical Insurance.*"	A pilot program of the URBMI was proposed, and it began to be established nationwide

(continued)

Table 3.3 (continued)

Year	Policy or event	Main content
October 25, 2008	The General Office of the State Council issued the "*Guiding Opinions on Including College Students into the Pilot Scope of Urban Resident Basic Medical Insurance.*"	It was proposed that, college students should be included in the pilot coverage of the URBMI
October 28, 2010	The 17th meeting of the Standing Committee of the 11th National People's Congress passed the "*Social Insurance Law of the People's Republic of China.*"	The UEBMI, and NRCMS have been upgraded to legal systems, causing that the social insurance system including medical insurance, to move from an experimental stage to a finalized, stable, and sustainable development stage
August 24, 2012	Six ministries and commissions, including the National Development and Reform Commission, jointly issued the "*Guiding Opinions on Carrying out Serious Illness Medical Insurance for Urban and Rural Residents.*"	Begin to establish a serious illness medical insurance system for urban and rural residents
March 5, 2013	The State Council issued the *State Council Government Work Report*	It was officially announced that "The universal basic medical insurance system has been established initially, with more than 1.3 billion people participating in public medical insurances, and universal medical insurance system has basically been established."
May 1, 2014	The "*Interim Measures for Social Assistance*" came into effect	It stipulates that the government will establish a medical aid system to ensure that recipients can receive basic healthcare services. To support persons in extreme poverty and recipients of medical aid system, the government subsidies for medical insurance pooling fund will be provided
April 21, 2015	The General Office of the State Council issued "*Notice on the Opinions on Comprehensively Carrying Out the Medical Assistance Work for Major and Serious Illnesses.*"	Promote the integration of medical aid system in urban and rural areas, and comprehensively carry out the serious illness medical insurance

(continued)

Table 3.3 (continued)

Year	Policy or event	Main content
January 3, 2016	The State Council issued the "*Opinions on Implementation on Integrating the Basic Medical Insurance System for Urban and Rural Residents*"	Promote the integration of the URBMI and the NRCMS
January 27, 2016	The General Office of the Ministry of Human Resources and Social Security issued the "*Guiding Opinions on the Pilot Program of Long-term Care Insurance System.*"	It was proposed to carry out long-term care insurance pilot projects, and 15 cities and two key contact provinces of Jilin and Shandong provinces were designated as the long-term care insurance pilot areas
June 19, 2017	The General Office of the State Council issued the "*Notice on the Implementation of the Pilot Plan for Integration of Maternity Insurance and Employee Basic Medical Insurance.*"	12 cities were designated as pilot projects for the project of integration of the maternity insurance and the UEBMI
June 20, 2017	The General Office of the State Council issued the "*Guiding Opinions on Further Deepening the Reform of Payment Methods in Basic Medical Insurance.*"	It was proposed to comprehensively establish and continuously improve a medical insurance payment system that conforms to national conditions of healthcare services
March 13, 2018	The State Council issued the *The State Council's institutional reform plan*	The National Medical Security Bureau, as an agency directly under the State Council, was established
February 25, 2020	The State Council issued the "*Opinions of the Central Committee of the Communist Party of China and the State Council on Deepening the Reform of the Medical Security System.*"	Clarify the blueprint for the development of medical insurance by 2025 and 2030, and put forward the "1 + 4 + 2" overall reform framework. This is the first top-level design specially formulated by the Party Central Committee and the State Council, for the reform of the medical insurance system, since the foundation of the PRC
September 10, 2020	The National Medical Insurance Administration and the Ministry of Finance jointly issued the "*Guiding Opinions on Expanding the Pilot Program of the Long-term Care Insurance System.*"	14 new cities were added to the pilot city list to expand the pilot project of LTCI
February 19, 2021	The State Council promulgated the first administrative regulation of the National Medical Security System "*Regulations on the Supervision and Administration of the Use of Medical Security Funds.*"	This law became the basis for the legalization of the medical insurance system. It came into effect on May 1, 2021

(continued)

Table 3.3 (continued)

Year	Policy or event	Main content
April 13, 2021	The General Office of the State Council issued the "*Guiding Opinions on Establishing and Improving the Outpatient Mutual Assistance Mechanism of Employee Basic Medical Insurance*"	It is required to establish and improve the pooling insurance mechanism of general outpatients in the UEBMI, reform personal accounts, and improve the payment mechanism compatible with the outpatient mutual assistance system

Source Created by the author based on government regulations, Han (2014), Feng (2021), and Guo and Zhang (2021)
Note UEBMI: urban employee basic medical insurance; URBMI: urban resident basic medical Insurance; NRCMS: new rural cooperative medical scheme; LTCI: long-term care insurance; PRC: People' Republic of China

References

Chen, L., Zhang, L., & Xu, X. (2020). Review of evolution of the public long-term care insurance (LTCI) system in different countries: Influence and challenge. *BMC Health Services Research, 20*(1057), 33218328.

Dai, W., & Yu, Y. (2021). The fragmentation and integration of the pilot policies of China' long-term care insurance system. *Journal of Jiangxi University of Finance and Economics, 2*(134), 55–65. (in Chinese).

Dong, Z., Li, Y., & Zhang, Y. (2019). Policy analysis and path improvement of long-term care insurance pilot program in Chengde City, Hebei Province. *Labor Security World, 9*, 43–44 and 50. (in Chinese).

Feng, P. (2021). From 1921 to 2021: A glimpse of China's medical insurance and commercial health insurance for a century. *Shanghai Insurance, 7*, 16–122. (in Chinese).

Guo, X., & Zhang, R. (2021). Memorabilia of 100 Years of Medical Insurance. *China Health Insurance, 7*, 16–21. (in Chinese).

Han, F. (2014). The historical evolution of medical insurance system in China. *China Medical Insurance, 6*, 20–24. (in Chinese).

Li, Y., & Ming, T. (2020). The financing mechanism of long-term care insurance: Practice, dilemma and countermeasures based on the analysis of 15 pilot cities' policies. *Financial Theory and Practice, 2*, 97–103. (in Chinese).

Lu, S., & Wu, J. (2015). Long-term care insurance in Qingdao: System effectiveness, implementation dilemma and policy optimization. *China Health Economic, 35*(8), 30–32. (in Chinese).

Ministry of Labor and Social Security Literature Research Office of the Central Committee of the Communist Party of China. (2002). *A selection of important documents on labor and social security in the new era*. China Labor and Social Security Press. (in Chinese).

Sheng, Z., Her, B., & Zhu, L. (2020). The pilot study of long-term care insurance system in Suzhou. *Chinese Medical Insurance, 2*, 37–40. (in Chinese).

Song, X. (2006). *Reform: Enterprise, labor and social security*. Social Science Literature Press. (in Chinese).

Song, X. (2009). Retrospect and prospect of China's medical insurance system in the 60 years since the founding of the People's Republic of China. *Chinese Journal of Health Policy, 2*(19), 6–14. (in Chinese).

Sun, J., & Xie, J. (2016). The divergence and policy recommendations of China's long-term care insurance financing and security policies: Based on the comparison of pilot schemes in 15 pilot cities. *Economic Affairs, 4*, 54–63. (in Chinese).

Wang, D. (2018). Policy framework, strategy, and institutional arrangement. In E. Glinskaya & Z. Feng (Eds.), *Options for aged care in China: Building an efficient and sustainable aged care system*. Washington DC: World Bank.

Yang, W., He, A., Fang, L., & Mossialos, E. (2016). Financing institutional long-term care for the elderly in China: A policy evaluation of new models. *Health Policy and Planning, 31*, 1391–1401.

Zhao, X. (2015). Qingdao: The latest operation status and evaluation of the long-term care insurance system price. *China Social Security, 35*(8), 30–32. (in Chinese).

Zou, C., Tian, Y., Xu, B., Sun, C., Yuan, B., Zhao, H., & Song, J. (2018). Historical evolution of the development of Chinese medical insurance system (1949–1978): Discussion on the history healthcare policy. *Medicine and Philosophy, 39*(6), 81–86. (in Chinese).

Chapter 4
Issues of Public Medical Insurance Reform in China

Abstract Using official data published by the Chinese government and survey data, this chapter reveals the problems of public medical insurance in China. This chapter mainly focuses on four issues: disparities between urban and rural areas, disparities between provinces, disparities in medical insurance coverage according to the income group, and disparities according to the employment sector (state-owned sector vs. non-state-owned sector), which are related to inequality in medical care.

Keywords Public medical insurance · Regional disparity · Employment sector · Income inequality · China

4.1 Introduction

The Chinese government has reformed public medical insurance since 1990. The government established and implemented the Urban Employment Basic Medical Insurance (UEBMI), the Urban Residents Basic Medical Insurance (URBMI), and the New Rural Cooperative Medical Scheme (NRCMS) as public medical insurances. Since 2017, the government promoted the integration of the URBMI and NRCMS to Urban and Rural Resident Basic Medical Insurance (URRBMI). These public medical insurances cover the entire population. Moreover, public medical insurance reforms aim to establish a universal medical insurance. However, because the medical insurance in China was established based on the conventional labor insurance medical care system, the publicly funded medical system, and the cooperative medical system (CMS) under the planned economy period, the operations of these schemes were conducted by the regional and varied employment sectors (e.g., state-owned sector, no-state-owned sector). Further, the benefits, medical insurance funds, and management between urban and rural areas differ. There maintain many problems in current public medical insurances in China.

This chapter uses official data published by the Chinese government and survey data collected by research institutes to discuss the problems in public medical insurance in China, while focusing on four issues: (i) disparities between urban and rural areas, (ii) disparities between provinces, (iii) disparities in medical insurance

X. Ma, *Public Medical Insurance Reforms in China*,
https://doi.org/10.1007/978-981-16-7790-8_4

coverage according to the income group, and (iv) disparities according to the employment sector (state-owned sector vs. non-stated-owned sector), which are related to inequality in medical care.

4.2 The Coverage of Public Medical Insurances in China

4.2.1 The Coverage of Public Medical Insurances in Urban China

Figure 4.1 shows the number of the UEBMI participants in urban China from 1994 to 2019. The UBEMI was implemented in1994 in pilot cities. After the implementation of the UEBMI in 1998 in entire urban areas, the total number of participants increased from 18.8 million in 1998 to 329.2 million in 2019; the enrollment rate increased from 5.29% in 1998 to 52.74% in 2019. However, it is important to note that in the future, as the population ages, the number of active workers will decrease while that of retirees will increase significantly; consequently, the number of beneficiaries and that of insurance payers will simultaneously increase and decrease, respectively. It is predicted that in the future, the Chinese government will suffer a insufficiency of medical insurance funds as in the presently developed countries, such as Japan.

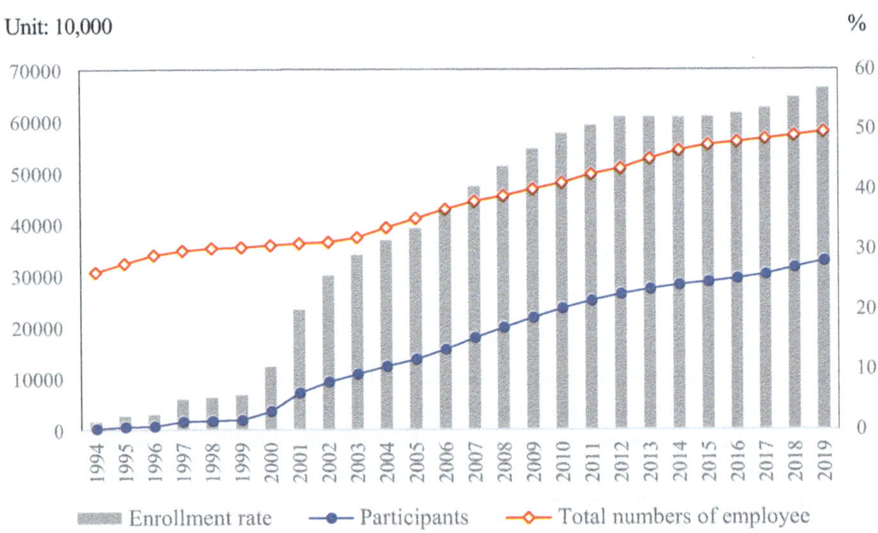

Fig. 4.1 Number of participants and enrollment rate of the UEBMI (1994–2019). *Source* Created by the author based on the data from *China Statistical Yearbook 2020*. *Note* Enrollment rate = number of participants of the UEBMI/total number of employees in secondary and tertiary industry

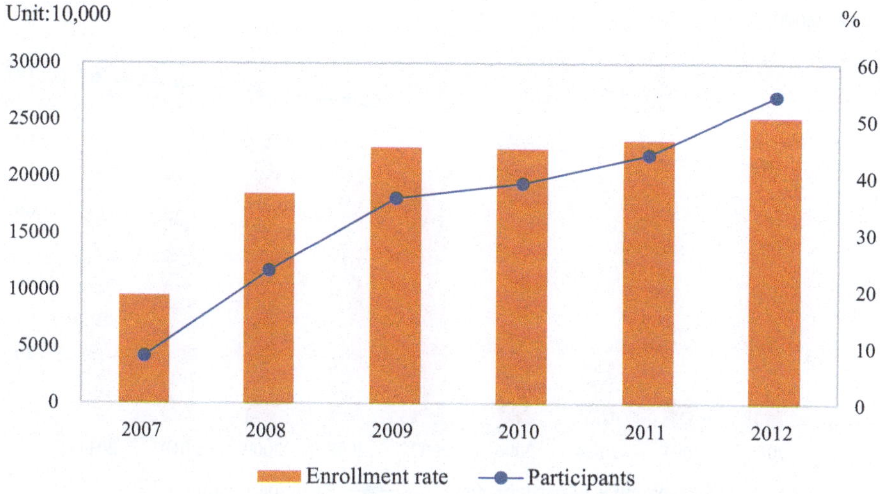

Fig. 4.2 Number of participants in the URBMI (2007–2012). *Source* Created by the author based on the data from *2012 China Hygiene Statistical Yearbook, China Statistical Yearbook 2012 and 2012 Labor and Social Security Business Development Statistics Bulletin*

Figure 4.2 summarizes the status of enrolling in the URBMI from 2007 to 2012. Enrolling in the URBMI is voluntary. However, the number of participants has increased annually, from 42.91 million in 2007 when the system was first implemented, to 271.56 million in 2012; the enrollment rate increased from 19.2% in 2007 to 50.9% in 2012.

4.2.2 The Coverage of Public Medical Insurances in Rural China

Figure 4.3 shows the changes in the number of participants and the enrollment rate in the NRCMS, which was implemented in 2003. The number of participants increased significantly, that is, from 179 million in 2005 to 823 million in 2011. Further, the enrollment rate (the ratio of the number of participants in the region where the NRCMS was implemented to the total number of rural residents in the region) increased significantly, that is from 75.7% in 2005 to 97.5% in 2011. Currently, the NRCMS covers almost all rural residents. Moreover, the enrollment rate is approximately 100%. NRCMS covers almost all rural residents. Moreover, the enrollment rate is approximately 100%.

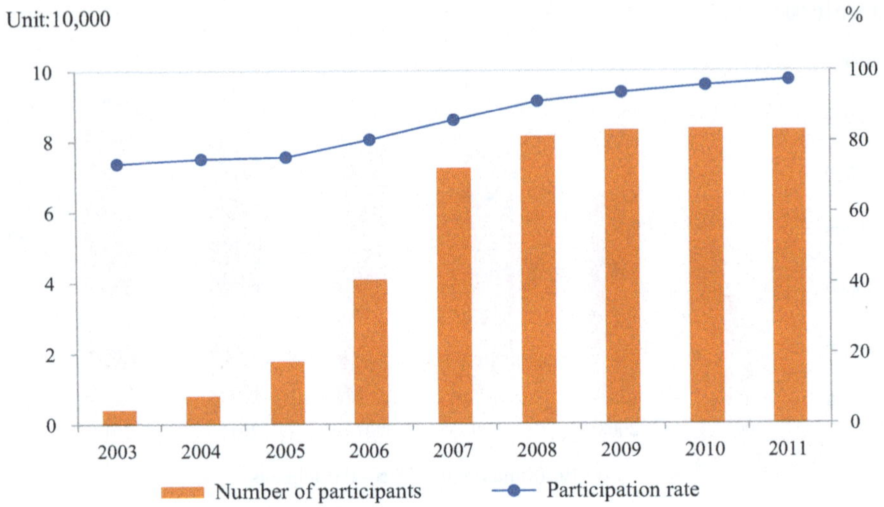

Fig. 4.3 Number of Participants in the NRCMS (2003–2011). *Source* Created by the author based on the data from *China Hygiene Statistical Yearbook of 2008 and 2011*

4.2.3 The Coverage of Public Medical Insurance Throughout China

The above sections focus on the coverage status of the UEBMI and the URBMI in urban areas and the NRCMS in rural areas, respectively. However, some individuals joined the NRCMS in urban areas (e.g., rural–urban migrants), while others joined the UEBMI in rural areas (e.g., workers who have urban *hukou* and are working in non-agriculture in rural areas). Additionally, some people enrolled in private medical insurance in both urban and rural areas. Table 4.1 summarizes the proportion of the members according to the type of medical insurance in consideration of these situations from a nationwide perspective of China.

Based on the Chinese nationwide statistics, in 2011, the proportion of the medical insurance participants was the highest, at 69.5% for the NRCMS. This was followed by proportions of 15.5% and 9.5% of the participants of the UEBMI and URBMI, respectively. The non-participants accounted for only 0.3%.

Further, the proportions of the participants of the UEBMI and URBMI were high at 49.6% and 25.1%, respectively, in urban areas, while that of the participants of the NRCMS was the highest at 89.9% in rural areas. It was shown that the enrollment status in various types of medical insurance between urban and rural areas differs.

The proportion of non-participants under any medical insurance nationwide decreased from 12.9% in 2008 to 5.2% in 2011. In the urban areas, the proportion decreased from 28.1% in 2008 to 10.9% in 2011, and in rural areas, it decreased from 7.5% in 2008 to 3.1% in 2011. The proportion of non-participant in medical

Table 4.1 Proportion of participants in medical insurances in China nationwide. Unit: %

	Nation		Urban		Rural	
	2008	2011	2008	2011	2008	2011
UEBMI	12.7	14.8	44.2	47.4	1.5	2.9
Publicly funded medical system	1.0	0.7	3.0	2.2	0.3	0.2
URBMI	3.8	9.5	12.5	25.1	0.7	3.8
NRCMS	68.7	69.5	9.5	13.4	89.7	89.9
Other insurance	1.0	0.3	2.8	0.9	0.4	0.1
Non-participation	12.8	5.2	28.0	11.0	7.4	3.1
Total	100.0	100.0	100.0	100.0	100.0	100.0

Source Created by the author based on the data from *China Medical Service Survey* of 2008 and *Medical Reform Evaluation Survey* of 2011
Note Other medical insurance: Commercial medical insurance, corporate subsidy insurance

insurance has decreased in recent years but is observed to be slightly higher in urban areas than in rural areas.

These results suggest that after the implementation of the UEBMI for urban workers, the URBMI for urban residents who did not join the UEBMI or the NRCMS, the number of participants increased significantly. The enrollment rate also increased over the years. The public medical insurance system implemented in China covers the entire population. Therefore, it can be concluded that the objective of universal medical insurance has been achieved in system designs. However, there are various problems in the operation of these schemes. The following section discusses these issues.

Figure 4.4 shows the changes in the number of participants of URRBMI and UEBMI and the total enrollment rate from 2007 to 2019. The number of participants of the URRBMI increased significantly, that is, from 184 million in 2007 to 1,354 million in 2019; the number of participants of the UEBMI increased from 180 million in 2007 to 329 million in 2019. Further, the total enrollment rate (the ratio of the number of participants of URRBMI and UEBMI to the total number of population) increased significantly, that is from 14.0% in 2007 to 96.7% in 2019. Currently, the public medical insurance covers almost all population in China, the enrollment rate is approximately 100%.

4.3 Issues in Public Medical Insurances in China

Regarding the current public medical insurance, problems such as inadequate individual account systems, insufficient medical insurance funds, and operation problems have been indicated.[1] This section mainly focuses on other three issues: (i) disparities between urban and rural areas; (ii) disparities between provinces; (iii) income

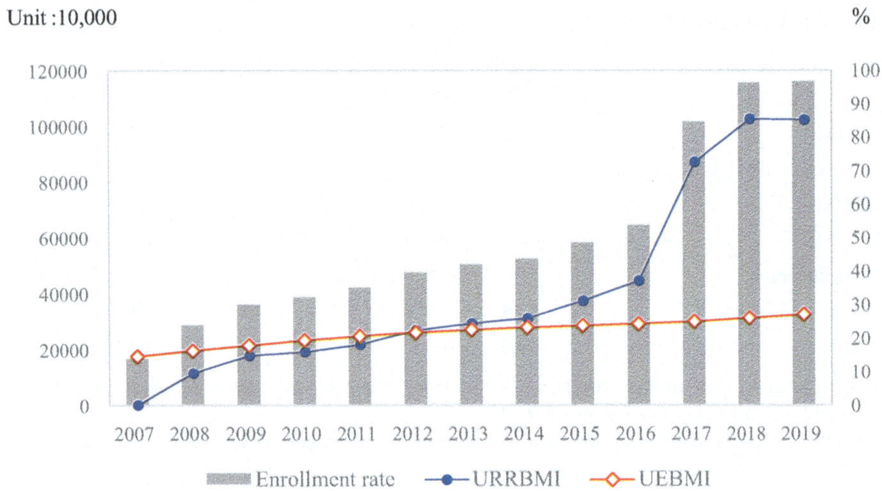

Fig. 4.4 Number of Participants in the public medical insurance (2007–2019). *Source* Created by the author based on the data from *China Statistical Yearbook 2020*. *Note* Enrollment rate = number of participants of URRBMI and UEBMI/total number of population

inequality and disparities in enrolling in public medical insurance; and (iii) disparities in medical insurance coverage between employment sectors, which is further related to the inequality in medical care, which the government should take heed of.

4.3.1 *Disparities Between Urban and Rural Areas*

(1) **Evidence Based on Government Official Data**

China's social security system, including public medical insurance, is divided according to the household registration (*hukou*) system. During the planned economy period, the government implemented a policy prioritizing the development of a heavy industry for military defense and modernization. To promote the development of the heavy industry sector located in urban areas, the government implemented a high welfare and low wage system for urban workers. Additionally, to guarantee the employment and social welfare of urban workers, a *hukou* system, which separated the rural and urban areas in China, was further implemented in 1958. *The hukou* system prevented people with rural *hukou* from moving to urban areas to work without government permission. Since the 1980s, a section of *the hukou* system has been deregulated and the number of migrant workers has gradually increased. However, the gap between rural and urban areas is still large in terms of income and consumption levels and social security (Ma, 2015; Peng & Yue, 2020; Tian, 2019; Wang et al., 2019; Yu, 2020). These conditions are confirmed below based on official statistical data.

Figure 4.5 shows changes in annual household income per capita in urban and rural areas. Over the years, income per capita has increased in both rural and urban areas. The range of increase is, however, larger in urban areas than in rural areas. Therefore, the income inequality between urban and rural areas is increasing. For example, when the ratio of urban to rural income per capita is used to indicate income inequality between urban and rural areas, the income inequality decreased from 2.56 times in 1978 to 1.82 times in 1983. The inequality further increased by 2.64 times in 2019.

Regarding the change in the population in urban and rural areas (see Fig. 4.6), before 2010, the rural population was larger than the urban population. Since 2010, the urban population has slightly increased than the rural population. However, the amount of medical insurance funds, including individual insurance contributions and government subsidies, is significantly higher in urban areas than in rural areas (see Fig. 4.7). For example, in 2010, the medical insurance fund was 395.54 billion yuan in urban areas, which was about three times that of rural areas (13.83 billion yuan). The public medical insurance expenditure totals 327.16 billion yuan in urban areas and 118.78 billion yuan in rural areas, which is 36.6% of that in urban areas. Evidently, the financial support of public medical insurance between urban and rural areas differs significantly.

Figure 4.8 displays the expenditure per capita on medical care in urban and rural areas. The medical care expenditure increased from 1990 to 2012. It was however lower in rural areas than in urban areas. The difference in the medical care expenditure between urban and rural areas increased from 1.35 (1990) to 3.63 (2000) times from 1990 to 2000. The difference narrowed slightly. In 2012, the per capita expenditure on medical care in urban areas was approximately twice as large as that in rural areas.

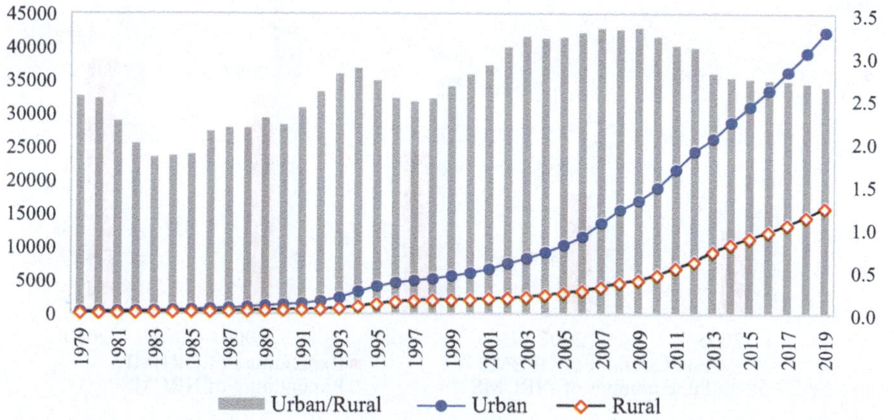

Fig. 4.5 Income inequality between urban and rural areas (1979–2019). *Source* Created by the author based on the data from *China Statistical Yearbook 2020*. *Note* Urban: disposable household income per capita; rural: net household income per capita

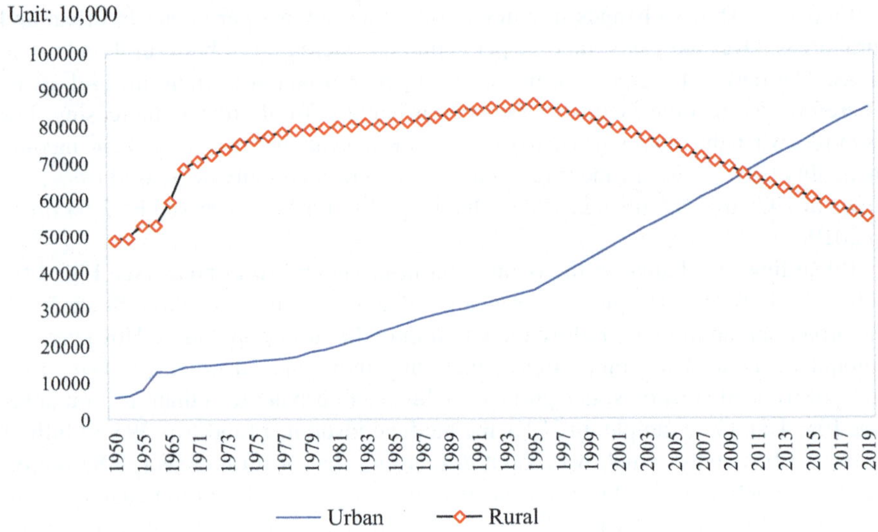

Fig. 4.6 Population in urban and rural areas (1950–2019). *Source* Created by the author based on the data from *China Statistical Yearbook 2020*. *Note*: (1) Data before 1981: hukou statistical data; data of 1982, 1990, 2000, 2010: China Population Census; other data: China Population Sampling Census. (2) Includes active military personnel (counted as urban population)

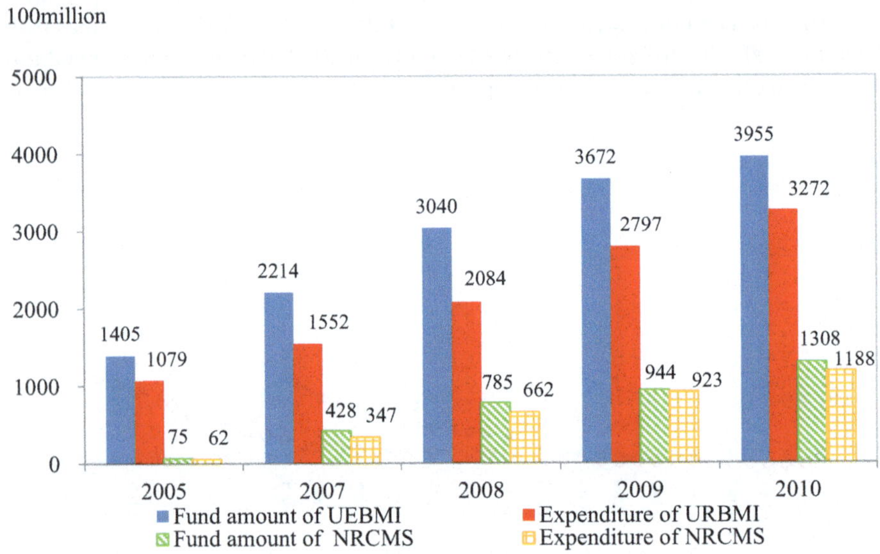

Fig. 4.7 Differences of medical insurance fund between urban and rural areas (2005–2010). *Source* Created by the author based on the data from *China Hygiene Statistical Yearbook 2012* and *China Statistical Yearbook 2012*

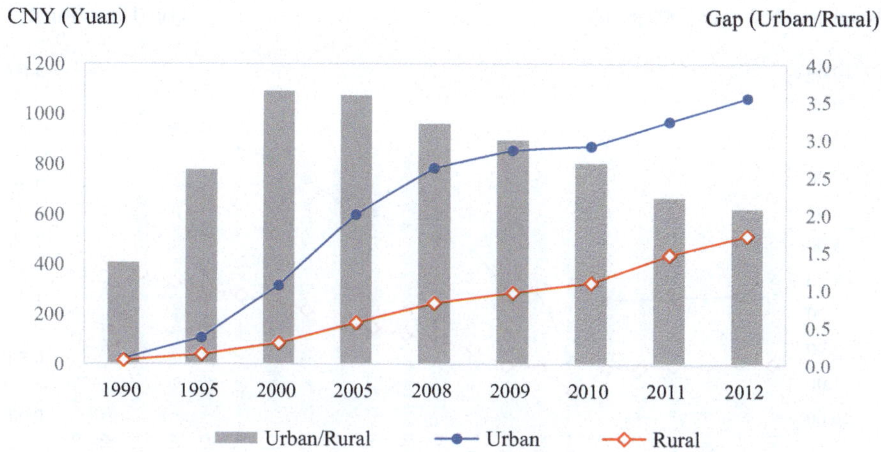

Fig. 4.8 Expenditure per capita on medical care in urban and rural areas (1990–2012). *Source* Created by the author based on the data from *China Hygiene Statistical Yearbook 2012* and *China Statistical Yearbook 2013*. *Note* Nominal value of expenditure for medical care in each year is used

This means that the inequality in medical care expenditures between the two areas was and is still large.

The difference in the expenditure per capita on medical care between urban and rural areas (Fig. 4.8) may be attributed to: (i) The income inequality between urban and rural areas shown in Fig. 4.5; (ii) the difference in the system design of public medical insurance between urban and rural residents, such as the difference in medical insurance funds between these two areas, as shown in Fig. 4.7; and (iii) the difference in the supply of healthcare services between urban and rural areas.

Figure 4.9 shows the number of beds per 1,000 people in hospitals or clinics in urban and rural areas. The number of beds is higher in urban areas than in rural areas between 1990 and 2019. Currently, the difference in the number of beds between the two areas has slightly decreased. However, the number of hospital beds in urban areas is twice as large as that in rural areas. Figures 4.10 and 4.11 shows the number of doctors and nurses per 1,000 people in urban and rural areas. The numbers of both doctors and nurses are higher for urban areas than for rural areas between 1980 and 2019. Furthermore, since 2014, the difference between the two areas has decreased slightly. However, as of 2019, the difference is still large; the numbers of doctors and nurses in urban areas are 2 times higher than that in rural areas. The results in Figs. 4.9, 4.10, and 4.11 suggest that the supply of healthcare services between urban and rural areas differ significantly, which may enlarge the inequality of medical care between the two areas.

Consequently, the health status of urban and rural residents differs. Table 4.2 shows the mortality rate in urban and rural areas. From 1991 to 2019, the maternal, under-five, infant, and newborn mortality rates have decreased for both urban and rural residents; the decrease is particularly greater for rural residents than for urban

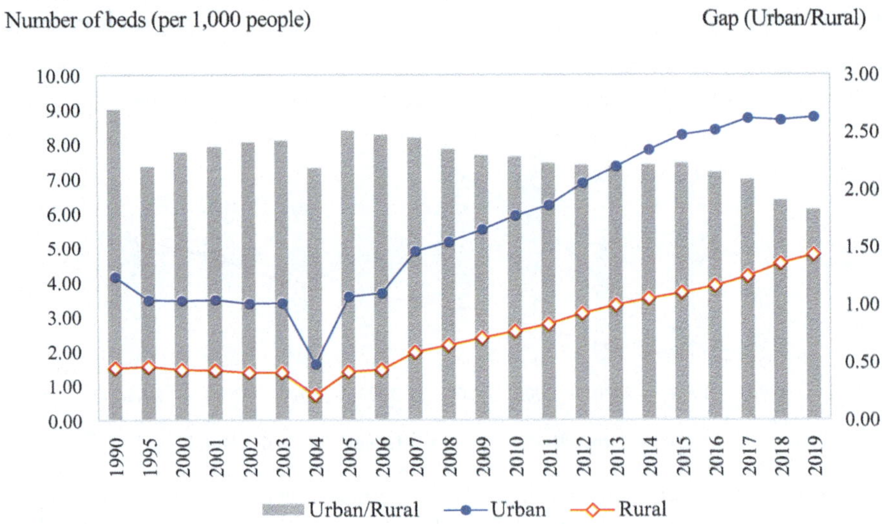

Fig. 4.9 Number of hospital beds per 1,000 people in rural and urban areas (1990–2019). *Source* Created by the author based on the data from *China Statistical Yearbook 2020*

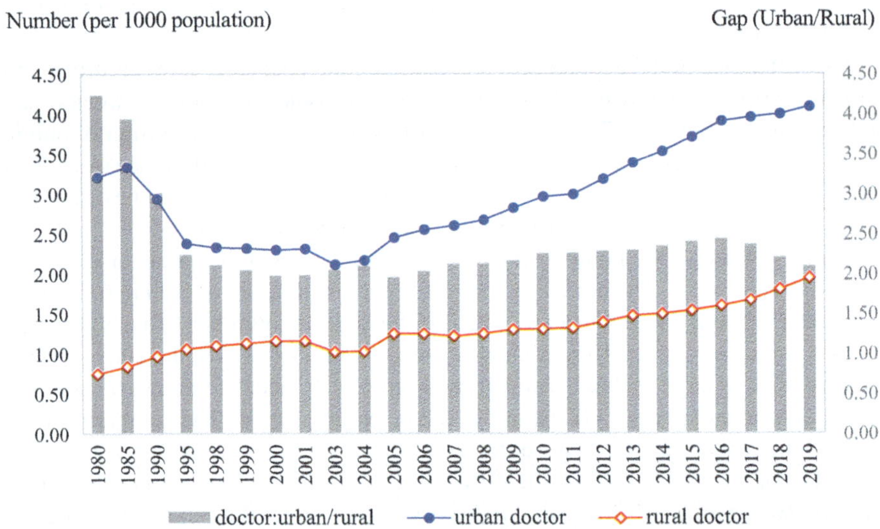

Fig. 4.10 Number of doctors in urban and rural areas (1980–2019). *Source* Created by the author based on the data from *China Statistical Yearbook 2020*

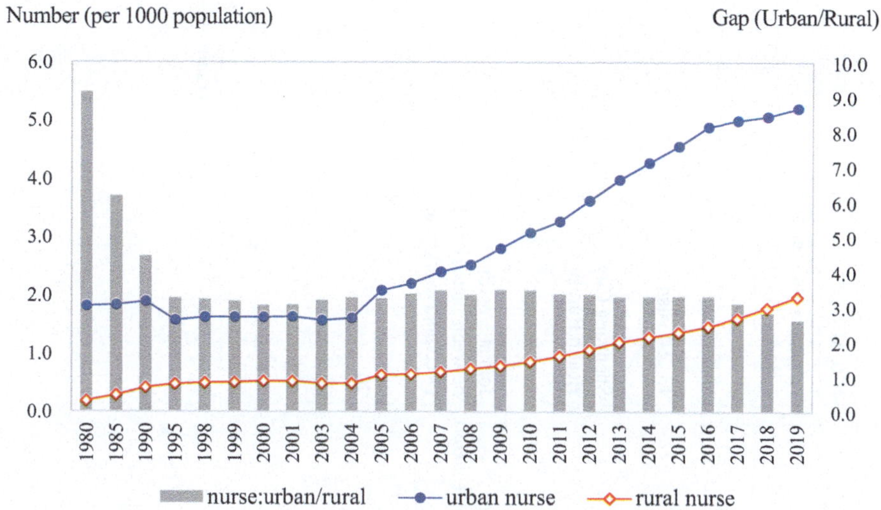

Fig. 4.11 Number of nurses in urban and rural areas (1980–2019). *Source* Created by the author based on the data from *China Statistical Yearbook 2020*

Table 4.2 Mortality rate in urban and rural areas (1991, 2000, 2010, and 2019)

	1991		2000		2010		2019	
	U	R	U	R	U	R	U	R
Maternal mortality rate (per 100,000 people)	46.3	100.0	29.3	69.6	29.7	30.1	16.5	18.6
Child mortality rate under 5 years old (per 1,000 people)	20.9	71.1	13.8	45.7	7.3	20.1	4.1	9.4
Infant mortality rate (per 1,000 people)	17.3	58.0	11.8	37.0	5.8	16.1	3.4	6.6
Newborn mortality rate (per 1,000 people)	12.5	37.9	9.5	25.8	4.1	10.0	2.0	4.1

Source Created by the author based on the data from *China Statistical Yearbook 2020*
Note U: urban; R: rural

residents. However, these mortality rates are higher for rural residents than for urban residents even in the current period; for example, in 2019, the under-five mortality rate of rural areas was 9.4 per 1,000 people, which is almost 2.3 times that of urban areas (4.1 per 1,000 people). This indicates that disparities in health status between urban and rural areas are still large in China.

(2) **Case Study of Shenyang City**

Table 4.3 summarizes the URCMS and the NRCMS implemented in Shenyang City Liaoning province, located in the Chinese Northeastern region.

Table 4.3 URBMI and NRCMS in Shenyang City in 2013

	URBMI				NRCMS	
Eligible	Elderly	Non-working	Aged under 18 and student	Children	Residents with rural *hukou*	
		Male aged 18–60				
		Female aged 18–55				
Annual income per capita (2012)		26,341 yuan			13,260 yuan	
Administration organization	Shenyang Social Medical Insurance Administration Bureau				Shenyang City Health Bureau	
Enrollment time	Join at any time between January and November every year	Join at any time between January and November every year	For students, unified enrollment depending on school	Household registration (*hukou*) location	Join at any time between January and December every year	
Funds (yuan)						
Individual contribution (yuan)	360	455	50	100	70	
Government subsidy (yuan)	240	240	240	240	280	
Total (yuan)	600	695	290	340	350	

(continued)

Table 4.3 (continued)

	URBMI				NRCMS	
Minimum limit of enjoy benefits (inpatients)						
First-level hospital (yuan)	200	200	100	100	Village designated hospital	0
District second-level hospital (yuan)	300	300	150	150	District designated hospital	0
City second-level hospital (yuan)	400	400	200	200	City designated hospital	500
Third-level hospital (yuan)	600	600	300	300	Province designated hospital	1,000
Third-level special hospital (yuan)	900	900	500	500		
Percentage of expenses paid by insurance						
First-level hospital	90%	90%	90%	90%	Village designated hospital	30% (0–200 yuan) 75% (201–3,000 yuan), 85% (3,001 yuan and above)

(continued)

Table 4.3 (continued)

	URBMI				NRCMS	
District second-level hospital	85%	85%	88%	88%	District designated hospital	30% (0–300 yuan) 70% (301–5,000 yuan) 80% (5,001 yuan and above)
City second-level hospital	80%	80%	85%	85%	City designated hospital	50%
Third-level hospital	75%	75%	78%	78%	Province designated hospital	50%
Third-level special hospital	70%	70%	73%	73%		
Maximum limit of enjoy benefits (inpatient) (thousand yuan)	180	180	225	225	150	

Source Created by the author based on https://www.jil.go.jp/foreign/jihou/2013_7/china_04/html
Information was published by Shenyang Social Medical Insurance Administration Bureau and Shenyang City Health Bureau in 2013

The eligible participants of the URCMS are the elderly and non-working, those aged 18 and under, and children, while the eligible participants of the NRCMS are those with rural *hukou*.

The administration organizations are different for the two insurances. The Shenyang Social Medical Insurance Administration Bureau manages the URBMI, while the Shenyang City Health Bureau manages the NRCMS. People can enroll any day of the year for both the URBMI and the NRCMS.

The medical insurance funds differ by insurance type and group within insurance. The total amounts of individual contributions and government subsidies are higher for the elderly and non-working participants in the URBMI than them in the NRCMS. For example, the individual contribution is 360 yuan, the government subsidy is 240 yuan for the elderly participants in the URBMI, while they are 70 yuan and 280 yuan for them in the NRCMS. In the URBMI, there are differences in the individual contributions between the elderly and unemployed participants (high fund group), and participants aged under 18/students and children (low fund group). It is indicated that there is a large difference in the insurance funds between the URBMI and the NRCMS, and large disparities within the URBMI by group.

Regarding the benefits of insurances, for city second-level and third-level hospitals, the minimum limit of medical care expenses paid by insurances is higher for the URBMI than for the NRCMS, while there is no minimum limit for participants of the NRCMS when they receive treatment in village- and district-designated hospitals. The maximum limit of insurance benefits is 180–225 thousand yuan for participants in the URBMI, which is higher than those in the NRCMS (150 thousand yuan). Moreover, the ratio of out-of-pocket (OOP) expenses is higher for the NRCMS than for the URBMI. For example, if we compare the ratio of OOP expenses between the first-level hospitals in the URBMI and village-designated hospitals in the NRCMS, which are the lowest-level of medical care facilities in urban and rural areas respectively, it is 10% for the URBMI participants, while it is 15–70% for the NRCMS participants. It is clear that the benefit is lower for the NRCMS than for the URBMI, and the ratio of OOP expenses is higher for participants in the NRBMI than those in the URCMS. There is a large insurance benefit disparity by insurance type, which may cause the inequality in utilization of healthcare services between urban and rural residents.

4.3.2 Disparities by Province

Regarding the disparities between provinces in rural areas, Fig. 4.12 shows the disparity between provinces in the NRCMS fund in 2012. The medical insurance funds per capita was higher in Shanghai (987.0 yuan) and Beijing (637.2 yuan), which are well-developed economies, and lower in Guizhou (225.4 yuan) and Anhui (229.8 yuan), which are less-developed economies.

Figure 4.13 shows the disparity in cumulative balance of the UEBMI between provinces in 2018. The insurance fund amount per capita was high in Beijing (7,422.2

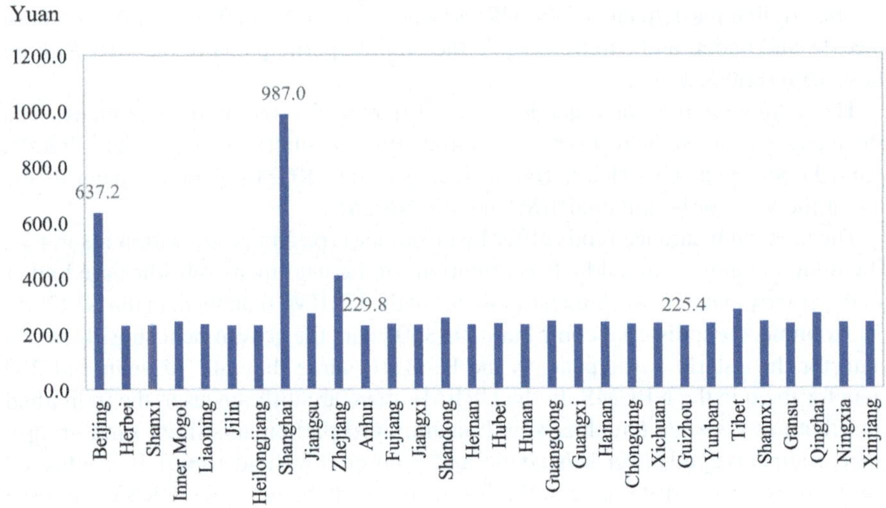

Fig. 4.12 Disparity between provinces in medical insurance fund of the NRCMS in 2012. *Source* Created by the author based on the data from *China Hygiene Statistical Yearbook 2012* and *China Statistical Yearbook 2013*

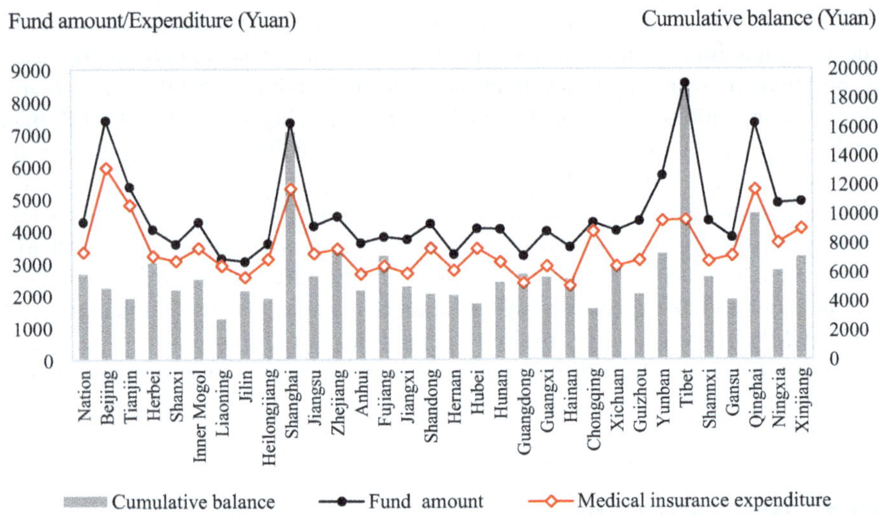

Fig. 4.13 Disparity between provinces in fund amount, medical insurance expenditure and cumulative balance of the UEBMI in 2018. *Source* Created by the author based on the data from *China Statistical Yearbook 2019*

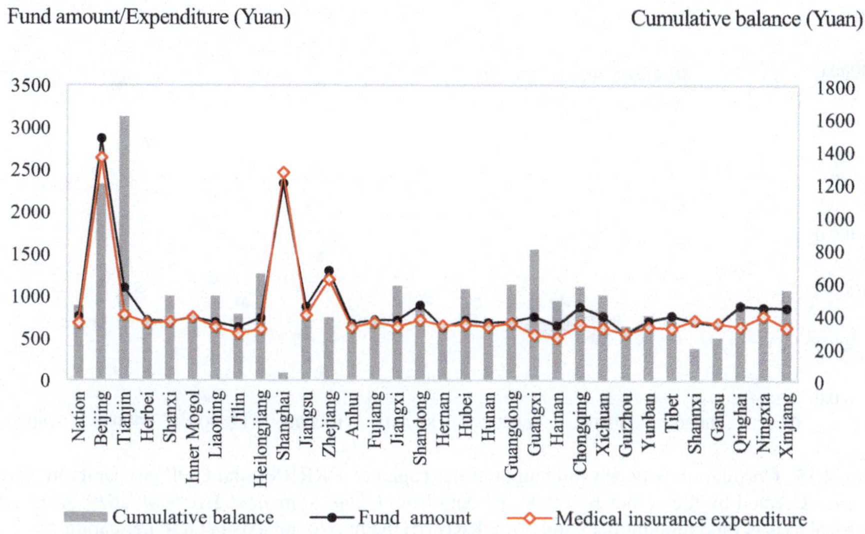

Fig. 4.14 Disparity between provinces in fund amount, medical insurance expenditure and cumulative balance of the URRBMI in 2018 *Source* Created by the author based on the data from *China Statistical Yearbook 2019*

yuan), Shanghai (7,347.9 yuan), and Qinghai (7,334.0 yuan) and low in Jilin (3,046.9 yuan) and Liaoning (3,141.8 yuan). The insurance expenditure per capita was high in Beijing (5,983.8 yuan), Qinghai (5,381.7 yuan), and Shanghai (5,314.1yuan), and low in Jilin (2,578.1 yuan) and Jiangxi (2,700.0 yuan).

Figure 4.14 shows the disparity of cumulative balance of the Urban and Rural Residents Basic Medical Insurance Scheme (URRBMI) between provinces in 2018. The insurance fund amount per capita was high in Beijing (2,870.7 yuan) and Shanghai (2,339.6 yuan) and low in Guizhou (566.9 yuan) and Hainan (653.9 yuan). The insurance expenditure per capita was high in Beijing (2,646.5 yuan) and Shanghai (2,470.8 yuan) and low in Hainan (514.7 yuan) and Guizhou (565.3 yuan).

The results indicate that both the insurance fund amount and insurance expenditures are high in well-developed provinces (e.g., Shanghai, Beijing) and special areas inhabited by ethnic minorities (e.g., Tibet), and low in less-developed provinces (e.g., Liaoning and Guizhou). The results suggest that economic development may affect the amount of insurance funds. The impact of economic development on the public medical insurance can be regarded as follows. First, considering the experience of well-developed countries, there are many cases in which the social security systems were improved with the progress of economic growth. Second, the microeconomic theory explains that a liquidity constraint[2] may influence the probability of enrolling in medical insurance. According to the liquidity constraints hypothesis, when enrollment in medical insurance is voluntary, it is necessary to pay the insurance premium. Unlike low-income groups, high-income groups are more likely to pay insurance premiums. Economic growth may increase the income levels of most

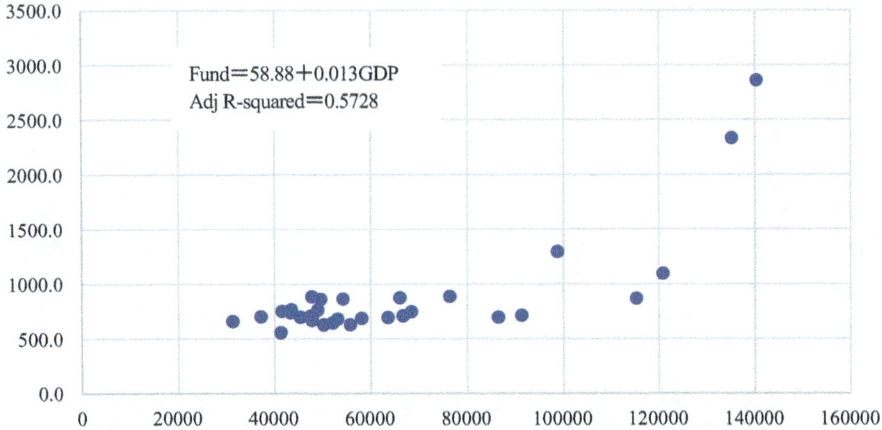

Fig. 4.15 Correlation between fund amount per capita of URRBMI and GDP per capita in 2018. *Source* Created by the author based on the data from *China Statistical Yearbook 2019*. *Note* The vertical axis is fund amount per capita of URRBMI; the horizontal axis is GDP per capita

people; therefore, the probability of enrolling in medical insurance may increase; this may consequently increase medical insurance funds.

Figure 4.15 shows the correlation between the fund amounts per capita of URRBMI and GDP per capita by province in 2018. The results of the regression analysis show that if GDP per capita increases by 1,000 yuan, the fund amounts per capita of medical insurance will increase by 13 yuan, which suggests that economic growth positively influences the amount of medical insurance funds among provinces in China.

Fiscal decentralization systems also influence the disparity in the fund amount of public medical insurance among provinces. The policies of the URBMI and NRCMS (or URRBMI) were instituted by the central government. The local government, however, mainly managed and operated these public medical insurances. Therefore, the operation status of public medical insurance (e.g., insurance premium, local government subsidy, benefits, etc.) in each region significantly depends on the local government's fiscal revenue. Owing to the decentralization reforms of the central and regional governments that took place in 1993, the taxes collected differ from region to region. It can be assumed that compared with the less-developed regions, the subsidies for medical insurance are more for the well-developed regions owing to the higher tax revenue collected by the local governments in well-developed regions.

Figures 4.16 and 4.17 show the correlation between the fund amount per capita of the URRBMI and government tax revenue/general fiscal revenue per capita in 2018. The results of the regression analysis indicate that if government tax revenue per capita increases by 1,000 yuan, the fund amount per capita of the URRBMI funds will increase by 685 yuan (Fig. 4.16), and if general fiscal revenue per capita increases by 1,000 yuan, the fund amount per capita of the URRBMI funds will increase by 617 yuan (Fig. 4.17).

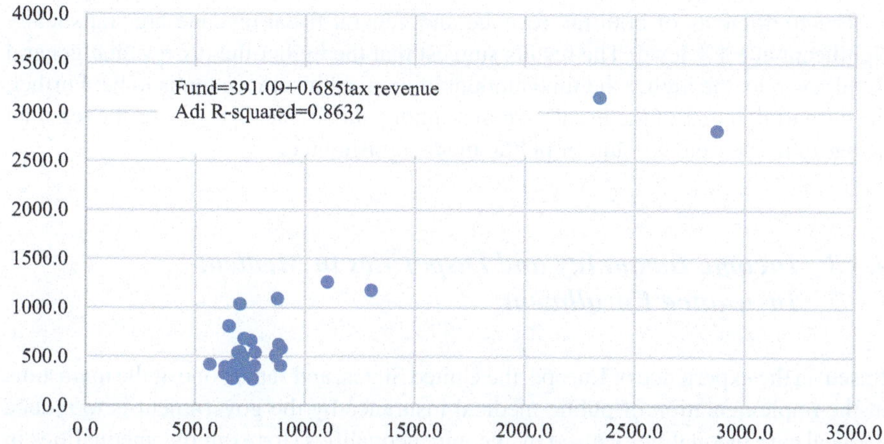

Fig. 4.16 Correlation between fund amount per capita of URRBMI and tax revenue per capita in 2018. *Source* Calculated by the author based on the data from *China Statistical Yearbook 2019*. *Note* The vertical axis is fund amount per capita of URRBMI; the horizontal axis is tax revenue per capita

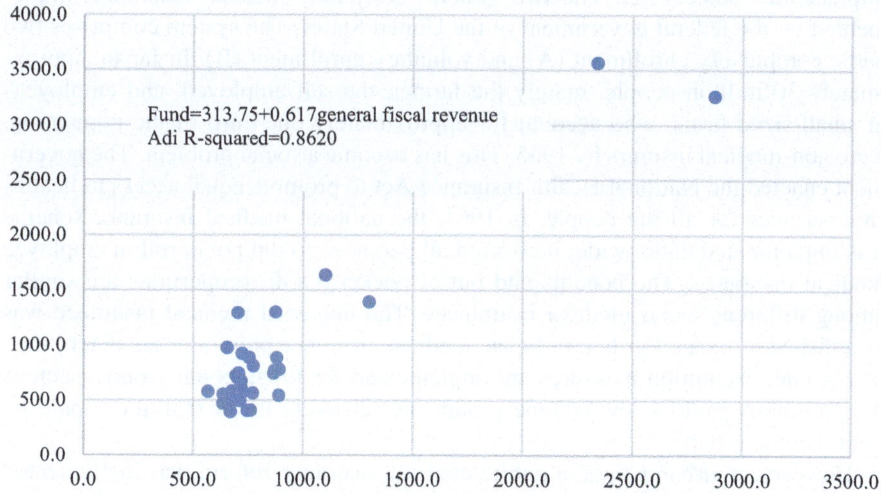

Fig. 4.17 Correlation between fund amount per capita of URRBMI and general fiscal revenue per capita in 2018. *Source* Calculated by the author based on the data from *China Statistical Yearbook 2019*. *Note* The vertical axis is fund amount per capita of URRBMI; the horizontal axis is general fiscal revenue per capita

The coefficients of both tax revenue and general fiscal revenue are statistically significant at a 1% level. The results suggest that the higher the tax revenue/general fiscal revenue, the higher the fund amount of medical insurance tends to be. Further, the decentralization of the fiscal system is among the factors that caused the regional disparity in the fund amount of public medical insurance.

4.3.3 Income Inequality and Disparities in Medical Insurance Enrollment

Based on the experience of Europe, the United States, and Japan, one of the main aims of the implementation of public medical insurance by the government is to reduce medical care inequalities caused by income inequalities (for example, inequalities in the utilization of healthcare services). In the United States and Japan, public medical insurance targeting low-income groups has been implemented. For example, in the United States, medical insurance systems for low-income earners (Medicaid) and the elderly aged 65 and above and individuals with disabilities (Medicare) have been implemented since 1965. The two systems are public medical insurance, implemented by the federal government of the United States. The system comprises two parts: compulsory enrollment (A) and voluntary enrollment (B). In Japan, approximately 30 million people, mainly the farmer, the self-employed, and employees in small-sized firms, who account for approximately one-third of the population, were non-medical insurers by 1955. This has become a social problem. The government enacted the National Health Insurance Act to promote equal access to healthcare services for all the people. In 1961, the national medical insurance scheme was implemented nationwide; it covered all people who did not enroll in employee medical insurance. The benefits and out-of-pocket (OOP) proportions are similar among different social medical insurances. The universal medical insurance was established in Japan. Further, in Japan, medical insurance premiums are determined by income; exemption measures are implemented for low-income groups, such as the premiums paid by low-income groups are relatively lower than those paid by high-income groups.

However, in urban China, a public medical insurance reform was implemented to change medical insurance from government to social insurance, which increases the proportions of OOP expenses on medical care. Although a medical aid system for low-income groups was implemented, the number of eligible people was small. Private medical insurance, such as commercial insurance, has developed since the 1980s. However, only high-income groups can enroll in private medical insurance. Consequently, compared to the high-income group, the majority of the low-income groups were not covered by any medical insurance. Table 4.4 shows the proportion of groups enrolled in each type of medical insurance according to the income group in urban areas in 2007. The proportion of those enrolled in UEBMI is the

Table 4.4 Proportion of participants in medical insurances by income group in urban areas. Unit: %

	First	Second	Third	Fourth	Fifth
UEBMI	50.2	58.8	60.1	63.4	60.1
Commercial MI	6.9	6.5	6.9	7.0	6.7
Other MI	4.4	3.2	2.6	4.5	4.0
Mixed MI	1.7	1.7	2.9	3.8	8.0
Non-MI	36.8	29.8	27.5	21.3	21.2

Source Calculated based on the data from Chinese Household Income Project survey of 2007 (CHIP 2007)

Note (1) UEBMI: only participated in the Urban Employee Basic Medical Insurance scheme; Commercial MI: only participated in commercial medial insurance (private medical insurance); Other MI: participated other medical insurances excluding UEBMI and commercial MI (e.g., firm medical subsidy system); Mixed MI: participated more than one kind of medical insurances; No-MI: non-participation in any medical insurance. (2) First-fifth: income quintile from first to fifth

highest at 63.4% for the fourth quintile-income group, followed by the fifth quintile-income group at 60.1%. However, the low-income group (first quintile-income group) accounted for the lowest proportion (50.2%). The proportion of those that were not covered by any medical insurance was the highest at 36.8% for the lowest- income group and the lowest at 21.2% for the highest-income group. Because the possibility of illness is higher for the low-income group than the high-income group, it can be assumed that there is an inequality in the utilization of healthcare services between income groups.

Table 4.5 summarizes the coverage rate by income groups based on a survey conducted in 2005 by the Survey and Evaluation Group on the Pilot of the NRCMS in 257 pilot areas. The enrollment rate of the NRCMS was 69.0% for the poor group and 74.2% for the extremely poor group, both of which were lower than the enrollment rate (76.6%) of the total sample. The same trend was observed in all the three regions (eastern, central, and western) with different levels of economic development. In rural areas, low-income groups were less likely to enroll in the NRCMS.

Table 4.5 Medical insurance coverage rate by income and region groups in rural areas. Unit: %

	Total	Poor	Extreme poor
Nation	76.6	69.0	74.2
East	81.8	69.4	72.5
Central	73.0	63.6	67.9
West	73.2	71.7	77.8

Source Created by the author based on data from the New Rural Collaborative Medical Pilot Work Survey Evaluation Group 2006

Table 4.6 Proportion of participants in medical insurances by employment sectors in urban China. Unit: %

	Gov	GO	SOE	COE	POE	FOE	Self	Non-work
UEBMI	64.0	61.7	64.1	56.3	54.5	65.1	40.3	46.6
Commercial MI	5.7	7.1	5.5	6.9	7.4	6.2	8.9	5.1
Other MI	2.8	3.4	3.3	5.6	4.0	2.4	5.5	3.8
Mixed MI	3.2	3.6	3.7	2.7	1.6	10.6	3.0	0.8
Non-participation	24.3	24.2	23.4	28.5	32.5	15.7	42.3	43.7

Source Calculated based on data from Chinese Household Income Project survey of 2007 (CHIP 2007)
Note (1) UEBMI: only participated in the Urban Employee Basic Medical Insurance scheme; Commercial MI: only participated in commercial medial insurance (private medical insurance); Other MI: participated other medical insurances excluding UEBMI and commercial MI (e.g., firm medical subsidy system); Mixed MI: participated more than one kind of medical insurances; No-MI: non-participation in any medical insurance. (2) Gov: government office; GO: government-related organization; SOE: state-owned enterprise; COE: collectively owned enterprise; FOE: foreign-owned enterprise; POE: privately-owned enterprise; Self: the self-employed

4.3.4 Disparities in Medical Insurance Enrollment Between Employment Sectors

Table 4.6 shows the proportion of participation in each medical insurance according to the employment sectors in urban China. The employment sectors are divided into eight types: (i) government office (Gov), (ii) government-related organization (GO), (iii) state-owned enterprise (SOE), (iv) collectively owned enterprise (COE), (v) foreign-owned enterprises (FOE), (vi) privately-owned enterprise (POE), (vii) self-employed and (viii) non-working. The state-owned sector comprises (i), (ii), and (iii), and the non-state-owned sector comprises (iv), (v), (vi), and (vii).

The proportion of those who only participated in the UEBMI is more for the groups in state-owned sector (64.0% for government office, 61.7% for government-related organization, 64.1% for SOE) than the groups in non-state-owned sector (56.3% for COE, 54.5% for POE, 40.3% for the self-employed), but it is the highest at 65.1% in FOE. The proportion of participation in the UEBMI is lowest for the self-employed and non-work groups (self-employed 40.3%, non-working 46.6%).

The difference in the enrollment status of public medical insurance depending on the employment sector is likely attributable to the following: First, the UEBMI, which was implemented in 2007 was established based on the public medical system implemented in the state-owned sector during the planned economy period. It had so far been implemented as a labor insurance medical system covering all the employers in SOEs. The publicly funded medical system covers all the employees of government offices and organizations. The labor insurance medical system was reformed and transitioned to the UEBMI in the 1990s. Therefore, the differences in the enrollment in public medical insurance between government offices, government-related organizations, and SOEs is small.

Second, it can be seen that there is a difference between enterprises in non-state-owned sector (FOE, COE/POE) in terms of the enrollment rate in the public medical insurance. Since 1998, when the UEBMI was implemented, workers in both FOEs and POEs were covered by the UEBMI. Compared to enterprises in the state-owned sector, both FOEs and POEs face fierce market competition. These enterprises further aim to maximize their profits. It is pointed out that there is a possibility of avoiding the burden of social insurance contributory payments (Nakagane, 2000; Ma, 2015). Nevertheless, the enrollment rate of public medical insurance is relatively higher in FOEs. This can be attributed to the fact that since the late 1990s, the government has increased administrative pressure on state-owned sector and FOEs to promote enrollment in the social security system, including public medical insurance (government compulsory factor). Additionally, factors such as the philosophy of complying with the law and the business conditions will also influence the insurance enrollment behavior of corporations (firm behavior factor). To clarify the effects of these factors, further analysis that considers firm attributes (e.g., years of establishment, number of employees, employee age structure, etc.) and their business conditions should be conducted in future research.

4.4 Conclusions

In China, three public medical insurance systems (the UEBMI in 1998, the URBMI in 2007, and the NRCMS in 2003) have been implemented since the late 1990s. Additionally, the number of members in these insurance systems has increased significantly over the years. These public medical insurances cover the entire population. Therefore, an universal medical insurance has been achieved from the perspective of institution establishment.

However, there are various problems in the operation and management of these insurance systems, which further result in system fragmentation and disparities between urban and rural areas, provinces, income groups, and employment sectors in public medical insurance in China. First, medical insurance differs between rural and urban areas. Further, the rural and urban areas in the public medical insurance system design differ in terms of benefits, the proportions of OOP expenses, and the amount of medical insurance funds. Second, provincial regions differ owing to the difference in the level of economic development and fiscal situations. Third, medical insurance coverage differs depending on the income group. The enrollment rate of both public medical insurance, private medical insurance (commercial insurance), and mixed medical insurance is higher for the high-income group than for the middle- and low-income groups. Fourth, the enrollment status in the public medical insurance system differs depending on the employment sectors. The proportion of those who enrolled in public medical insurance was higher for workers in FOEs and state-owned sector (i.e., government offices, government-related organizations), and less for the self-employed and non-working groups. These results suggest that public medical insurance differs significantly according to *the hukou* system, region, income, and employment sector in China. The issue to establish a realistic universal medical insurance such as that implemented in developed countries has become crucial for the Chinese government (Ma, 2015, 2019; Peng & Yue, 2020; Tian, 2019; Wang et al., 2019; Yu, 2020).

Notes

1. He (2005), Li (2010) and Lu (2013) argued the issues in public medical insurances, such as designing personal accounts and the higher risk of social polling funds from a long-term perspective persist.
2. For the empirical studies on the liquidity constraints hypothesis, please refer to Wolfe and Goddeeris (1991), Shaefer et al. (2011) for the United States, and Lin et al. (2009), Ma (2015) for China. Their results supported the hypothesis. For the detail analyses and discussions on the issue, please refer Chaps. 5–6 in this book.

References

He, P. (2005). Medical insurance system evaluation and perspectives of medical insurance in China. *Social Security Research, 2005*(2), 146–151 (in Chinese).

Li, H. (2010). Exploration of medical insurance reform in China. *Modern Trade Economy, 2010*(7), 66–67 (in Chinese).

Lin, W., Liu, G., & Chen, G. (2009). The urban resident basic medical insurance: A landmark reform towards universal coverage in China. *Health Economics, 18*(2), 83–96.

Lu, F. (2013). Issues and problems in current medical insurance system reform. *Northern Economy, 2013*(2), 84–85 (in Chinese).

Ma, X. (2015). *Public medical insurance reform in China*. Kyoto University Press. (in Japanese).

Ma, X. (2019). Public medical insurance system reform and issues in China. In L. Hu, T. Yuan, & X. Ma (Eds.), *Research on social security system in Japan after the cold war: Enlightenment to China*. Shanghai: Shanghai' People Press.

Nakagane, K. (2000). Issues and focuses on Chinese social security system research. *Overseas Social Security Research Journal, 132*, 2–12. (in Japanese).

Peng, H., & Yue, J. (2020). Integration of China's basic medical insurance system: Theoretical controversy, practical progress and future prospects. *Academic Monthly, 52*(11), 55–65. (in Chinese).

Shaefer, H. L., Groganm, C. M., & Pollack, H. A. (2011). Who transitions from private to public health insurance? Lessons from expansions of the State Children's Health Insurance Program. *Journal of Health Care for the Poor and Underserved, 22*(1), 59–370.

Tian, W. (2019). From "fragmentation" to "integration": China's urban and rural medical insurance system reform path. *Henan Social Sciences, 27*(5), 103–107. (in Chinese).

Wang, Q., Li, L., & Xue, H. (2019). Review, evaluation and prospect of China' s medical security system reform in the past 40 years since the reform and opening-up. *Economy System Reform, 1*, 25–31. (in Chinese).

Wolfe, J. R., & Goddeeris, J. H. (1991). Adverse selection, moral hazard, and wealth effects in the Medigap insurance market. *Journal of Health Economics, 10*(4), 433–459.

Yu, B. (2020). The design and thinking of China's medical security system in the next 5–10 years. *Health Economic Research, 37*(4), 3–7. (in Chinese).

Part II
Impacts of Public Medical Insurance Reform in China: Evidence Based on Empirical Studies

Chapter 5
Determinants of Medical Insurance Participation of Urban Residents

Abstract Using data from the Chinese Household Income Project Survey, this chapter presents an empirical analysis to verify the determinants of participation in medical insurance of urban residents. Several major conclusions emerge. Both adverse selection and liquidity constraints hypotheses were supported. The probability of participation in medical insurance was higher for the middle- and high-income groups than for the low-income group. Some low-income groups were not covered by either public or private medical insurance in 2007, indicating that income inequality results in disparities in medical insurance coverage. Additionally, medical insurance participation differs between state- and non-state-owned sectors. The findings have important policy implications for developing an equitable public medical insurance in China.

Keywords Medical insurance · Liquidity constraints hypothesis · Adverse selection · Hypothesis · Urban residents · China

5.1 Introduction

Over the years, China's old social security system has transformed, and many new types of medical insurance schemes have been implemented (see Appendix Table 5.7). For example, the main public medical insurance for residents with urban household registration (*hukou*) (hereinafter referred to as "urban residents") mainly comprises the Urban Employee Basic Medical Insurance (UEBMI), which covers urban employees, and the Urban Residents Basic Medical Insurance (URBMI), which covers non-working residents with urban *hukou*. Private medical insurance

---

This chapter is a revised and developed version of two published papers as follows: Ma, X. (2015). Determinants of participation in medical insurance in urban China. In Ma, X. *Public Medical Insurance Reform in China*, Chapter 4, Kyoto: Kyoto University Press (in Japanese), copyright © Kyoto University Press, and Ma, X. (2014). The determinants of participation in Chinese urban public health insurance: Empirical analysis using 2008 Chinese Household Income Project Survey. *Asian Economic (AJIA KEIZAI)*, 55(2), 62–94 (in Japanese), copyright © Institute of Developing Economies, Japan External Trade Organization (IDE-JETRO).

X. Ma, *Public Medical Insurance Reforms in China*,
https://doi.org/10.1007/978-981-16-7790-8_5

(i.e., commercial insurance), and corporate subsidy medical insurance, were also implemented to subsidize public medical insurance.

While diverse medical insurance systems can meet the various demands of individuals, two problems arise. First, the participation status in medical insurance differs across employment sectors (e.g., state- and non-state-owned sectors). For example, the UEBMI requires firms to pay medical insurance premiums. State-owned enterprises (SOEs) implemented the public medical system in the planned economy period, and most of them paid the social medical insurance premium. However, the non-state-owned sector (i.e., small and medium-sized privately-owned enterprises: POEs) faces a fiercely competitive market and tends to avoid the medical insurance premium burden to reduce labor costs (Ma & Cheng, 2019; Nagakane, 2000). Second, income inequality may lead to disparity in medical insurance enrollment. In developed countries such as the U.S. and Japan, public medical insurance targeting low-income groups addresses the disparity in medical care due to income inequality. In other words, public medical insurance is implemented as a means of income redistribution. However, until 2007, only a small proportion of the poor in urban areas were covered by public medical insurance, and neither public nor private medical insurance targeted low-income groups. Therefore, low-income groups experienced a situation of "non-medical insurance" and "non-medical care" (due to high medical expenses and difficult access to healthcare services), in contrast to free medical care in the past. Serious inequalities in medical care due to employment sector disparity and income inequality can lead to social instability. The implementation of the URBMI in 2007, for individuals not covered by the UEBMI, aimed to address inter-group medical care inequality for urban residents.

How do household income and employment sector affect public medical insurance enrollment in urban China? Using data from the Chinese Household Income Survey of 2007 (CHIP2007), this chapter investigates the determinants, including household income and employment sector, on public medical insurance participation, and explores medical insurance participation behavioral mechanisms for urban residents in China.

The remainder of this chapter is organized as follows. Section 5.2 reviews the economic theory and existing empirical studies on the issue. Section 5.3 describes the medical insurance enrollment situation in urban China. Section 5.4 introduces the data, models, and analytical methods used in this study. Section 5.5 presents the econometric analysis results of the determinants of medical insurance participation. Section 5.6 concludes.

5.2 Literature Review

5.2.1 *Research Hypotheses*

Ideally, both the supply side (e.g., government, workplace, insurance company) and the demand side (individual) factors driving medical insurance participation should be considered. However, due to data constraints, this study focuses on the demand-side factors.

Two demand-side hypotheses can explain the present issue. First, according to the adverse selection hypothesis, there is information asymmetry in the insurance market, implying that an insurance company cannot obtain complete information on potential customers. Medical care expense is assumed to be higher for the group with poor health than for the healthy group. Therefore, the poor health group is more likely to participate in medical insurance to decrease the risk of high out-of-pocket (OOP) expenses on medical care.

Second, based on the liquidity constraints hypothesis, the high-income group is more likely to participate in medical insurance than the low-income group because they can afford insurance premium payments.

5.2.2 *Empirical Literature on the Issue*

Empirical studies on the two hypotheses have yielded mixed results. For developed countries, Wolfe and Goddeeris (1991) and Shaefer et al. (2011) found that the probability of changing from private to public medical insurance was higher for poor health and low-income groups in the U.S. and reported that the adverse selection and the liquidity constraints hypotheses were supported. However, other studies (Bograd et al., 1997; Drehr et al., 1996; Long & Marquis, 2002; Madden et al., 1995; Swartz & Garnick, 2000; Swartz & Garnick, 2000) did not find a statistically significant effect of health status on public medical insurance participation, which indicates that the adverse selection hypothesis was not supported.

For developing countries, Kimani et al. (2012) analyzed urban residents in Kenya and found that high-income groups of regular employees were more likely to opt for public medical insurance, thereby validating the liquidity constraints hypothesis. However, Hofter (2006) and Pardo and Schott (2012) found that poor health, low-income, less educated, and self-employed groups in Chile were more likely to participate in public medical insurance, indicating that the adverse selection hypothesis was supported, but the liquidity constraints hypothesis was not.

There are only a few empirical studies in the Chinese context. Using survey data from the Guangdong Province Social Transition Basic Survey conducted by the Zhongshan University Development Research Center in 2000, Zhou (2003) focused on the group that voluntarily joined the 1998 UEBMI (including owners of individual firms or privately-owned enterprises (POEs) and their employees and freelance workers) and found that the probability of medical insurance participation is lower for the healthy, younger, and non-working groups compared with the others, indicating that both adverse selection and liquidity constraints hypotheses were supported. Using data from a survey conducted by Peking University in 2008, Lin et al. (2009) found that low-income and high-income groups had higher enrollment probabilities than middle-income groups, which showed a U-shaped relationship, and chronic diseases in the past year made individuals more likely to join the 2007 URBMI, supporting the adverse selection hypothesis.

The existing studies have certain limitations. First, unlike the developed European countries and the U.S., the labor market in urban China during the transition period was segmented by the employment sector (the state- and non-state-owned sectors), and the UEBMI was a medical insurance based on the public medical care system in the public sector in the planned economy period. However, previous studies did not consider the differences between the state- and non-state-owned employment sectors. The influence of the employment sector on the probability of participation in public medical insurance and on the effect of each factor remains under-researched.

Second, during the transition period, medical insurance was diversified in urban areas and classified into four categories for urban residents: Those who (a) only participated in public medical insurance; (b) only participated in private medical insurance; (c) participated in both (mixed medical insurance); (d) did not participate in any medical insurance. Specifically, private medical insurance has evolved since the 1990s. Existing studies focus only on public medical insurance participation behavior, and the determinants of participation in private medical insurance remain ambiguous.

Using survey data from CHIP2007, this study employed an empirical study to explore three questions:

(i) Can the adverse selection and liquidity constraints hypotheses explain participation behavior in medical insurance among urban residents in China? (issue1)
(ii) Which factors influence the participation in public medical insurance (in this study, the UEBMI[1]), private medical insurance, and mixed medical insurance? (issue2)
(iii) Does the influence of these factors differ across employment sectors? (issue3).

The main contributions of this study are as follows: First, this study employed an analysis considering four types of medical insurance enrollment; specifically, the analysis of the determinants of private medical insurance is the first. Second, the results for issue 1 and issue 2 are comparable with those of previous studies. The result for issue 3 provides new evidence from China to complement the existing empirical research.

5.3 Methodology and Data

5.3.1 *Model*

A probit regression model was used[2], as expressed in Eq. (5.1).

$$\begin{aligned} y_i^* &= a + \beta X_i + u_i \\ P_{ij} &= Pr(y_i = 1) = Pr(y_i^* > 0) = Pr(u_i > -a - \beta X_i), \end{aligned} \tag{5.1}$$

where the subscript i denotes an individual; X is each factor that influences the probability of medical insurance participation (e.g., health status, age, income); β is the estimated coefficient of each factor. Additionally, y_i^* is a continuous but unobservable latent variable defined as follows:

$$y_i = \begin{cases} 1 \; if \; y_i^* > 0 \\ 0 \; if \; y_i^* \leq 0 \end{cases}$$

An appropriate sample was necessary for hypothesis testing. Two conditions were considered: (i) Whether individuals voluntarily participated in medical insurance, and (ii) whether the insurance company accepted refusal behavior (risk avoidance).

As shown in Table 5.1, the self-employed and employees in small POEs (Group I), who decide whether to participate in the UEBMI, met both criteria. This did not hold for the other groups: (i) For Group II, comprising employees in firms or organizations (e.g., government office, government organization, POE, foreign-owned enterprise: FOE), UEBMI participation is compulsory; (ii) for Group III, although private medical insurance (i.e., commercial insurance) enrollment is voluntary, the enrollment behavior may potentially be affected by the commercial insurance company's prior refusal behavior. For example, as commercial insurance is private and subject to the market mechanism, insurance companies that aim at maximizing profits may exclude individuals likely to incur higher expenses on medical care (such as the unhealthy group)[3]; (iii) For Group IV, wherein individuals decide whether to participate in both public and private medical insurance, public medical insurance is compulsory, and the insurance company may undertake risk avoidance behavior to exclude some individuals. None of these groups (Groups II–IV) meet the two conditions required for hypothesis testing. Thus, only Group I is used to test the hypotheses. Health status, age, and income variables are used as indicators. Employment sector dummy variables are used to compare the employment-based differences

Table 5.1 Samples selected for hypotheses testing: comparison between groups

		Demand side Voluntary	Supply side Risk aversion behavior	Group type	Relation with Hypothesis testing
UEBMI	(a) Self-employed, employees in small POEs	Voluntary	No	Group I	Analyzed group
	(b) Employees in SOEs, FOEs or middle- and large POEs	Compulsory	No	Group II	Comparison group
Commercial		Voluntary	Yes	Group III	Comparison group
Mixed		Voluntary/forced	Yes/No	Group IV	Comparison group

Source Created by the author
Note Commercial: Commercial insurance; Mixed: Mixed medical insurance, including two types of medical insurance (participation in both public and private medical insurance); SOEs: State-owned enterprises; POEs: Privately-owned enterprises; FOEs: Foreign-owned enterprises

in medical insurance participation. Finally, the hypotheses for different employment sector groups are tested to investigate the differences in underlying mechanisms.

5.3.2 Data

CHIP2007 was used in this study. The CHIP2007 was conducted by the Beijing Normal University, the Institute of Economic Research, the Chinese Academy of Social Sciences, and the National Bureau of Statistics (NBS), China in 2008. The survey subjects comprised three groups: urban *hukou* residents, rural *hukou* residents, and rural–urban migrants. The individual and household survey data for urban *hukou* residents is used. The CHIP2007 covers nine representative Chinese regions (Shanghai, Jiangsu, Zhejiang, Anhui, Henan, Hubei, Guangdong, Chongqing, and Sichuan). Based on the resident register used in the National Census conducted by the NBS, a multi-step random sampling method was used. The sample size is 19,748. The CHIP covers a wide range of representative regions and is considered a highly reliable data source. This study uses CHIP2007 data on medical insurance, income, health status, and individual characteristics, such as age and education, to perform an empirical analysis.

5.3.3 Variable Setting

The dependent variable was determined based on the question item: "Did you participate in the following medical insurance in 2007?" The respondents chose one out of the five types of insurance: (i) UEBMI; (ii) commercial insurance; (iii) new rural cooperative medical insurance scheme (NRCMS); (iv) other medical insurance; and (v) no medical insurance. Owing to the study's focus on urban residents, the sub-sample of those who selected (iii) was deleted. It is presumed that "other medical insurance" included the medical aid system, urban residents medical insurance, and firm subsidy medical insurance; however, these medical insurance systems could not be identified. Utilizing these options, the following binary variables were constructed: (a) Participation in commercial insurance only (1 = when only participating in commercial insurance, and 0 = when not participating in any medical insurance); (b) participation in the UEBMI only (1 = when only participating in the UEBMI, and 0 = when not participating in any medical insurance); (c) participation in mixed insurance (1 = when participating in either commercial insurance and the UEBMI/ the UEBMI and other medical insurance/ commercial insurance and other medical insurance, and 0 = when not participating in any medical insurance).

The independent variables were constructed as follows (see Appendix Table 5.8): First, to test the adverse selection hypothesis, health status[4] and age group dummy variables were used as indicators. Four types of subjective health status dummies—very good, good, fair, and poor—were constructed. Five age groups were considered—16–19, 20–29, 30–39, 40–49, and 50–59 years—and five age group dummy variables were constructed.[5]

Setting the unhealthy and the 50–59 years groups as the baseline, the negative values of the other dummy variables indicated that the group with poor health and the older age group are more likely to participate in medical insurance, thereby validating the adverse selection hypothesis.

Second, to test the liquidity constraints hypothesis, the dummy variables of household income excluding the respondent's labor income were used.[6, 7, 8] When the results showed that the probability of medical insurance participation is lower for low-income group, the liquidity constraints hypothesis is supported.

Third, regarding the differences in medical insurance participation between employment sectors, eight kinds of employment dummy variables were constructed: (i) government office; (ii) government-related organization (*Shiye Danwei*); (iii) SOE[9]; (iv) collectively owned enterprise (COE); (v) POE; (iv) FOE; (iv) self-employed; and (iv) others (including the non-working individuals).

Fourth, the definitions of regular and non-regular work, which have not been standardized in China so far, were based on the following choices: (i) lifetime employment; (ii) long-term labor contract (the employment period is one year or more); (iii) short-term labor contract (the employment period is less than one year); (iv) short-term workers without a labor contract; (v) family workers; (vi) self-employed; (vii) other short-term employees. The regular work dummy was constructed as 1 = for options (i) or (ii), and 0 = for the other options. It was assumed that most regular employees worked in the state-owned sector and were more likely to participate in public medical insurance because the government enforces public medical insurance implementation in the state-owned sector.

Fifth, a local urban *hukou* dummy was introduced, with a value of 1 = the group with a local urban *hukou*, and 0 = otherwise.

Sixth, public medical insurance management and establishment differs across regions as do economic development, health status, culture, and lifestyle. Nine regional dummy variables were used to control for such regional disparities for Shanghai, Jiangsu, Zhejiang, Anhui, Henan, Hubei, Guangdong, Chongqing, and Sichuan.[10]

Seventh, existing researchers such as Madden et al. (1995), Drehr et al. (1996), Bograd et al. (1997), Swartz and Garnick (2000), Long and Marquis (2002), and Swartz and Garnick (2000) have reported that individual attributes other than age and health status also influence medical insurance participation. Therefore, male, having spouse, having a child, and education dummies were also used.

Urban *hukou* samples were used in this study. It should be noted that migrant workers and their dependents (e.g., children) in urban areas were not included in the analysis. Considering the impact of the mandatory retirement system, the age range was limited to 16–59 years.[11] In addition, the non-respondents for each of the above variables, and the missing values for all variables were excluded.

Appendix Table 5.8 summarizes the descriptive statistics for each variable.

5.4 Descriptive Statistic Results

5.4.1 Proportion of Participants in Medical Insurance by Age

Table 5.2 presents the proportion of participants in medical insurance by age group. Compared with the group aged 16–29, the percentage of UEBMI participants is higher in the group aged 30 and above (65.08% for the group aged 30–39, 70.73% for the group aged 40–49, 67.84% for the group aged 50–59). By contrast, the percentage

Table 5.2 Proportion of participants in medical insurance by age group (Unit: %)

	UEBMI	Commercial	Other	Mixed	Non-participant
Age 16–19	16.22	15.56	6.92	1.46	59.84
Age 20–29	49.36	7.13	2.84	3.63	37.04
Age 30–39	65.08	6.81	3.67	3.81	20.63
Age 40–49	70.73	3.82	3.76	3.85	17.84
Age 50–59	67.84	3.01	2.16	2.85	24.14

Source Calculated based on the data from CHIP2007
Note Other: Medical insurance except the UEBMI and commercial medical insurance

Table 5.3 Proportion of participants in medical insurance by health status (Unit: %)

	UEBMI	Commercial	Other	Mixed	Non-participant
Very good	51.74	8.17	4.49	2.07	33.53
Good	55.24	6.67	3.77	2.54	31.78
Fair	60.43	4.34	3.14	3.14	28.95
Poor	57.34	2.34	3.08	1.60	35.64
Very poor	53.70	5.56	5.56	1.85	33.33

Source Calculated based on the data from CHIP2007
Note Other: Medical insurance except the UEBMI and commercial insurance

of non-participants is higher in the group aged 16–29 compared with the group aged 30 and above (59.84% for the group aged 16–19, 37.04% for the group aged 20–29). The percentage of middle-aged and older people who participated in public medical insurance is higher than that of the younger generation, and the percentage of those who did not participate in medical insurance is small. Thus, the status of participation in public medical insurance differs by age group.

5.4.2 *Proportion of Participants in Medical Insurance by Health Status*

Table 5.3 summarizes the proportion of participants in medical insurance by subjective health status. The percentage of the UEBMI participants is highest in the group that answered "fair" at 60.43% and lowest in the group that answered "very good" at 51.74%. In addition, the percentage of those who did not participate in the medical insurance is the lowest at 28.95% in the group that answered 'fair" and highest at 35.64% in the group that answered "poor". The relationship between health status and participation in medical insurance is thus unclear.

5.4.3 *Proportion of Participants in Medical Insurance Participation by Educational Background*

Table 5.4 presents the proportion of participants in medical insurance by educational background. The percentage of UEBMI participants is higher among individuals graduated from senior high school (56.38%), college (60.05%), and university (61.41%) than individuals graduated from elementary school and below (48.71%) and junior high school. By contrast, the percentage of those who did not participate in medical insurance is lower in the senior high school (31.22%), college (26.90%), and university (23.39%) groups than for elementary school and below (42.41%) and

Table 5.4 Proportion of participants in medical insurance by educational background (Unit: %)

	UEBMI	Commercial	Other	Mixed	Non-participant
Elementary and below	48.71	4.10	4.04	0.74	42.41
Junior high	52.55	5.88	3.59	1.93	36.05
Senior high	56.38	5.76	3.99	2.65	31.22
College	60.05	6.55	3.44	3.06	26.90
University	61.41	7.89	3.25	4.06	23.39

Source Calculated based on the data from CHIP2007
Note Other: Medical insurance except the UEBMI and commercial medical insurance

junior high school (36.05%) counterparts. The results indicate that the higher the educational level, the higher the percentage of those who participated in the UEBMI and the lower the percentage of those who did not participate in medical insurance. The income level can be assumed to be higher for the well-educated group than for the less-educated group. The descriptive results suggest that the lower the income, the lower the percentage of those who participated in the public medical insurance (here, the UEBMI) implying that the effect of public medical insurance on reducing income inequality may be smaller.

5.4.4 Proportion of Participants in Medical Insurance by Working and Non-Working Groups

Figure 5.1 shows the proportion of participants in medical insurance for working and non-working groups. The percentage of UEBMI participants is higher in the working group (62.83%) than in the non-working group (48.86%). By contrast, the percentage of participants who did not participate in medical insurance is higher in the non-working group (38.96%) than in the working group (23.97%). It can be observed that the medical insurance participation differs depending on whether an individual is employed or not.

5.4.5 Proportion of Participants in Medical Insurances by Employment Sector

In the working group, SOEs (enterprises wholly owned by the government), state-owned joint-stock enterprises (in which the share of assets owned by the government is 50% or more of the total asset amount), and state-owned joint-stock enterprises

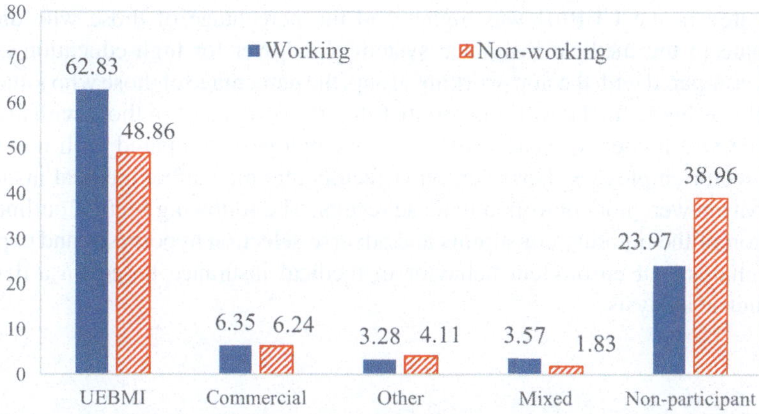

Fig. 5.1 Proportion of participants in medical insurance by working and non-working groups. *Source* Calculated based on the data from CHIP2007. *Note* Other: Medical insurance except the UEBMI

(listed corporates whose main shareholder is the government) were designated as state-owned sector; POEs and the self-employed were designated as non-state-owned sector. One of the reasons for public medical insurance reforms in urban areas is to establish a social insurance system that unifies the publicly funded medical system for civil servants and the labor insurance medical system for employees in corporates. However, a part of civil servants still applied to publicly funded medical system which is supported by government in the 2007. Figure 5.2 shows the results for state- and non-state-owned sector groups.

The proportion of workers who participated in the UEBMI is higher in the state-owned sector (58.18%) than in the non-state-owned sector (53.45%), while the percentage of those who did not participate in medical insurance was higher in the non-state-owned sector (35.93%) than in the state-owned sector (28.20%). The results thus suggest that medical insurance enrollment differs according to the type of employment sector.

To summarize: First, compared with the younger generation, the percentage of those who joined the public medical insurance was higher for the middle-aged and older groups. Second, there was no clear relationship between subjective health status and participation in medical insurance. Third, the percentage of those who participated in the UEBMI was higher and the percentage of those who did not participate in the medical insurance system was lower for high-education group. Fourth, compared with the non-working group, the percentage of those who joined the UEBMI was higher in the working group. Fifth, the percentage of those with medical insurance was higher for state-owned sector employees compared with non-state-owned sector employees. However, other factors that may affect medical insurance participation were not controlled in these results. The following section outlines the validation of the liquidity constraints and adverse selection hypotheses and explores the mechanism of enrollment behavior in medical insurance based on a detailed econometric analysis.

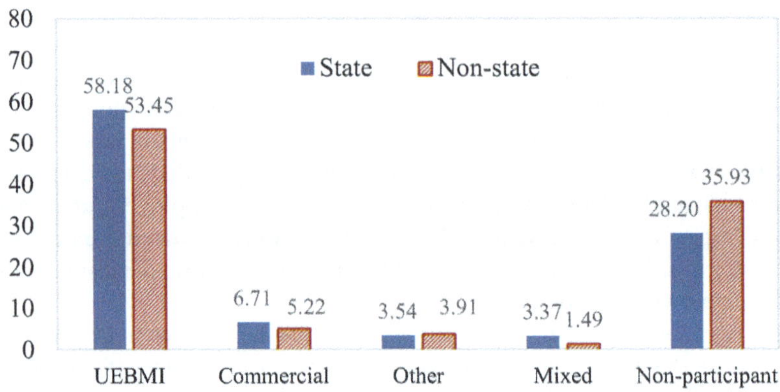

Fig. 5.2 Proportion of participants in medical insurance by employment sector. *Source* Calculated based on the data from CHIP2007. *Note* (1) Other: Medical insurance except the UEBMI. (2) State: state-owned sector (i.e., government offices, SOEs, etc.); non-state: no-state-owned sector (i.e., POEs, FOEs, and the self-employment sector, etc.)

5.5 Econometric Analysis Results

5.5.1 *Testing Results of Adverse Selection and Liquidity Constraints Hypotheses*

Table 5.5 summarizes the results for the probability of participation in medical insurance.

First, to test the adverse selection hypothesis, based on the results of Model 1 (UEBMI), compared with the unhealthy group, the probability of UEBMI participation is 29.8 percentage points higher in the healthy group (the group that answered "very good"). Although the level of statistical significance is 10%, the participation probability is 21.1 percentage points higher in the group that answered "good." These results do not support the adverse selection hypothesis. Moreover, compared with the group aged 50–59 years, the probability of medical insurance participation is 54.6, 48.6, 19.6, and 13.7 percentage points lower for the groups aged 16–19, 20–29, 30–39, and 40–49 years, respectively, all of which are significant at the 1% level. The group aged 50–59 years is found more likely to participate in the UEBMI than those below 50. The results may differ based on the reference (age) group. We also performed the estimations using the group aged 30–39, whose work and life are relatively stable, as the reference group. Compared with this reference group, the probability of medical insurance participation is 45.4 percentage points lower for the group aged 16–19, and 33.2 percentage points lower for the group aged 20–29; it is 5.3 percentage points higher for the group aged 40–49 and 18.68 percentage points higher for the group aged 50–59; these results are significant at the 1% level. The results confirm that the probability of public medical insurance participation increases with age and support the adverse selection hypothesis.

Second, regarding the liquidity constraints hypothesis, the results of Model 1 show that, compared with the low-income (first quintile) income group, the probability of medical insurance participation is higher at 10.1, 15.2, 13.1, and 16.7 percentage points for the second, third, fourth, and fifth quintile income groups, respectively, and the results are all significant at the 1% or 5% level, supporting the liquidity constraints hypothesis. The results from Model 3 (commercial insurance) and Model 4 (mixed insurance) also indicate that, compared with the low-income group, the probability of medical insurance participation is higher for middle- and high-income groups, validating the liquidity constraints hypothesis.

5.5.2 *Results for Other Factors*

First, the results of Model 2 showed that, compared with those employed in government offices, the probability of UEBMI participation was lower for COEs (9.6 percentage points), POEs (7.2 percentage points), the self-employed (9.8 percentage

Table 5.5 Probability of medical insurance participation in urban China

	(1) UEBMI		(2) UEBMI		(3) Commercial		(4) Mixed	
	dy/dx	SE	dy/dx	SE	dy/dx	SE	dy/dx	SE
Health status (poor)								
Very good	0.298***	0.303	0.044	0.125	0.067	0.242	−0.016	0.288
Good	0.211*	0.293	0.006	0.120	0.019	0.236	−0.035	0.274
Fair	0.181	0.299	0.008	0.122	0.030	0.241	−0.013	0.280
Age (Age 50–59)								
Age 16–19	−0.546***	0.292	−0.507***	0.109	0.166***	0.164	−0.043***	0.289
Age 20–29	−0.486***	0.209	−0.130***	0.074	0.070*	0.144	0.008	0.200
Age 30–39	−0.196**	0.152	0.016	0.055	0.173***	0.108	0.019	0.147
Age 40–49	−0.137**	0.142	0.064***	0.052	0.067**	0.112	0.037**	0.139
Income (First quintile)								
Second quintile	0.101**	0.123	0.049***	0.051	0.061**	0.088	−0.003	0.154
Third quintile	0.152***	0.147	0.073***	0.056	0.103***	0.095	0.045***	0.151
Fourth quintile	0.131**	0.162	0.097***	0.058	0.127***	0.101	0.084***	0.149
Fifth quintile	0.167**	0.179	0.098***	0.066	0.138***	0.112	0.202***	0.154
Employment sector (Government office)								
Government organization			−0.003	0.074	0.032	0.133	−0.020	0.177
SOE			0.014	0.079	−0.032	0.146	−0.006	0.187
COE			−0.096***	0.097	0.010	0.168	−0.036***	0.237
POE			−0.072***	0.079	0.000	0.141	−0.048***	0.207
FOE			0.000	0.126	0.039	0.231	0.052*	0.248
Self			−0.098***	0.090	0.044	0.154	0.017	0.220
Other			−0.087**	0.119	0.005	0.204	0.017	0.270
Employment status								
Regular worker	0.178***	0.120	0.133***	0.048	0.042**	0.080	0.064***	0.139
Hukou (Non-local *hukou*)								
Local *hukou*	0.485***	0.274	0.339***	0.098	0.114***	0.150	0.056***	0.410
Region (Shanghai)								
Jiangsu	−0.341***	0.306	−0.182***	0.091	−0.155***	0.184	−0.053***	0.187
Zhejiang	−0.299***	0.290	−0.139***	0.093	−0.107***	0.173	−0.054***	0.211
Anhui	−0.506***	0.289	−0.362***	0.089	−0.127***	0.157	−0.080***	0.225

(continued)

Table 5.5 (continued)

	(1) UEBMI		(2) UEBMI		(3) Commercial		(4) Mixed	
	dy/dx	SE	dy/dx	SE	dy/dx	SE	dy/dx	SE
Hernan	−0.581***	0.294	−0.440***	0.091	−0.132***	0.158	−0.065***	0.168
Hubei	−0.421***	0.295	−0.359	0.096	−0.100***	0.167	−0.063***	0.264
Guangdong	−0.382***	0.292	−0.354***	0.090	−0.097***	0.151	−0.066***	0.163
Chongqing	−0.570***	0.267	−0.543***	0.094	−0.137***	0.164	−0.078***	0.246
Sichuan	−0.473***	0.287	−0.354***	0.088	−0.108***	0.154	−0.069***	0.170
Male	0.061*	0.095	0.063***	0.037	0.034**	0.063	0.023***	0.093
Married	−0.013	0.175	0.114***	0.066	0.043	0.119	0.054***	0.187
Having child	−0.277***	0.284	−0.104***	0.093	−0.093**	0.157	−0.036	0.227
Education (Elementary and below)								
Junior high	0.031	0.161	0.045**	0.082	0.080*	0.149	0.039	0.277
Senior high	0.159***	0.159	0.082***	0.080	0.070*	0.146	0.061**	0.270
College	0.267***	0.221	0.134***	0.087	0.120**	0.158	0.164***	0.277
University	0.114	0.240	0.131***	0.091	0.112**	0.165	0.185***	0.280
Observations	930		7,175		2,303		2,172	
Log likelihood	−484.890		−3110.639		−1084.246		−498.305	
Pseudo R2	0.242		0.237		0.071		0.471	

Source Calculated based on the data from CHIP2007
Note
(1) ***$p < 0.01$, **$p < 0.05$, *$p < 0.10$
(2) SE: standard error; dy/dx: marginal effect

points), and the non-working group (8.7 percentage points). However, the differences in the probability of UEBMI enrollment among government offices, SOEs, government organizations, and FOEs was not significant.

The reasons for this are as follows: The UEBMI was reformed based on the public medical system instituted in the state-owned sector during the planned economy period, which had already been implemented as the labor insurance medical system covering employees in SOEs and COEs, and the publicly funded medical system that covered civil servants in government offices and government-related organizations; therefore, the differences between government offices, government-related organizations, and SOEs were minor. However, in the non-state-owned sector, the results indicated a difference between FOEs and POEs. The UEBMI implemented in 1998 covered enterprises in both state-owned and non-state-owned sectors, including FOEs and POEs. Both FOEs and POEs face fierce market competition and aim to maximize profits; thus, both may prefer to avoid the financial burden of medical insurance premiums. Nevertheless, the differences in the probability of medical insurance participation between FOEs and POEs may be attributable to the government monitoring and management of both SOEs and FOEs since the late 1990s for social insurance participation, including public medical insurance (government mandate factor). In addition, other factors, such as the philosophy of legal compliance and the business conditions may also affect firms' joining behavior. Future research can consider the effect of firm attributes (such as years of establishment, employee size, and employee age structure) and business conditions.

Second, compared with those without a local urban *hukou*, the probability of medical insurance participation was higher (33.9–48.5 percentage points for UEBMI, 11.4 percentage points for commercial medical insurance, and 5.6 percentage points for mixed medical insurance) for the group with a local urban *huk*ou. The decentralization of financial resources may explain this result. Currently, the central government determines the main rules of social insurance operation, while the local governments manage and implement it. The implementation of medical insurance depends on the local government's fiscal revenue. When the local government implements a policy that prioritizes residents with local urban *hukou*, the probability of enrolling in medical insurance may be higher for the local urban *hukou* group.

Third, compared with non-regular worker group (non-regular workers and self-employed), the probability of medical insurance participation was higher for the regular worker group (13.3–17.8 percentage points for UEBMI, 4.2 percentage points for commercial insurance, and 6.4 percentage point for mixed medical insurance). This is because the urban labor market is segmented by the employment sectors. According to the labor market segmentation hypothesis, the Chinese urban labor market includes the primary market, in which both the wage level and welfare are low, and the secondary labor market, in which both the wage level and welfare are high. Most of the regular employees work in the primary labor market, while non-regular and self-employed people work in the secondary labor market. Therefore, medical insurance participation differed by employment sectors.

Fourth, compared with women, the probability of medical insurance participation was higher for men (6.1–6.3 percentage points higher for UEBMI, 3.4 percentage points higher for commercial insurance, and 2.3 percentage points higher for mixed medical insurance). Keeping other factors constant, the probability of non-participation in medical insurance was higher for females than for males. A detailed analysis of the gender gap in medical insurance enrollment should be conducted in the future.

Fifth, the probability of participation in commercial insurance and mixed medical insurance was higher in senior high school, college, and university groups than in the elementary school group. The educational background results are consistent with those of previous studies in Europe and the U.S. According to health capital model (Grossman, 1972, 2000), the stock of health capital depends on the health investment, the potential for healthy behavior, and the efficiency of health-improving behavior (e.g., medical insurance participation, exercise) and is higher for the highly educated group than for the less-educated group. The present results confirm Grossman's model.

Sixth, the probability of participation in the UEBMI and mixed medical insurance was 11.4 percentage points and 5.4 percentage points higher for those with a spouse and for single individuals, respectively. In addition, the probability of participation in the UEBMI, and commercial medical insurance was 10.4–27.7 percentage points and 9.3 percentage points lower in the group with children and the group without children, respectively. Thus, family factors also affect medical insurance enrollment. Since family responsibilities increase in the group with spouses, the probability of medical insurance participation may be high to avoid household risks such as high medical care expenses. In addition, given household budget constraints, the group with children will prioritize their children over themselves, resulting in more investment for their children (by reducing medical insurance payments) and medical care. Thus, the probability of medical insurance participation was low.

Seventh, compared with those living in Shanghai, the probability of medical insurance participation (UEBMI, commercial insurance, and mixed medical insurance) was lower for those who lived in the other regions (Jiangsu, Zhejiang, Anhui, Henan, Hubei, Guangdong, Chongqing, and Sichuan). From the experience of developed countries, social security policies, including medical insurance, tend to emerge with economic growth. As a result of the promotion of regional economic policies such as let some of the people "get rich first" (*Xianfu Lun*)[12] in China during the transition period, the eastern region developed, but the economic development of the western and central regions was delayed. As Shanghai has the highest level of economic development in China, it follows that the region also had the highest medical insurance enrollment for the study period.

5.5.3 Heterogenous Group: Results by Employment Sector

To explore the different mechanisms of medical insurance participation by employment sector, the probability of participation in the UEBMI was analyzed for four types of sectors: (i) Model 5: Government agencies (government office and government-related organization); (ii) Model 6: SOE; (iii) Model 7: POE; and (iv) Model 8: FOE. The results are summarized in Table 5.6.

First, the health status dummy estimates are not statistically significant for any of the groups, and the adverse selection hypothesis is not supported. This is because UEBMI enrollment is compulsory, and the adverse selection mechanism does not apply; the influence of health status on enrollment probability is small.

Second, in the state-owned sector, compared with the group aged 50–59, the probability of enrolling in the UEBMI is higher for the groups aged 30–39 and 40–49 and lower for the groups aged 16–19 and 20–29. An intergenerational disparity

Table 5.6 Results for the probability of UEBMI participation by state and non-state-owned sectors

	(5) State (Government)		(6) State (SOE)		(7) Non-state (POE)		(8) Non-state (FOE)	
	dy/dx	SE	dy/dx	SE	dy/dx	SE	dy/dx	SE
Health status (Poor)								
Very good	−0.050	0.245	0.011	0.323	0.082	0.243	−0.992	0.548
Good	−0.083	0.236	0.008	0.312	0.078	0.235	−0.898	0.548
Fair	−0.041	0.241	−0.004	0.314	0.032	0.240	−0.990	0.548
Age (Age 50–59)								
Age 16–19	−0.423***	0.186	−0.517***	0.260	−0.478***	0.226	−0.239	0.910
Age 20–29	−0.106***	0.132	−0.050	0.196	−0.479***	0.139	0.009	0.461
Age 30–39	0.032	0.093	0.100***	0.145	−0.030	0.106	0.016	0.398
Age 40–49	0.074***	0.090	0.111***	0.131	0.053	0.103	−0.092	0.405
Income (First quintile)								
Second quintile	0.035*	0.094	0.043*	0.127	0.053*	0.097	−0.094	0.412
Third quintile	0.059***	0.099	0.058**	0.137	0.053	0.108	−0.045	0.476
Fourth quintile	0.051**	0.099	0.103***	0.150	0.109***	0.113	0.033	0.485
Fifth quintile	0.079***	0.112	0.075**	0.169	0.042	0.126	0.007	0.441
Employment status								
Regular worker	0.131***	0.098	0.040	0.152	0.150***	0.075	0.118**	0.354
Hukou (Non-local *hukou*)								
Local *hukou*	0.359***	0.189	0.279**	0.361	0.287***	0.153	0.464***	0.479
Region (Shanghai)								
Jiangsu	−0.112**	0.188	−0.316***	0.215	−0.103**	0.150	−0.095	0.440

(continued)

Table 5.6 (continued)

	(5) State (Government)		(6) State (SOE)		(7) Non-state (POE)		(8) Non-state (FOE)	
	dy/dx	SE	dy/dx	SE	dy/dx	SE	dy/dx	SE
Zhejiang	−0.157***	0.187	−0.229***	0.228	−0.050	0.155	0.003	0.503
Anhui	−0.376***	0.166	−0.319***	0.201	v0.233***	0.163	–	
Hernan	−0.406***	0.170	−0.405***	0.202	−0.415***	0.171	−0.773***	0.898
Hubei	−0.415***	0.174	−0.479***	0.229	−0.215***	0.199	−0.115***	0.528
Guangdong	−0.408***	0.166	−0.442***	0.254	−0.243***	0.157	−0.159**	0.430
Chongqing	−0.561***	0.182	−0.573***	0.211	−0.521***	0.162	−0.635***	0.569
Sichuan	−0.344***	0.166	−0.416***	0.211	−0.281***	0.156	−0.270**	0.499
Male	0.059***	0.064	0.081***	0.092	0.020	0.070	0.077***	0.282
Married	0.140***	0.120	0.091**	0.176	0.154***	0.124	0.007	0.445
Having child	−0.123***	0.198	−0.141***	0.477	−0.060	0.148	0.237**	0.469
Education (Elementary and below)								
Junior high	0.073**	0.165	−0.043	0.213	0.091*	0.165	−0.002	0.625
Senior high	0.056*	0.157	0.040	0.210	0.126**	0.162	0.027	0.582
College	0.114***	0.162	0.055	0.224	0.195***	0.176	0.019	0.598
University	0.106***	0.164	0.076*	0.244	0.189***	0.190	0.028	0.599
Observations	2,724		1,412		1,772		266	
Log likelihood	−1021.858		−496.156		−879.728		−68.872	
Pseudo R^2	0.251		0.300		0.187		0.369	

Source Calculated based on the data from CHIP2007

Note

(1) $^{***}p < 0.01$, $^{**}p < 0.05$, $^{*}p < 0.10$

(2) SE: standard error; dy/dx: marginal effect

emerges in the public medical insurance participation rate in the state-owned sector. With age, the out-of-pocket (OOP) expenses on medical care for the group aged 50–59 that did not participate in the UEBMI would increase, leading to a greater risk of poverty and illnesses. In POEs, the probability of joining the UEBMI is 47.8 and 10.4 percentage points lower in the groups aged 16–19 and 20–29, respectively, compared with the group aged 50–59 years; however, the difference between the groups aged 50–59 and 30–49 is not remarkable. Moreover, in FOEs, the differences in the probability of UEBMI participation between the age groups are not statistically significant. The adverse selection hypothesis is supported partly for both SOEs and POEs, but not for FOEs. Although UEBMI enrollment is stipulated by law, the differences in the probability of enrollment between age groups in SOEs and POEs should be explored at the firm level in future.

Third, in both government offices and SOEs, compared with the low-income group (first quintile), the probability of UEBMI participation is higher in the middle- and high-income groups (third–fifth quintiles). In COEs and POEs, compared with the low-income group (first quintile), the probability of UEBMI participation is 10.9 percentage points higher in the fourth quintile income group. In FOEs, there is no significant difference in the probability of joining the UEBMI among various income groups. The liquidity constraints hypothesis is supported for government offices, SOEs, COEs, and POEs, but not for FOEs.

The results indicate that in 2007, the urban labor market was polarized into high-income/high-welfare and low-income/low-welfare groups. The URBMI, which was implemented in 2007, did not perform the function of income redistribution, but widened the existing disparities instead. This can be attributed to the fact that the UEBMI, implemented in 1998, was not aimed at reducing inequality. Specifically, the main purpose of the reform of the public medical insurance system in urban China was to reduce the government's fiscal burden for medical care expenditures. Therefore, even in the state-owned sector, which emphasizes equality, a disadvantaged low-income–low-welfare group emerged.

5.6 Conclusions

Using CHIP2007 data, this study tested the adverse selection and the liquidity constraints hypotheses for the determinants of medical insurance participation behavior among urban residents in China.

The main conclusions are as follows: First, the probability of participation in the UEBMI increased with age for the self-employed group and employees in POEs. The adverse selection hypothesis was thus supported. The probability of medical insurance participation was higher in the middle- and high-income groups than in the low-income group, and the liquidity constraints hypothesis was also supported.

Second, compared with low-income groups, middle- and high-income groups were found more likely to participate in the UEBMI, commercial insurance, and mixed medical insurance. The results indicated that some low-income groups were covered by neither the public nor the private medical insurance system in 2007, which suggests that there were disparities in medical insurance coverage caused by income inequality.

Third, medical insurance coverage differed across groups. The probability of medical insurance participation was lower for workers in the non-state-owned sector (e.g., COEs, POEs, self-employed, and non-working group), the group with no local urban *hukou*, non-regular workers, low-income and less-educated groups, the group with children, and groups in less-developed regions compared with their counterparts.

Fourth, the impact of each factor on UEBMI participation differed by employment sector. For example, (1) the influence of age on the probability of joining the UEBMI was smaller in the non-state-owned sector than in the state-owned sector. (2) In government offices and government organizations, SOEs, COEs, and POEs, the probability of participation in public medical insurance was higher in middle- and high-income groups than in low-income groups, while in FOEs, the difference among income groups was small.

This study offers the following policy implications: In 2007, public medical insurance coverage differed across low- and high-income groups and state-owned versus non-state-owned employment sectors in urban China, and a group, including low-income individuals, emerged, that was not covered by either the public or the private medical insurance system. To reduce medical care inequality, a medical insurance system targeting the disadvantaged groups—low-income, less-educated, self-employed, and small POEs workers, and non-working individuals—should be implemented. This study provides evidence to support the URBMI scheme that was implemented by the Chinese government in 2007 to cover those who did not participate in the UEBMI (such as those under the age of 18 and non-working groups). However, the financial fund and insurance premiums differ between the UEBMI and the URBMI; thus, the inequality of public medical insurance by group (working and non-working groups) has not been completely eliminated. In addition, there is a difference in public medical insurance coverage and OOP expenses between regular and non-regular workers. Policymakers may consider a system wherein the proportion of OOP expenses is the same regardless of the type of public medical insurance that an individual subscribes to. The true realization of universal medical insurance should be an important issue for the Chinese government.

Notes

1. There are two types of public medical insurance systems for urban *hukou* residents: the UEBMI scheme covering urban employees implemented in 1998, and the URBMI scheme, implemented in 2007, covering urban residents who could not be covered by the UEBMI. As the survey data is from the CHIP2007, the UEBMI is analyzed as public medical insurance. For the analysis including both the UEBMI and the URBMI, please refer to Chap. 6 of this book.
2. A multinomial logit model, under the assumption of independence of irrelevant alternatives (IIA), can also be used to analyze the probability of each medical insurance. The IIA test results for (i) the UEBMI only, (ii) commercial medical insurance only, (iii) other medical insurance only, (iv) mixed medical insurance, and (v) not covered by medical insurance did not confirm the IIA between the five kinds of insurance. Therefore, this study used a binary probit regression model.
3. Although commercial medical insurance companies cannot refuse insurance purchase applications from consumers, they may try to avoid the problem of adverse selection by setting payments and limiting contract conditions. For example, the premiums of a certain commercial medical insurance sold by the China Life Insurance Company (China Life), a large-scale commercial insurance company, are summarized in Appendix Table 5.9. The premiums for men and women living in Beijing are observed to increase with age. Specifically, for men aged 60–69 years, the total premium is the same as the maximum premium. It is assumed that the middle-aged and older age groups (50 and 60 s) are excluded by setting such high insurance premiums. In addition, according to the authors' field survey, the types of illnesses for which insurance is provided are limited in commercial medical insurance contracts, and a prior medical examination is required; the contract contents differ for the type of diseases.
4. For the question item on subjective health status, since the number of respondents who answered "poor" and "very poor" was small, the two groups were combined into one group with poor health for the analysis.
5. In the age group analysis, the following two points are the main reasons for selecting the 50–59 years category as the reference group. First, the proportion of the sample aged 50–59 years was the largest. When the group with a large number of samples is used as the reference group, robust estimation results can be obtained. Second, the results are easier to understand if a scale is used to compare the lowest and the highest age groups. We performed estimations using the lowest and the highest age groups as reference groups, and the results were similar. Due to space limitations, only the results using the highest age group (50–59 years) as the reference group have been provided.
6. To avoid the problem of multicollinearity, household income excluding individual labor income, was used as a proxy variable for liquidity constraints.

7. Income groups were categorized based on the per capita household equivalent income. The per capita household equivalent income is the household income, excluding the individual working income, divided by the number of family members.
8. Although factors such as savings, debt, and inheritance are considered to be proxy indicators for liquidity constraints, only household income was used as a proxy indicator in this study as these data could not be obtained from the CHIP2007.
9. Based on the CHIP2007 questionnaire items, central government/provincial government SOEs, local government SOEs, and enterprises wherein the government became the main shareholder through equity conversion reforms are collectively defined as SOEs.
10. The Shanghai dummy was designated as the reference group for the following reasons: First, individual workers' awareness of insurance coverage generally differs with the level of economic development. Shanghai had the highest economic development among the nine regions, with a GDP per capita of 73,124 yuan in 2007, making it the ideal reference group. Second, according to the officer data from *2008 China Hygiene Statistics Yearbook* and *China Statistical Yearbook 2008*, in 2007, Shanghai's public medical insurance enrollment rate (UEBMI and URBMI) was the highest, at 66.6% (24.1%–52.7% in the other eight regions).
11. According to public pension regulations, the mandatory retirement age for blue-collar workers is 55 years and 50 years for male and female workers, respectively, and the mandatory retirement age for white-collar workers (executives and university graduates) is 60 and 55–60 years for male and female workers, respectively.
12. The "let some of the people get rich first" is one of the basic principles of the reform and opening-up policy that has been advocated by Deng Xiaoping since 1985. This principle implied that areas that developed first (eastern areas) would eventually influence the development of other areas (central and western areas). As a result, regional disparities have grown since the 1990s.

Appendix

See Appendix Tables 5.7, 5.8, and 5.9.

Table 5.7 Types of medical insurance in urban China and analyzed targets in empirical studies

	Type		Target	Premium	Implemented year	Analyzed in this study	Analyzed in previous study
Public medical insurance	UEBMI		Employees in Corporates including SOEs, COEs, POEs and FOEs, Social organization, NPO organization	Fixed rate system Corporate: 6% of total wage bill Employee: 2% of wage Government: fund operating and Management costs	1998	Yes	Yes Zhou (2003)
	URBMI		Urban residents who did not covered by the UEBMI (those who younger than 18 years and non-work urban residents)	Government: per capita 120 yuan yearly Individual: differ by region	2007	No	Yes Lin et al. (2009)
Private medical insurance	Commercial insurance		Urban residents	Flat rate system	Since 1980s	Yes	No
Other medical insurance	Other	Medical aid	Low-income individual	Exemption system	Since1950s	Yes	No
		Corporate subsidy medical insurance	A part of employee	Differ by Corporates	Since 1980s	Yes	No

Source Created by the author

Note UEBMI: urban employee basic medical insurance; URBMI: urban resident basic medical insurance; SOEs: state-owned enterprises; COEs: collectively owned enterprises; POEs: privately owned enterprises; FOEs: foreign owed enterprises; NPO: no-profit organization

Table 5.8 Descriptive statistics of variables

	Total		UEBMI		Mixed		Commercial		Non-participant	
	Mean	SD	Mean	SD	Mean	SD	Mean	SD	Mean	SD
Health status (Poor)										
Very good	0.195	0.396	0.190	0.393	0.154	0.361	0.233	0.423	0.201	0.401
Good	0.543	0.498	0.540	0.499	0.490	0.501	0.562	0.497	0.557	0.497
Fair	0.239	0.426	0.247	0.431	0.319	0.467	0.189	0.392	0.219	0.414
Poor	0.023	0.151	0.023	0.151	0.037	0.191	0.016	0.124	0.023	0.149
Age (Age 50–59)										
Age16–19	0.060	0.238	0.016	0.124	0.026	0.161	0.193	0.395	0.156	0.363
Age20–29	0.175	0.380	0.142	0.349	0.188	0.391	0.229	0.421	0.261	0.440
Age30–39	0.255	0.435	0.269	0.444	0.276	0.448	0.304	0.460	0.192	0.394
Age40–49	0.284	0.451	0.321	0.467	0.310	0.463	0.166	0.372	0.197	0.397
Age50–59	0.226	0.418	0.252	0.434	0.200	0.401	0.108	0.311	0.194	0.396
Income										
First quintile	0.215	0.411	0.183	0.387	0.109	0.312	0.208	0.406	0.325	0.469
Second quintile	0.223	0.416	0.220	0.415	0.112	0.316	0.225	0.418	0.257	0.437
Third quintile	0.189	0.391	0.197	0.398	0.165	0.371	0.191	0.394	0.174	0.379
Fourth quintile	0.197	0.398	0.215	0.411	0.229	0.421	0.206	0.405	0.138	0.345
Fifth quintile	0.176	0.380	0.185	0.388	0.385	0.487	0.170	0.376	0.106	0.309
Employment sector										
Government office	0.084	0.277	0.091	0.288	0.082	0.275	0.070	0.256	0.067	0.250
Government organization	0.294	0.456	0.316	0.465	0.300	0.459	0.289	0.454	0.231	0.422
SOE	0.192	0.394	0.211	0.408	0.218	0.413	0.125	0.331	0.155	0.362
COE	0.063	0.243	0.062	0.240	0.053	0.224	0.070	0.256	0.065	0.247

(continued)

Table 5.8 (continued)

	Total		UEBMI		Mixed		Commercial		Non-participant	
	Mean	SD	Mean	SD	Mean	SD	Mean	SD	Mean	SD
POE	0.181	0.385	0.171	0.376	0.085	0.280	0.204	0.403	0.225	0.418
FOE	0.040	0.197	0.043	0.204	0.126	0.333	0.032	0.176	0.021	0.143
Self	0.115	0.318	0.078	0.269	0.106	0.308	0.176	0.381	0.197	0.398
Other	0.031	0.172	0.028	0.163	0.030	0.169	0.034	0.181	0.039	0.194
Employment status										
Regular worker	0.765	0.424	0.820	0.384	0.868	0.339	0.692	0.462	0.623	0.485
Non-regular	0.162	0.368	0.131	0.337	0.097	0.296	0.170	0.376	0.249	0.432
Other	0.073	0.261	0.049	0.216	0.035	0.185	0.138	0.345	0.128	0.334
Local *hukou*	0.971	0.168	0.982	0.134	0.991	0.094	0.960	0.197	0.936	0.245
Regions										
Shanghai	0.124	0.330	0.142	0.349	0.441	0.497	0.091	0.288	0.038	0.192
Jiangsu	0.115	0.319	0.139	0.346	0.076	0.266	0.047	0.211	0.081	0.273
Zhejiang	0.119	0.324	0.146	0.353	0.053	0.224	0.074	0.263	0.070	0.255
Anhui	0.127	0.333	0.123	0.329	0.018	0.132	0.130	0.336	0.147	0.354
Hernan	0.110	0.313	0.089	0.285	0.094	0.292	0.121	0.326	0.152	0.350
Hubei	0.074	0.262	0.068	0.252	0.021	0.142	0.093	0.291	0.096	0.359
Guangdong	0.127	0.333	0.109	0.312	0.185	0.389	0.183	0.387	0.135	0.294
Chongqing	0.074	0.261	0.056	0.230	0.024	0.152	0.093	0.291	0.131	0.342
Sichuan	0.130	0.336	0.128	0.333	0.088	0.284	0.168	0.374	0.150	0.339
Male	0.497	0.500	0.516	0.500	0.503	0.501	0.501	0.501	0.443	0.497
Married	0.788	0.409	0.866	0.341	0.826	0.379	0.614	0.487	0.608	0.488
Having child	0.940	0.238	0.931	0.253	0.932	0.252	0.926	0.263	0.966	0.181
Education										
Elementary and below	0.046	0.210	0.036	0.187	0.015	0.121	0.038	0.192	0.081	0.273
Junior high	0.220	0.414	0.200	0.400	0.135	0.343	0.257	0.437	0.283	0.451
Senior high	0.359	0.480	0.350	0.477	0.332	0.472	0.350	0.478	0.384	0.487
College	0.209	0.407	0.230	0.421	0.253	0.435	0.195	0.397	0.146	0.353
University	0.166	0.371	0.184	0.387	0.265	0.442	0.160	0.366	0.106	0.308
Observations	8,209		5,341		340		471		1,832	

Source Calculated based on the data from CHIP 2007
Note Mean: mean value; SD: standard deviation

Table 5.9 China Life Insurance Company's Guoshou kangning lifetime serious illness insurance premium (Beijing). Unit: CNY(Yuan)

	Age 30–39	Age 40–49	Age 50–59	Age 60–69
Women				
Premium yearly	7,800	9,900	12,900	27,500
Number of payment year	20	20	20	10
Total amount	156,000	198,000	258,000	275,000
Maximum amount of payment	300,000	300,000	300,000	300,000
Men				
Premium yearly	8,700	11,200	14,600	30,000
Number of payment year	20	20	20	10
Total amount	174,000	224,000	292,000	300,000
Maximum amount of payment	300,000	300,000	300,000	300,000

Source Creation by the author based on the materials published on the website of China Life Insurance Company. http://www.e-chinalife.com/product/benefitshow/indexlis.jsp?RiskCode=432 (accessed on October 20, 2016)

References

Bograd, H., Ritzwoller, D. P., Calonge, N., Shields, K., & Hanrahan, M. (1997). Extending health maintenance organization insurance to the uninsured. *Journal of the American Medical Association, 277*(13), 1067–1072.

Drehr, P., Madden, C. W., Cheadle, A., Martin, D. P., Patrick, D. L., & Skillman, S. (1996). Will uninsured people volunteer for voluntary health insurance? Experience from Washington State. *American Journal of Public Health, 86*(4), 529–532.

Grossman, M. (1972). On the concept of health capital and the demand for health. *Journal of Political Economy, 80*, 223–255.

Grossman, M. (2000). The human capital model. In A. J. Culyer & J. P. Newhouse (Eds). *Handbook of health economics Volume 1B*. Elsevier.

Hofter, R. H. (2006). Private health insurance and utilization of health services in Chlie. *Applied Economics, 38*, 423–439.

Kimani, J. K., Ettarh, R., Kyobutungi, C., Mberu, B., & Muindi, K. (2012). Determinants for participation in a public health insurance program among residents of urban slums in Nairobi, Kenya: Results from a cross sectional survey. *BMC Health Services Research, 12*(66), 2–11.

Long, S. H., & Marquis, M. S. (2002). Participation in a public insurance program: Subsidies, crowd-out, and adverse selection. *Inquiry, 39*(3), 243–257.

Lin, W., Liu, G. G., & Chen, G. (2009). The urban resident basic medical insurance: A landmark reform towards universal coverage in China. *Health Economics, 18*, 83–96.

Madden, C. W., Cheadle, A., Diehr, P., Martin, D. P., Patrick, D. L., & Skillman, S. (1995). Voluntary public health insurance for low-income families: The decision to enroll. *Journal of Health Politics, Policy and Law, 20*(4), 955–972.

Ma, X., & Cheng, J. (2019). The influence of social insurance on wages in China: An empirical study based on Chinese Employee-Employer Matching Data. *Emerging Markets Finance and Trade*. https://doi.org/10.1080/1540496X.2019.1693363

Nagakane, K. (2000). The issues and the points of social security research in China. *Journal of Social Security Research, 132*, 2–12. (in Japanese).

Pardo, C., & Schott, W. (2012). Public versus private: Evidence on health insurance selection. *Journal Health Care Finance Economics, 12*, 39–61.

Shaefer, H. L., Grogan, C. M., & Pollack, H. A. (2011). Who transitions from private to public health insurance? Lessons from expansions of the state children's health insurance program. *Journal of Health Care for the Poor and Underserved, 22*, 359–370.

Swartz, G., & Garnick, D. (2000). Adverse selection and price sensitivity when low-income people have subsidies to purchase health insurance in the private market. *Inquiry, 37*(1), 45–60.

Wolfe, J. R., & Goddeeris, J. H. (1991). Adverse selection, moral hazard, and wealth effects in the Medigap insurance market. *Journal of Health Economics, 10*, 433–459.

Zhou, Y. (2003). No-participants of medical insurance and household health care expenditure: Based on Guangdong Province Household Survey data in China. *Journal of Social Security Research, 143*, 80–92. (in Japanese).

Chapter 6
Determinants of Participation in Public Medical Insurance Systems: A Comparison Between Urban and Rural Residents

Abstract Using the data from the China Health and Retirement Longitudinal Study of 2011, this study tests three hypotheses and verifies the determinants of participation in public medical insurances in rural and urban areas. Several major conclusions have been drawn. First, we find differences in the participation probability between rural and urban residents. This is because the establishment and implementation of public medical insurance programs differ between rural and urban areas. Second, the liquidity constraints hypothesis is rejected, whereas the adverse selection hypothesis is supported. Lastly, education, gender, and drinking behavior affect participation probabilities as well; however, the effects vary between rural and urban residents.

Keywords Medical insurance · Liquidity constraints hypothesis · Adverse selection hypothesis · Rural and urban residents · China

6.1 Introduction

Since the 1980s, China has witnessed a decline in fertility rate and an increase in the aging population due to the implementation of the population control policy (e.g., the one-child policy). Thus, the implementation of social security systems has become an important issue for the Chinese government. Along with the transition from a planned economy to a market-oriented economy, public medical insurance has been reformed since the 1990s (see Appendix Tables 6.5 and 6.6).

Currently, a variety of public medical insurance programs are being implemented in current China. For example, the Urban Employee Basic Medical Insurance

---

This chapter is a revised and developed version of Ma (2016) Public medical insurance system reform and the determinants of participation to the medical insurance systems in the aging China. *Journal of Population Problems*, 72(3), 236–255. copyright © National Institute of Population and Social Security Research, Japan.

I would like to thank Dr. Toru Suzuki (National Institute of Population and Social Security Research), Dr. Keita Suga (National Institute of Population and Social Security Research), Professor Hiroshi Kojima (Waseda University), and Professor Naoko Soma (Yokohama National University) for their comments at the 2014 International Conference "Comparative Studies on Population Aging Policies in the Eastern Asian" held in Tokyo and Kyoto. I am very grateful to Dr. Toru Suzuki for his extremely helpful suggestions.

X. Ma, *Public Medical Insurance Reforms in China*,
https://doi.org/10.1007/978-981-16-7790-8_6

(UEBMI), which covers employees in urban areas, the majority of whom have an urban *hukou* (household registration),[1] has been implemented since 1998; the Urban Resident Basic Medical Insurance (URBMI), which covers non-working individuals with urban *hukou*, was introduced in 2007, and the New Rural Cooperative Medical Scheme (NRCMS), initiated in 2003, provides coverage to individuals with a rural *hukou*. In addition, since the 1990s, private medical insurance (e.g., commercial insurance), and corporate medical insurance, which is purchased by a corporate as part of its welfare system for its employees, have been implemented to complement the public medical insurances. Moreover, the medical aid system (MA) has been implemented to assist low-income groups since the 1950s. Currently, these public and private medical insurances cover the entire population in rural and urban areas.

However, the implementation of these public medical insurances faces some problems; this study focuses on two issues. First, the extents of participation and offerings differ according to the type of medical insurance system. For instance, public medical insurances vary in urban and rural areas. Although individuals working in urban corporates are eligible to participate in the UEBMI, the enrollment rate of rural–urban migrant workers in this scheme is low. One of the reasons for this is that corporates do not prefer to pay the medical insurance premiums for rural-urban migrant workers. Thus, there is a disparity in medical insurance participation between rural and urban residents. Moreover, the implementation of public medical insurance systems varies by employment sector. For example, the regulations of the UEBMI mandate that corporates (employers) must pay medical insurance premiums (amounting to 6% of the wage bill) for their employees. However, as Nakagane (2000) and Ma (2014, 2015) point out, compared with corporates in the state-owned sector (i.e., stare-owned enterprise: SOE, etc.), the possibility of corporates in non-state-owned sector (i.e., privately-owned enterprise: POE, etc.) not paying medical insurance premiums for their employees might be higher as they seek to gain more profits, and the medical insurance premium is a part of the labor cost in corporates. Consequently, participation in public medical insurance might differ by employment sector (i.e., state-owned sector vs. no-state-owned sector).

Second, growth in income inequality is accompanied by a disparity in medical insurance participation. To rectify the inequality in medical care caused by income inequality, the public medical insurance in developed countries, such as the U.S. and Japan, is implemented as a means of income redistribution, and it covers low-income groups as well. However, in China, the main purpose of public medical insurance reforms, which have been instituted since the 1990s, is to reduce the insurance fund burden on the government and SOEs, and most private medical insurance companies focus only on the middle- and high-income groups. Thus, income inequality in China may have given rise to disparities in public medical insurance participation.

Does participation in each kind of medical insurance differ by rural and urban *hukou* or employment sectors? Does income affect an individual's participation in public medical insurance? This study attempts to answer these research questions through empirical analysis. We use data from the China Health and Retirement Longitudinal Study (CHARLS) conducted in 2011 (CHARLS 2011).

The remainder of this chapter is structured as follows. Section 2 reviews the public medical insurance reforms in China and previous empirical studies. Section 3 describes the data, models, and analytical methods. Section 4 analyzes participation in medical insurance via statistical analysis. Section 5 presents the results of the quantitative analysis. Finally, Sect. 6 concludes the study.

6.2 Literature Review

First, we review previous studies on the determinants of participation in medical insurance from the demand side perspective.[2] Specifically, we analyze the adverse selection and liquidity constraints hypotheses. Regarding the adverse selection hypothesis based on microeconomic theory, there exists an information asymmetry problem in the insurance market. For example, insured individuals often have relatively more information about their health status than insurers. When one in poor health guesses that one will have to pay more toward one's medical care expenses in the future, one tries to hedge the risk by participating in medical insurance. Consequently, the probability of participation in medical insurance is relatively higher for groups in poor health as compared to those in good health. According to the liquidity constraints hypothesis, since a medical insurance premium needs to be paid, the possibility that an individual cannot purchase the insurance premium is higher in the low-income group than in the high-income group, and thus, the probability of participation in medical insurance is lower for the low-income group.

However, the estimated results for these two hypotheses have been inconsistent. For example, some empirical studies in the U.S., such as Wolfe and Goddeeris (1991) and Shaefer et al. (2011), analyzed the probability of switching from private medical insurance to public medical insurance. They found that the probability of such a change is higher for groups with low income and poor health and indicate that the estimated results support both the liquidity constraints and adverse selection hypotheses. However, Madden et al. (1995), Drehr et al. (1996), Bograd et al. (1997), Swartz and Garnick (2000), and Long and Marquis (2002) found that health status does not affect the participation probability in the U.S. and that the adverse selection hypothesis is rejected.

Then, we review the empirical studies on developing countries, excluding China. Kimani et al. (2012) conducted an empirical study on Kenya's public medical insurance reforms and found that the probability of participation in public medical insurance is higher for regular workers as compared to those working in the informal sector. Their results indicate the existence of a liquidity constraints problem in Kenya. Hofter (2006) and Pardo and Schott (2012) analyzed the case of Chile and demonstrated that the probability of participation in public medical insurance is higher for the poor, healthy, low-income, less educated, and self-employed worker groups. Therefore, both adverse selection and liquidity constraints hypotheses are supported in this case.

Related empirical studies on China are scarce. Zhou (2003) analyzed the determinants of voluntary participation in the UEBMI (e.g., she considered the self-employed workers and free workers who can adjust their work hours by themselves and are not employed by companies and organizations) using data from the Social Change Basic Survey conducted by the Development Center at Zhongshan University in 2000. She found that participation probabilities are lower for the poor, younger generation, and unemployed workers. Further, she points out that both adverse selection and liquidity constraints hypotheses are supported. Lin et al. (2009) analyzed the probability of participation in the URBMI using data from a survey conducted by Peking University in 2008. Their findings show that the relationship between income and participation probability is U-shaped (i.e., compared to the middle-income group, the participation probability is relatively higher for the low- and high-income groups) and the participation probability is higher for the group that suffered from a chronic disease in the past year. Thus, they show that the adverse selection hypothesis is supported, and the liquidity constraints hypothesis is partly supported. Ma (2014) analyzed the determinants of participation of local urban residents in the UEBMI and the private medical insurance using data from the Chinese Household Income Project Survey conducted in 2008 and found that both adverse selection and liquidity constraints hypotheses are supported. In addition, she points out that compared with the public sector, the probability of participation in the UEBMI was lower for employees in the non-state-owned sector (e.g., collectively owned enterprise: COE, POE, and self-employment sector), and non-working individuals in 2007.

Currently, the lack of empirical evidence on the determinants of participation in public and private medical insurance in China prevents us from comprehending the mechanism of participation behavior. In particular, the significant income inequality between rural and urban areas, and differences in lifestyles, medical care facilities, and public medical insurance contents make it likely that the determinants of participation in public medical insurance will vary between urban and rural areas. In addition, the implementation of public medical insurance might vary by employment sector, and thus, it is assumed that the determinants of participation in public medical insurance systems vary by employment sector. However, none of the empirical studies focus on comparisons between rural and urban residents and between employment sectors in China. This study aims to fill this gap in the literature.

Based on previous studies and China's special situation, this study tests the following three hypotheses (H1, H2, and H3):

H1: Participation in public medical insurance differs by rural and urban *hukou* (segmentation by the *hukou* hypothesis).

H2: Participation in public medical insurance differs by income group (liquidity constraints hypothesis).
H3: The adverse selection problem exists when an individual decides to participate in public medical insurance (adverse selection hypothesis).

The estimated results of H1 are particularly applicable to China, and these results are useful for an in-depth understanding of the problems related to social security systems in China. The results of the analyses for H2 and H3 can be compared with those of previous related studies on developed and other developing countries.

6.3 Methodology and Data

6.3.1 Model

Probit regression models, expressed as Eqs. (6.1)–(6.3), are utilized to measure the probability of participation in a medical insurance.

$$Y_i^* = a + \beta X_i + u_i \tag{6.1}$$

$$Y_i^* = \begin{cases} 1 \text{ if } Y_i^* \geq 0 \\ 0 \text{ if } Y_i^* < 0 \end{cases} \tag{6.2}$$

$$P(Y_i = 1) = P(1 - a - \beta X_i > u_i) \tag{6.3}$$

Here, i denotes individuals, $P(Y_i = 1)$ indicates the dependent variable (which is equal to 1 if the individual subscribes to public or private medical insurance, and 0 otherwise), Y_i^* is a continuous but unobservable latent variable (we only observe the actual variable, as expressed in Eq. (6.3)), a is a constant, and u_i is the random error term. β refers to the factors affecting participation behavior, and the index variables of H1–H3 are utilized to test these hypotheses. β refers to the estimated parameters. If β is statistically significant, the hypotheses are supported.

6.3.2 Data and Variable Setting

Data from the CHARLS of 2011 (CHARLS 2011) are used for the analysis. The survey was conducted in August 2011 by the China Center for Economic Research, Peking University. It covers individuals aged 45 years and above and their family members in rural and urban regions. The total sample comprises 17,780 individuals. The survey data includes information on participation in medical insurance, health status, household income and consumption, demographic factors, health behavior, and employment status. Nationwide samples and subsamples, namely, the rural group (the group with rural *hukou*) and the urban group (the group with urban *hukou*), are utilized in the analysis. The objects of the analysis in this study are individuals aged 45 years and above, including workers and non-working individuals in urban and rural areas.

In the participation probability function, the dependent variable is the binary variable (equal to 1 if the individual has participated in any medical insurance system, and 0 otherwise).

Based on CHARLS 2011, medical insurance is classified into 10 categories as follows: 1. UEBMI, 2. URBMI, 3. new rural cooperative medical scheme (NRCMS), 4. urban and rural resident basic medical insurance (URRMI), 5. publicly funded medical system (PFMS), 6. medical aid system (MA), 7. private medical insurance purchased by firms (PMI-1), 8. private medical insurance purchased by individuals (PMI-2), 9. other (other medical insurance not listed above), and 10. No insurance (i.e., the individual has not participated in any medical insurance).

To test H1–H3, the independent variables are constructed as follows: First, the urban *hukou* dummy is constructed based on two questions, namely, "What is your current *hukou* (registration) status?" and "What is the location of your current *hukou*?" This dummy variable takes the value of 1 when the answers are "non-agriculture" and "province or city," respectively, and 0 otherwise. Holding the other factors (individual characteristics) constant, when the coefficients of the urban *hukou* dummies are statistically significant, it reveals that participation probabilities differ between the urban and rural *hukou* groups, and thus, H1 (segmentation by *hukou* hypothesis) is supported.

Second, to test H2 (liquidity constraints hypothesis), the indicator of liquidity constraints is calculated. CHARLS 2011 provides information on both household income and consumption for the previous year. Considering the permanent income effect, household consumption is a better index than temporary income (information on a single year's household income can be obtained from the survey). Therefore, total household consumption, excluding medical care expenses, is utilized as the indicator of liquidity constraints. The household consumption variables are divided into five groups, one for each quintile. The first quintile group has the lowest income, and the fifth quintile group has the highest income. When the liquidity constraints problem exists, the participation probability is higher for the high-income group as compared to the low-income group. Thus, the estimated results for household income are positively significant.

Third, to analyze H3 (adverse selection hypothesis), two indicators are constructed. First, the occurrence of disease in the past year's dummy variables[3] (equals 1 when the individual suffers from a disease, and 0 otherwise) is used. Based on CHARLS, there are 14 types of diseases as follows: 1. Hypertension; 2. Dyslipidemia (elevation of low-density lipoprotein, triglycerides (TGs), and total cholesterol, or a low high-density lipoprotein level); 3. Diabetes or high blood sugar levels; 4. Cancer or malignant tumors (excluding minor skin cancers); 5. Chronic lung diseases such as chronic bronchitis and emphysema (excluding tumors and cancer); 6. Liver disease (except fatty liver, tumors, and cancer); 7. Heart attack, coronary heart disease, angina, congestive heart failure, or other heart problems; 8. Stroke; 9. Kidney disease (excluding tumors or cancer); 10. Stomach or other digestive diseases (excluding tumors or cancer); 11. Emotional, nervous, or psychiatric problems, 12. Memory-related disease; 13. Arthritis or rheumatism; and 14. Asthma. Second, five types of age dummy variables (age 45–49, age 50–59, age 60–69, age 70–79, and age 80 and older) are used.

Lastly, regarding the other factors, we construct dummies for married respondents, children, and males to control for the influence of individual attributes and family factors. Further, the following employment sector dummies are used to control for the influence of the employment sector, which is explored in Chap. 4: (i) government office; (ii) government-related organization (*Shiye Danwei*); (iii) SOE (including 100% SOEs and state-controlled enterprises); (iv) COE (including 100% collective-owned firms and collective-controlled firms); (v) POE including 100% private enterprise, privately controlled enterprises, 100% foreign-owned enterprise (FOE), joint venture enterprises, and other joint-ownership enterprises; (vi) self-employed [4]; and (vii) others.

As stated earlier, the regulations of the UEBMI mandate that firms need to pay a portion of the public medical insurance premiums for their employees. Thus, there should be no disparity between employment sectors with different ownership types. If other factors comprising individual attributes are held constant, when the coefficients of the ownership dummies are statistically significant, it suggests that the participation probabilities vary by ownership types, which might cause disparities among the employment sectors.

In addition, because behaviors such as smoking and drinking can affect health status, they might influence participation in the medical insurance system. Therefore, we introduce a smoking status dummy (no smoking, smoking now, smoking in the past) and drinking fequency dummies (no drinking, drinking once a month, drinking more than once a month).

Appendix Table 6.7 shows sample statistical descriptions by nationwide, urban, and rural areas. Excluding the missing values, the total sample that is utilized for the econometric analysis has 16,778 observations, of which 3,763 are for the urban group, and 13,015 are for the rural group.

6.4 Descriptive Statistic Results

6.4.1 Proportion of Participants in Medical Insurance by Hukou Group

Table 6.1 summarizes the proportion of participants in medical insurance systems by nation, rural, and urban *hukou* groups.

First, the overall proportion of participants in public medical insurance (including participation in the UEBMI, URBMI, NRCMS, PMFS, or MA) is 90%, and the proportion of non-participation (i.e., the respondents subscribe to none of the above-mentioned medical insurance systems) is only 6.7%. Thus, it can be said that China virtually achieved "universal medical insurance" in 2011 (the survey year).

Table 6.1 Proportion of participants in medical insurance by medical insurance type

Medical Insurance Categories	Nation		Urban		Rural	
	Num	%	Num	%	Num	%
1. UEBMI	1,772	10.2	1,690	43.7	82	0.6
2. URBMI	740	4.3	647	16.7	93	0.7
3. NRCMS	12,568	72.3	471	12.2	12,097	89.5
4. URRBMI	212	1.2	93	2.4	119	0.9
5. PFMS	352	2.0	324	8.4	28	0.2
6. MA	14	0.1	7	0.2	7	0.1
7. PMI (1)	117	0.7	75	1.9	42	0.3
8. PMI (2)	314	1.8	122	3.2	192	1.4
9. Other	130	0.7	46	1.2	84	0.6
10. No insurance	1,162	6.7	396	10.1	766	5.7
Total	17,381	100.0	3,871	100.0	13,510	100.0

Source Calculated based on the data from CHARLS 2011
Note UEBMI: Urban Employee Basic Medical Insurance; URBMI: Urban Resident Basic Medical Insurance; NRCMS: New Rural Cooperative Medical Scheme; URRMI: Urban and Rural Resident Basic Medical Insurance; PFMS: publicly funded medical system; MA: medical aid; PMI-1: private medical insurance purchased by firms; PMI-2: private medical insurance purchased by individuals; Others: other medical insurance not listed above; no insurance: the individual has not participated in any medical insurance

Moreover, the proportion of participants in the NRCMS is the highest (72.3%) nationwide, owing to the high proportion of rural residents. It is noteworthy that although the percentage of urban residents is nearly 50% in 2011, the proportion of participants in the NRCMS is 72.3%, which is higher than the proportion of rural residents. This indicates that a section of the rural–urban migrants[5] has not been covered by urban public medical insurance (e.g., UEBMI and URBMI), which indicates that public medical insurance is segmented by urban and rural *hukou*.

Second, the proportion of participants in public medical insurance differs between urban and rural residents; specifically, the proportion of participants in the NRCMS (89.5%) is the highest for rural residents, whereas that in the UEBMI (43.7%) is the highest for urban residents.

6.4.2 Proportion of Participants in Medical Insurance by Income, Health Status and Age Groups

Table 6.2 reports the proportion of participants in medical insurance by income, health status and age groups.

First, for urban residents, the proportion of participants in the public medical insurance system is greater for the high-income group (UEBMI: 51.3%, URBMI:

Table 6.2 Proportion of participants in medical insurance by group

Medical insurance categories	Urban			Rural		
	Low	Middle	High	Low	Middle	High
(a) by income group (unit: %)						
1. UEBMI	48.6	44.5	51.3	0.9	0.7	0.9
2. URBMI	14.9	14.9	15.9	0.5	0.4	0.7
3. NRCMS	9.8	8.6	7.4	89.0	90.7	87.5
4. URRBMI	1.5	1.8	1.7	1.1	1.5	1.3
5. PFMS	5.9	9.7	6.4	0.2	0.4	0.1
6. MA	0.3	0.2	0.0	0.1	0.1	0.0
7. PMI (1)	5.1	2.0	0.5	0.6	0.4	0.1
8. PMI (2)	4.4	3.8	3.6	1.1	0.7	1.5
9. Other	0.5	1.4	1.0	1.1	0.4	0.7
10. No insurance	9.0	13.1	12.2	5.4	4.7	7.2
Total	100.0	100.0	100.0	100.0	100.0	100.0
Medical insurance categories	Urban			Rural		
	Good	Fair	Poor	Good	Fair	Poor
(b) by SRH group (unit: %)						
1. UEBMI	23.5	47.8	7.5	4.0	0.8	6.1
2. URBMI	9.1	15.4	5.0	1.5	0.7	3.7
3. NRCMS	45.5	13.3	75.6	82.7	89.2	79.3
4. URRBMI	1.4	1.5	1.6	0.7	1.1	1.4
5. PFMS	5.4	7.5	1.2	0.9	0.1	1.1
6. MA	0.1	0.0	0.1	0.1	0.0	0.1
7. PMI (1)	2.2	1.2	0.6	1.1	0.3	0.5
8. PMI (2)	2.6	3.3	1.5	1.8	1.5	1.4
9. Other	1.0	1.3	0.8	0.6	0.5	0.7
10. No insurance	9.2	8.7	6.1	6.8	5.7	5.7
Total	100.0	100.0	100.0	100.0	100.0	100.0
Medical insurance categories	Urban			Rural		
	40–49	50–59	60+	40–49	50–59	60+
(c) by age group (unit: %)						
1. UEBMI	39.7	42.6	46.1	0.6	0.6	0.6
2. URBMI	17.7	17.8	15.6	0.6	0.8	0.7
3. NRCMS	14.5	13.7	10.2	87.9	89.1	90.8
4. URRBMI	2.2	2.5	2.4	0.8	0.8	1.0
5. PFMS	3.5	6.2	11.9	0.1	0.3	0.2
6. MA	0.0	0.2	0.3	0.1	0.0	0.1

(continued)

Table 6.2 (continued)

Medical insurance categories	Urban			Rural		
	40–49	50–59	60+	40–49	50–59	60+
7. PMI (1)	2.0	1.7	2.1	0.6	0.3	0.2
8. PMI (2)	6.8	3.5	1.4	2.9	1.8	0.3
9. Other	0.9	0.9	1.5	0.7	0.8	0.4
10. No insurance	12.7	10.9	8.5	5.7	5.5	5.7
Total	100.0	100.0	100.0	100.0	100.0	100.0

Source Calculated based on the data from CHARLS 2011
Note UEBMI: Urban Employee Basic Medical Insurance; URBMI: Urban Resident Basic Medical Insurance; NRCMS: New Rural Cooperative Medical Scheme; URRMI: Urban and Rural Resident Basic Medical Insurance; PFMS: publicly funded medical system; MA: medical aid; PMI-1: private medical insurance purchased by firms; PMI-2: private medical insurance purchased by individuals; Others: other medical insurance not listed above; no insurance: the individual has not participated in any medical insurance

15.9%). In contrast, for the rural residents, the proportion of participants in the public medical insurance (NRCMS) is marginally lower for the high-income group (87.5%) as compared to the low-income group (89.0%) and middle-income group (90.7%). These results indicate that the effects of household income on participation in public medical insurance differ between rural and urban residents.

Second, regarding the effect of health status (SHR: subjective reported health) on participation in public medical insurance systems, in both urban and rural groups, the proportion of participants is greater for groups that indicate their health status as being "Fair" as compared to those who answered "Good" and "Poor". For example, in the urban group, the proportion of participants in the UEBMI is 47.8% for the "Fair" group, which is greater than that of the "Good" group (23.5%). Moreover, the proportion of participants in the NRCMS is 89.2% for the "Fair" group, which exceeds that of the "Good" group (82.7%) slightly.[6]

Finally, compared to the relatively younger group (groups aged 40–49 and 50–59), the proportion of participants in public medical insurance (UEBMI or NRCMS) is greater for the elderly group (aged 60 and over). For example, the proportion of participants in the UEBMI is 46.1% for the elderly group, which exceeds that of the younger group in the urban residents, while the proportion of participants in the NRCMS is 90.8% for the elderly group, which is slightly greater than that of the younger groups in the rural residents.

6.5 Econometric Analysis Results

Tables 6.3 and 6.4 present the probabilities of participation in the UEBMI, and the NRCMS, and URBMI, respectively. We use the results of the urban *hukou* dummy

Table 6.3 Results of probabilities of participation in the UEBMI

	(1)			(2)		
	Coef	z-value	dy/dx	Coef	z-value	dy/dx
Urban	1.678***	22.26	0.599	1.179***	5.58	0.288
Diseases						
Hypertension	0.142*	1.93	0.052	−0.063	−0.29	−0.010
Dyslipidemia	0.375***	3.77	0.130	1.030**	2.34	0.095
Diabetes or high blood sugar	0.170	1.42	0.061	1.021	1.54	0.085
Cancer or malignant tumor	0.639*	1.76	0.198	0.661	0.54	0.066
Chronic lung diseases	−0.046	−0.41	−0.017	0.156	0.43	0.022
Liver disease	0.171	1.08	0.061	−0.347	−0.76	−0.068
Heart disease	0.091	0.97	0.033	−0.009	−0.03	−0.001
Stroke	0.156	0.80	0.056	(omitted)		
Kidney disease	0.170	1.25	0.061	-0.066	−0.17	−0.011
Stomach or other digestive disease	−0.014	−0.17	−0.005	0.470*	1.88	0.059
Emotional, nervous, or psychiatric problems	−0.475	−1.58	−0.185	–	–	–
Memory-related disease	-0.011	−0.05	−0.004	−0.999	−0.75	−0.272
Arthritis or rheumatism	-0.216***	−3.00	−0.081	−0.557***	−2.60	−0.112
Asthma	-0.185	−1.09	−0.070	0.867	0.85	0.076
Age categories (age 45–49)						
Age 50–59	0.214**	2.56	0.078	−0.009	−0.05	−0.001
Age 60–69	0.564***	5.87	0.194	−0.176	−0.60	−0.031
Age 70–79	0.839***	7.03	0.263	−0.228	−0.43	−0.042
Age 80 and older	0.683***	3.61	0.211	-0.078	−0.07	−0.013
Income categories (first quintile)						
Second quintile	−0.054	−0.57	−0.020	−0.318	−1.14	−0.058
Third quintile	−0.138	−1.26	−0.052	−0.198	−0.67	−0.035
Fourth quintile	−0.148	−1.57	−0.056	−0.321	−1.19	−0.057
Fifth quintile	−0.129	−1.37	−0.048	−0.233	−0.85	−0.040
Ownership categories (government office)						
Public organization				0.237	0.60	0.035
SOE				−0.249	−0.65	−0.044
COE				−0.007	−0.01	−0.001
POE				−0.220	−0.56	−0.039
Self-employed				−1.730***	−4.60	−0.490

(continued)

Table 6.3 (continued)

	(1)			(2)		
	Coef	z-value	dy/dx	Coef	z-value	dy/dx
Other				−1.352***	−3.34	−0.387
Education categories (no education)						
Dropping out of primary school	0.414***	3.27	0.141	0.816*	1.61	0.078
Primary school	0.650***	5.50	0.214	0.478	1.04	0.058
Junior high school	1.169***	9.91	0.361	1.179***	2.72	0.133
Senior high school	1.440***	11.46	0.410	1.409***	3.16	0.186
College and higher	2.082***	11.01	0.410	1.374***	2.79	0.134
Married	0.390***	3.56	0.150	0.517	1.51	0.110
Male	0.029	0.34	0.011	−0.135	−0.61	−0.021
Number of children	0.019	0.60	0.007	0.296**	2.48	0.047
Smoking (no smoking)						
Smoking now	−0.093	−1.05	-0.035	−0.238	−1.05	−0.040
Smoking in the past	−0.078	−0.65	-0.029	−0.027	−0.08	−0.004
Drinking (no drinking)						
Drinking once a month	0.197*	1.63	0.070	0.098	0.37	0.015
Drink more than once a month	0.304	3.61	0.109	0.610***	2.83	0.087
Constants	−2.578***	−14.29		−0.955	−1.49	
Observations	2,940			715		
Log likelihood	−1098.122			−171.456		
Pseudo R2	0.437			0.521		

Source Calculated based on the data from CHARLS 2011
Notes
(1) ***$p < 0.01$, **$p < 0.05$, *$p < 0.10$
(2) dy/dx: marginal effect

from Table 6.3 to test H1. In addition, because participation in the NRCMS and URBMI is voluntary, the results shown in Table 6.4 are used to test H2 and H3.

First, the participation probability in public medical insurance systems differs by rural and urban groups; specifically, the participation probabilities in the UEBMI (Table 6.3) are 28.8–59.9 percentage points higher for the urban group. Thus, H1 (segmentation by *hukou* hypothesis) is supported.

Second, based on the results shown in Table 6.4 (for the NRCMS and the URBMI), the results of household consumption quintiles are statistically non-significant. Therefore, H2 (liquidity constraints hypothesis) is rejected for public medical insurance.

The results of the test for H2 for the UEBMI and NRCMS are not consistent with those of Zhou (2003) and Lin et al. (2009). This indicates that increased government

Table 6.4 Results of probabilities of participation in the NRCMS and URBMI

	(1) NRCMS			(2) URBMI		
	Coef	z-value	dy/dx	Coef	z-value	dy/dx
Diseases						
Hypertension	0.090*	1.87	0.010	0.176*	1.82	0.065
Dyslipidemia	0.132	1.54	0.013	0.263**	1.97	0.095
Diabetes or high blood sugar	0.034	0.35	0.004	0.018	0.11	0.007
Cancer or malignant tumor	0.519*	1.84	0.038	0.352	0.75	0.122
Chronic lung diseases	−0.014	−0.21	−0.002	0.019	0.13	0.007
Liver disease	0.032	0.32	0.003	0.200	0.90	0.072
Heart disease	−0.014	−0.23	−0.002	0.282**	2.33	0.102
Stroke	−0.081	−0.64	−0.010	0.117	0.45	0.043
Kidney disease	0.114	1.37	0.012	0.207	1.22	0.075
Stomach or other digestive disease	0.103**	2.23	0.011	0.033	0.30	0.012
Emotional, nervous, or psychiatric problems	0.061	0.37	0.006	−0.520	−1.47	−0.204
Memory-related disease	0.006	0.04	0.001	−0.135	−0.45	−0.052
Arthritis or rheumatism	0.028	0.69	0.003	0.050	0.54	0.019
Asthma	−0.111	−1.14	−0.013	−0.246	−1.07	−0.095
Age categories (age 45–49)						
Age 50–59	0.039	0.77	0.004	0.093	0.83	0.035
Age 60–69	0.181	3.12	0.019	0.200	1.55	0.073
Age 70–79	−0.014	−0.20	−0.002	0.108	0.67	0.040
Age 80 and older	0.040	0.39	0.004	0.267	1.12	0.095
Income categories (first quintile)						
Second quintile	0.029	0.49	0.003	0.019	0.14	0.007
Third quintile	0.109*	1.86	0.012	0.157	0.96	0.058
Fourth quintile	0.043	0.69	0.005	0.063	0.49	0.023
Fifth quintile	−0.064	−1.09	−0.007	0.056	0.42	0.021
Education categories (no education)						
Dropping out of primary school	0.020	0.36	0.002	0.031	0.20	0.011
Primary school	0.005	0.09	0.001	0.133	0.92	0.049
Junior high school	0.101	1.56	0.011	0.234*	1.64	0.086
Senior high school	0.033	0.36	0.004	0.221	1.44	0.080
College and higher	0.162	0.34	0.016	0.138	0.49	0.050

(continued)

Table 6.4 (continued)

	(1) NRCMS			(2) URBMI		
	Coef	z-value	dy/dx	Coef	z-value	dy/dx
Married	0.400***	6.37	0.056	0.032	0.24	0.012
Male	0.003	0.06	0.000	−0.314***	−2.64	−0.118
Number of children	0.014	0.83	0.002	−0.032	−0.75	−0.012
Smoking (no smoking)						
Smoking now	0.025	0.46	0.003	−0.038	−0.31	−0.014
Smoking in the past	−0.033	−0.43	−0.004	0.140	0.85	0.051
Drinking (no drinking)						
Drinking once a month	−0.008	−0.11	−0.001	0.318*	1.86	0.112
Drink more than once a month	−0.013	−0.26	−0.001	0.351***	2.92	0.125
Constants	1.058***	11.37		−0.107	-0.48	
Observations	12,593			1,041		
Log likelihood	−2716.170			−654.409		
Pseudo R2	0.022			0.044		

Source Calculated based on the data from CHARLS 2011
Notes
(1) ***$p < 0.01$, **$p < 0.05$, *$p < 0.10$
(2) dy/dx: marginal effect

assistance in public medical insurance and the enforcement of participation in the system by the government has helped to reduce the disparities in insurance enrollment caused by income inequality.

Third, we consider the results for H3 (adverse selection hypothesis). Compared with the group without diseases, the participation probabilities in the NRCMS are 1.1 percentage points higher for the subgroups with stomach or other digestive diseases (excluding tumors or cancers). The participation probabilities in the URBMI are 9.5 and 10.2 percentage points higher for the subgroups with dyslipidemia (elevation of low-density lipoprotein, TGs, and total cholesterol, or a low high-density lipoprotein level), and heart attack, coronary heart disease, angina, congestive heart failure, or other heart problems.

Furthermore, in most cases, compared with the younger group (aged 40–49 years), the participation probabilities in medical insurance systems are higher for the elderly group. For example, the participation probability in the NRCMS is 1.9 percentage points higher for the group aged 60–69 years.

Therefore, these results support H3(adverse selection hypothesis). Moreover, these estimated results are consistent with the findings of previous studies (Lin et al., 2009; Ma, 2014; Zhou, 2003).

Lastly, we consider the other factors. Firstly, compared with the group with the lowest education, the participation probabilities in the UEBMI are 13.3–36.1

percentage points (junior high school), 18.6–41.0 percentage points (senior high school), and 13.4–41.0 percentage points (college and higher) higher for the groups with middle- and high-level education. However, the differentials of the participation probabilities in the NRCMS and the URBMI between these education groups are lower (Table 6.4).

Secondly, compared with the unmarried group, the probabilities of participation of the married group in the UEBMI and NRCMS are 15.0 percentage points and 5.6 percentage points higher, respectively. In contrast, the differentials of participation in the URBMI between the unmarried and married groups are statistically insignificant.

Thirdly, the gender gaps in participation probabilities differ according to the type of medical insurance system. For example, the participation probability in the URBMI is 11.8 percentage points lower for males as compared to that of females, whereas the gender gaps in the participation probabilities in the UEBMI and NRCMS are statistically insignificant.

Fourthly, compared with the group without a child, the probabilities of participation in the UEBMI are higher for the group with children. If the number of children increases by one, the probability of participation in the UEBMI increases by 4.7 percentage points. In contrast, the effect of the number of children on participation in the NRCMS and URBMI is not statistically significant.

Fifthly, compared with the government group, the probability of participation in the UEBMI (Table 6.3) is 49.0 and 38.7 percentage points lower for the self-employed worker group and the other work sector groups, respectively. However, the differentials among government office, public organization, SOE, COE, and POE are comparatively lower. The results show that although disparities in participation between the ownership types in the formal sector have reduced, they continue to exist between the formal and informal sectors. This reveals that there is a large difference in enrollment of medical insurance by employment sectors (e.g., workplace ownership type, and formal and informal sector), which is consistent with the results in Chap. 4. Accordingly, the government must consider policies to promote self-employed workers' participation in the UEBMI.

Finally, the results for all smoking behavior dummies are not statistically significant. However, drinking behavior affects the participation probability. Specifically, the probability of participation in the UEBMI and the URBMI is 8.7 and 12.5 percentage points higher for the group that drank more than once a month, respectively.

6.6 Conclusions

China's rapidly aging population caused the government to introduce reforms in the public medical insurance system in the 1990s. By the end of the 2000s, the UEBMI, URBMI, and NRCMS were implemented, covering the entire population of China. Thus, it can be said that universal medical insurance has been implemented in China from an institutional establishment perspective. Using CHARLS 2011 survey data, we have conducted an empirical analysis to test three hypotheses to verify the determinants of participation in public medical insurance. Several major conclusions have been drawn.

First, we note differences in participation probabilities between the rural and urban residents, and thus, H1 (segmentation by the *hukou* hypothesis) is supported.

Second, the results of household consumption quantiles are statistically insignificant, and thus, H2 (liquidity constraints hypothesis) is rejected.

Third, compared with the group without chronic diseases, the probabilities of participation in public medical insurance systems are higher for the group with chronic diseases. Compared with the younger group, the probabilities of participation in medical insurance systems are higher for the older generation group. These results support H3 (adverse selection hypothesis).

Finally, education, gender, drinking behavior, and work status (e.g., workplace ownership type, formal and informal sector, etc.) affect participation probabilities as well, although these effects vary between rural and urban residents.

The estimated results indicate that the establishment and implementation of public medical insurance systems are segmented by the rural and urban *hukou* systems, as well as the employment sectors. The following policy implications can be considered. First, compared with the government worker group, the participation probabilities are lower for the self-employed group. Thus, the government must consider policies to promote the participation of workers in the informal sector in the UEBMI.

Second, we revealed differences in the participation probability between the rural and urban residents. This might be caused due to the public medical insurance systems being segmented by the rural and urban *hukou* system. The proportions of out-of-pocket expenses are relatively higher for the participants in the NRCMS as compared to that of those in the UEBMI and the UREMI. This may lead to inequalities in healthcare service utilization between rural and urban residents (Liu, 1995; Ma, 2015; Cheng et al., 2015). To address this problem, it is vital that the Chinese government increases the benefits of NRCMS and unifies NRCMS, UEBMI, and URBMI in the future.

Notes

1. In China, the *hukou* system is mainly divided into two types: urban *hukou* and rural *hukou*. Most individuals with rural *hukou* live and work in rural areas (villages or the countryside). Workers with rural *hukou* working in urban areas (provinces or cities) are called "rural–urban migrant workers."
2. Regarding the participation behavior in medical insurance, it is necessary to consider the factors influencing both the supply side (government, employer, and insurance companies) and the demand side (individuals). Owing to data limitations, the analysis in this chapter only analyzed the demand-side factors.
3. Although the total CHARLS 2011 sample comprises 17,780 observations, only 8,866 respondents answered the questions on self-reported health. In response to the sample bias problem, the disease dummy is utilized as the index of health status to test the hypotheses in the following analysis.

4. Based on the firm classification rules published by the Chinese government, an individual firm in the self-employed sector is defined as a small firm with less than eight workers including the employer (owner of a firm) or firms made up entirely of self-employed workers and unpaid family members.

Appendix

See Tables 6.5, 6.6 and 6.7

Table 6.5 Medical insurances in urban and rural areas during the planned economy period

	Insurance	Participant	Premium	Promulgated year
Public medical insurance	Labor insurance	Employees and their dependent family members with urban *hukou* in corporates	• Premiums paid by an employer: 6% of total wage bills • Part of medical care expenses was supported by government	1956
	Publicly funded medical system	Civil servants with urban *hukou* in government offices and organizations	• Premium and medical care expenses were paid by government	1960s
	CMS	Rural *hukou* residents	• Funds were established by people's communes	1960s
Others	Medical aids	Low-income group	• Exemption system	1950s

Source Created by the author

Table 6.6 Medical insurances in urban and rural areas during the market-oriented reform period

	Classifications	Participants	Premiums	Promulgated Year
Public medical insurance	UEBMI	Employees in corporates	• Fixed-rate system • Combination of social pooling fund and personal account system • Premium paid by an employer: 7% of total wage bills • Premium paid by an employee: 3% of an employee' basic wages	1998
	ERBMI	Non-working residents with the urban *hukou*	• Premiums paid by government: differ by region • Premiums paid by a resident: differ by region	2007
	NRCMS	Residents with the rural *hukou*	• Premium paid by central government (e.g. per capita 380 yuan yearly in 2015) • Premium paid by a resident (e.g. per capita 120Yuan yearly in 2015)	2003
Private medical insurance	Commercial insurance	All population	Proportional-rate system	1990s
Others	• Medical aids	Low-income group	Exemption system	1950s
	• Enterprise replenishment medical insurance	Employees in corporates	By companies	1980s

Source Created by the author

Table 6.7 Descriptive statistics of variables

	Nation		Urban		Rural	
	Mean	SD	Mean	SD	Mean	SD
Urban	0.224	0.417				
Diseases						
Hypertension	0.246	0.431	0.320	0.467	0.224	0.417
Dyslipidemia	0.092	0.289	0.172	0.378	0.069	0.253
Diabetes or high blood sugar	0.057	0.232	0.100	0.300	0.045	0.206
Cancer or malignant tumor	0.010	0.100	0.013	0.115	0.009	0.096
Chronic lung diseases	0.102	0.302	0.099	0.299	0.102	0.303
Liver disease	0.039	0.194	0.043	0.204	0.038	0.191
Heart disease	0.121	0.326	0.184	0.388	0.102	0.303
Stroke	0.023	0.151	0.032	0.177	0.021	0.142
Kidney disease	0.064	0.244	0.065	0.246	0.063	0.244
Stomach or other digestive disease	0.223	0.417	0.177	0.381	0.237	0.425
Emotional, nervous, or psychiatric problems	0.013	0.113	0.011	0.104	0.014	0.116
Memory-related disease	0.015	0.120	0.022	0.146	0.013	0.112
Arthritis or rheumatism	0.332	0.471	0.258	0.437	0.354	0.478
Asthma	0.036	0.186	0.035	0.183	0.036	0.187
Age categories						
Age 40–49	0.214	0.410	0.196	0.397	0.219	0.413
Age 50–59	0.345	0.475	0.327	0.469	0.350	0.477
Age 60–69	0.273	0.446	0.278	0.448	0.272	0.445
Age 70–79	0.130	0.336	0.158	0.365	0.121	0.327
Age 80 and older	0.038	0.192	0.041	0.196	0.038	0.190
Income categories						
First quintile	0.195	0.396	0.185	0.388	0.198	0.398
Second quintile	0.198	0.399	0.179	0.383	0.204	0.403
Third quintile	0.205	0.403	0.118	0.323	0.230	0.421
Fourth quintile	0.205	0.404	0.263	0.440	0.188	0.391
Fifth quintile	0.197	0.398	0.255	0.436	0.181	0.385
Education categories						
No formal education illiterate	0.277	0.448	0.095	0.294	0.330	0.470
Did not finish primary school	0.179	0.383	0.096	0.295	0.203	0.402
Primary school	0.214	0.410	0.172	0.378	0.226	0.418
Junior high school	0.204	0.403	0.279	0.448	0.183	0.386
Senior high school	0.101	0.302	0.258	0.437	0.056	0.230

(continued)

Table 6.7 (continued)

	Nation		Urban		Rural	
	Mean	SD	Mean	SD	Mean	SD
College and higher	0.025	0.154	0.100	0.299	0.002	0.051
Married	0.871	0.335	0.881	0.324	0.869	0.338
Male	0.463	0.499	0.502	0.500	0.453	0.498
Number of children	0.684	1.285	0.602	1.125	0.708	1.327
Smoking						
No smoking	0.627	0.484	0.638	0.481	0.623	0.485
Smoking in the past	0.084	0.278	0.107	0.309	0.078	0.268
Smoking now	0.289	0.453	0.255	0.436	0.299	0.458
Drinking						
No drinking	0.681	0.466	0.680	0.467	0.682	0.466
Drinking once a month	0.077	0.266	0.082	0.275	0.075	0.263
Drink more than once a month	0.242	0.428	0.238	0.426	0.243	0.429
Observations	16,778		3,763		13,015	

Source Calculated based on the data from CHARLS 2011
Note Mean: mean value; SD: standard deviation

References

Bograd, H., Ritzwoller, D. P., Calonge, N., Shields, K., & Hanrahan, M. (1997). Extending health maintenance organization insurance to the uninsured. *Journal of the American Medical Association, 277*(13), 1067–1072.

Cheng, L., Liu, H., Zhang, Y., Shen, K., & Zeng, Y. (2015). The impact of health insurance of health outcomes and spending of the elderly: Evidence from China's New Cooperative Medical Scheme. *Health Economics, 24*(6), 672–691.

Drehr, P., Madden, C. W., Cheadle, A., Martin, D. P., Patrick, D. L., & Skillman, S. (1996). Will uninsured people volunteer for voluntary health insurance? Experience from Washington State. *American Journal of Public Health, 86*(4), 529–532.

Hofter, R. H. (2006). Private health insurance and utilization of health services in Chile. *Applied Economics, 38*(4), 423–439.

Kimani, J. K., Ettarh, R., Kyobutungi, C., Mberu, B., & Muindi, K. (2012). Determinants for participation in a public health insurance program among residents of urban slums in Nairobi, Kenya: Results from a cross sectional survey. *BMC Health Services Research, 12*(66), 2–11.

Lin, W., Liu, G., & Chen, G. (2009). The urban resident basic medical insurance: A landmark reform towards universal coverage in China. *Health Economics, 18*(S2), 83–96.

Liu, Y., Hsiao, W. C. L., Li, Q., Liu, X., & Ren, M. (1995). Transformation of China's rural health insurance financing. *Social Science & Medicine, 41*(8), 1085–1093.

Long, S. H., & Marquis, M. S. (2002). Participation in a public insurance program: Subsidies, crowd-out, and adverse selection. *Inquiry, 39*(3), 243–257.

Ma, X. (2014). Determinants of participation in medical insurance of urban residents in China. *Asian Economics, 55*(2), 62–93. (in Japanese).

Ma, X. (2015). *Public medical insurance systems reform in China*. Kyoto University Press. (in Japanese).

Madden, C. W., Cheadle, A., Diehr, P., Martin, D. P., Patrick, D. L., & Skillman, S. (1995). Voluntary public health insurance for low-income families: The decision to enroll. *Journal of Health Politics, Policy and Law, 20*(4), 955–972.

Nakagane, K. (2000). The issues and the points of social security research in China. *Journal of Social Security Research, 132*, 2–12. (in Japanese).

Pardo, C., & Schott, W. (2012). Public versus private: Evidence on health insurance selection. *Journal Health Care Finance Economics, 12*(1), 39–61.

Shaefer, H. L., Grogan, C. M., & Pollack, H. A. (2011). Who transitions from private to public health insurance? Lessons from expansions of the State Children's Health Insurance Program. *Journal of Health Care for the Poor and Underserved, 22*(1), 359–370.

Swartz, G., & Garnick, D. (2000). Adverse selection and price sensitivity when low-income people have subsidies to purchase health insurance in the private market. *Inquiry, 37*(1), 45–60.

Wolfe, J. R., & Goddeeris, J. H. (1991). Adverse selection, moral hazard, and wealth effects in the Medigap insurance market. *Journal of Health Economics, 10*(4), 433–459.

Zhou, Y. (2003). No-participants of medical insurance and household health care expenditure: Based on Guangdong Province Household Survey data in China. *Journal of Social Security Research, 143*, 80–92. (in Japanese).

Chapter 7
New Rural Cooperative Medical Scheme and Its Effects on the Utilization of Healthcare Services

Abstract This study conducts an empirical analysis using longitudinal survey data from the China Health and Nutrition Survey to estimate the impact of the New Rural Cooperative Medical Scheme (NRCMS) on the utilization of healthcare services. It is found that, first, predisposing factors, enabling factors, health care needs factors, and lifestyle factors affect the utilization of healthcare services. Second, results of the difference-in-differences method analysis indicate that NRCMS did not affect the utilization of healthcare services (e.g., outpatient and inpatient) of ill persons. However, it might increase the possibility of getting a health examination. Third, the utilization of healthcare services (both outpatient and inpatient) between the NRCMS enrollment and non-enrollment groups in both the working age (15–59) and the elderly groups (60 and over) did not differ. However, NRCMS positively affected disease prevention behavior in the working age group. Fourth, from a long-term perspective, the NRCMS did not affect the utilization of healthcare services (outpatient or inpatient). Further, its positive effect on health examination dissipated.

Keywords New Rural Cooperative Medical Scheme · Utilization of healthcare service · Rural China

7.1 Introduction

The Cooperative Medical Scheme (CMS) in rural China contributed significantly to preventing infectious diseases and providing primary medical care as part of the people's commune system in the planned economy period from 1949 through 1977. However, during the market-oriented reform period, the CMS enrollment rates decreased significantly—from 90% in 1981 to merely 5–10% in the 1990s—as the people's communes were eliminated and the Household Contract Responsibility System was implemented (Liu et al., 1995; Wagstaff & Linedelow, 2008; Song, 2006, 2009; Cheng et al., 2015). Additionally, since the 1990s, the Chinese government has enforced reforms in the healthcare services market, moving from unified management systems to a competitive market. Consequently, the medical care expense has increased significantly (Song, 2006, 2009; Ma, 2015) and persons with serious illness risk poverty from high medical care expenses. Thus, inequality in the utilization of

X. Ma, *Public Medical Insurance Reforms in China*,
https://doi.org/10.1007/978-981-16-7790-8_7

healthcare services resulting from income inequality has become a pressing dilemma in China (Ma, 2015). To address this issue, the Chinese government introduced a new public medical insurance scheme in rural areas, the New Rural Cooperative Medical Scheme (NRCMS), which was implemented in 2003. Enrollment in the NRCMS is optional and it covers all the rural residents. Although the NRCMS is financially supported by the central and local governments, its members have to pay medical insurance premiums. Moreover, the majority of medical care expenses are incurred by the patients themselves because the local medical insurance funds are insufficient. Therefore, rural residents may still not access healthcare services when required despite joining the NRCMS due to the concern that the high out of pocket (OOP) expenses on medical care could drive their families into poverty. Accordingly, an empirical study evaluating the impact of NRCMS on the utilization of healthcare services has become crucial.

Previous empirical studies[1] for example, Wagstaff et al. (2009), Shi et al. (2010), You and Kobayashi (2011), Lu et al. (2012), Li and Zhang (2013), and Li et al. (2014), used cross-sectional data to investigate the impact of NRCMS on the utilization of healthcare services (i.e., the probability of visting a hospital and medical care expense). Additionally, Wagstaff and Lindelow (2008), Lei and Lin (2009), and Cheng et al. (2015) used longitudinal data to address the heterogeneity problem in the impact of NRCMS on utilization of healthcare services. However, the estimated results from the different measurement methods and datasets were inconsistent. Moreover, some problems remain unanswered. First, although the difference-in-differences (DID) method analysis is an appropriate method for policy assessment and is widely used in empirical studies, it is rarely used to address this issue. Second, regarding the determinants of health care demand and healthcare service utilization behavior, the Anderson model (Anderson & Newman, 1973; Anderson, 1995) is generally used in studies pertaining to health economics. However, this model has not been used to address this issue in China.[2]

Using the data from the China Health and Nutrition Survey (CHNS), this study investigates the impact of NRCMS on utilization of healthcare services based on two aspects: the probability of accessing a hospital (inpatient and outpatient) and the probability of taking a health examination. For the analysis, this study used a DID method based on the Anderson model. These results provide new evidence on this issue in rural China.

The remainder of this chapter is organized as follows. Section 7.2 introduces the framework of the empirical analysis, including models and datasets. Section 7.3 presents the estimation results. Section 7.4 summarizes the conclusions.

7.2 Methodology and Data

7.2.1 Model

Probit regression model was used to measure the probability of the utilization of healthcare services.

We used a random effects (FE) probit regression model to address the heterogeneity problem. These are expressed as Eqs. (7.1) – (7.3).

$$y_{it}^* = a_t + \beta_1 NRCMS_{it} + \beta_2 X_{it} + u_i + v_{it} \tag{7.1}$$

$$Y_i^* = \begin{cases} 1\ if\ Y_i^* \geq 0 \\ 0\ if\ Y_i^* < 0 \end{cases} \tag{7.2}$$

$$P(Y_{it} = 1) = p_{it} = P(1 - a_{it} - \beta_1 NRCMS_{it} - \beta_2 X_{it} > u_i + v_{it}) \tag{7.3}$$

In Eqs. (7.1)– (7.3), i denotes individuals; t expresses the survey year (2000, 2004, 2006, and 2011); $P(Y_{it} = 1)$ indicates the dependent variable which equals 1 if the individual visited a hospital for inpatient or outpatient services when ill in the previous year and 0 otherwise; y_{it}^* is a continuous but unobservable latent variable; we only observe the actual variable as expressed in Eq. (7.3); a is a constant, v_{it} is the true error term, u_i is the error related to individual heterogeneity. Using the RE probit regression model, the bias resulting from u_i can be addressed. X are factors affecting the healthcare service utilization behavior introduced in the Anderson model; $NRCMS$ expresses the enrollment into the NRCMS, which equals 1 if the individual joined the NRCMS and 0 otherwise; β is the estimated parameter. If β_1 is positively and statistically significant, it indicates that compared with the group that did not join the NRCMS, the enrollment group is more likely to visit hospital for outpatient or inpatient services.

Further, the estimations may contain measurement bias resulting from the differentials of the utilization of healthcare services by heterogeneous groups and various periods. To address such problems (e.g., enrollment selection bias based on group attributes differences, time series bias), we used the DID method to investigate the causality relationship between the NRCMS and utilization of healthcare service, the DID method is expressed in Eq. (7.4)

$$y_{it}^* = a_t + \gamma_1 Treat_{it} + \gamma_2 Year_t + \gamma_3 DID_{it} + \gamma_4 X_{it} + \varepsilon_{it} \tag{7.4}$$

In Eq. (7.4), $Treat$ denotes the treatment group dummy. Using the CHNS longitudinal survey data, the treatment and control groups were constructed as follows. The control group represents the group that did not join the NRCMS in 2000 when the NRCMS had not been implemented and in 2004 (or 2006, 2011) when the NRCMS was implemented. The treatment group represents the group that did not join the

NRCMS in 2000 but joined the NRCMS in 2004, 2006, or 2011 when the NRCMS was implemented. *Year* represents the year dummy when the NRCMS was implemented (2004, 2006 or 2011 dummies). *DID* is the interaction of *Treat* and *Year*. X are factors that affect the utilization of healthcare services. γ represents the estimated coefficients. When γ_3 is positive and statistically significant, it indicates that compared with the group that did not join the NRCMS, the enrollment group is more likely to visit hospital for outpatient or inpatient services. Equation (7.4) is the most important assessment method for evaluating the impact of NRCMS.

7.2.2 Data

This study uses CHNS longitudinal data from 2000 to 2011, which is approximately the period before and after the year in which the NRCMS was implemented. The CHNS is a national longitudinal survey conducted by the Carolina Population Center at the University of North Carolina and the National Institute for Nutrition and Health at the Chinese Center for Disease Control and Prevention. The survey was conducted by an international team of researchers whose backgrounds included nutrition, public health, economics, sociology, Chinese studies, and demography. The survey was conducted over a 7-day period using a multistage, random cluster process to draw a sample of approximately 7,200 households with over 30,000 individuals in 15 provinces and municipal cities that vary substantially in geography, economic development, public resources, and health indicators. We used 11 provinces, covered from 2000 to 2011. The three waves of survey data from 2000, 2004, and 2006 were mainly used in the analysis. Further, two waves of survey data from 2000 and 2011 were used to conduct robustness checks from a long-term perspective.

7.2.3 Variable Setting

The independent variables of the utilization of healthcare services are a set of binary variables: (i) utilization including inpatients and outpatients, which equals 1 if the individual visited a hospital for inpatient or outpatient services when ill in the previous year and 0 otherwise; (ii) outpatient, which equals 1 if the individual visited a hospital for outpatient services when ill in the previous year and 0 otherwise; (iii) inpatient, which equals 1 if the individual visited a hospital for inpatient services when ill in previous year and 0 otherwise; (iv) health examination, which equals 1 if the individual visited hospital for a health examination in the previous year and 0 otherwise.

Anderson and Newman (1973) and Andersen (1995) indicated four kinds of factors that affect healthcare service utilization behavior: predisposing factors[3], enabling factors, health care needs factors, and lifestyle factors. The independent variable settings based on the Anderson model are as follows (see Appendix Table 7.5).

First, age and the dummy variables of education and sex are used to indicate "predisposing factors". Based on Grossman's health capital model (Grossman, 1972), the elderly and higher education groups are more likely to utilize healthcare services (or seek health care services). Using the male dummy, gender gaps in healthcare demand can be controlled for.

Second, medical insurance, household income, and healthcare service supply status variables were used to indicate "personal enabling factors" in previous studies. NRCMS is a binary dummy. The income variable is the household income per capita, which divides the total household income[4] by the number of family members. Province dummies are used to control for the regional disparity of healthcare services supply (e.g., the number of hospitals per capita or the quality of medical facilities may differ by region).

Third, the dummy variables of self-reported health status, hypertension, and diabetes were used to indicate the healthcare service need factors. It is presumed that the probability of visiting the hospital will be higher in groups with hypertension or diabetes, and in the group who reported a poor health status.

Finally, smoking status (equals 1 if the individual is smoking during the year of the survey or has smoked in the past and 0 otherwise), the drinking frequency dummies (no drinking, less 2 times monthly, 1-2 times weekly, 3-4 times weekly, everyday, don't know), performing health exercises (equals 1 if the individual is performing health exercises during the year of the survey and 0 otherwise), and living environment variables[5] are used to indicate "lifestyle factors."

7.3 Econometric Analysis Results

7.3.1 Determinants of the Utilization of Healthcare Services

A RE probit regression model was used to estimate the determinants of the utilization of healthcare services. We distinguished the four types of models using various independent variables as follows: Model 1 (the probability of utilization of healthcare services including outpatient and inpatient services), Model 2 (the probability of using only outpatient services), Model 3 (the probability of using only inpatient services), and Model 4 (the probability of undergoing a health examination). Table 7.1 summarizes the results. The main findings are as follows.

First, the coefficients of the NRCMS in Model 1 (outpatient and inpatient), Model 2 (outpatient), and Model 4 (health examination) are positively significant; the coefficient in Model 3 (inpatient) is however insignificant. These results indicate that after addressing the heterogeneity problem and controlling for the other factors, the

Table 7.1 Determinants of utilization of healthcare service

	(1) Outpatient + Inpatient		(2) Outpatient		(3) Inpatient		(4) Health examination	
	Coef	z-value	Coef	z-value	Coef	z-value	Coef	z-value
NCMS	0.099**	2.19	0.092**	2.01	0.108	1.03	0.405***	3.29
Years (2000)								
2004	0.488***	10.21	0.490***	10.08	0.156	1.27	0.340**	2.01
2006	0.413***	7.97	0.416***	7.90	0.104	0.79	0.468***	2.70
Age category (Age 30–39)								
Age 20–29	0.183*	1.93	0.117	1.19	0.536**	2.45	−0.171	−0.64
Age 40–49	0.041	0.67	0.040	0.64	0.015	0.08	−0.475***	−2.61
Age 50–59	0.108*	1.77	0.107*	1.75	0.032	0.18	−0.182	−1.16
Age 60–69	0.196***	3.08	0.175***	2.72	0.231	1.28	−0.264	−1.50
Age 70–79	0.299***	4.14	0.281***	3.84	0.248	1.26	−0.398*	−1.79
Age 70 and over	0.411***	5.01	0.416***	5.03	0.039	0.17	0.012	0.06
Education category (Not enrollment)								
Primary school	0.074	1.56	0.075	1.56	−0.002	−0.02	−0.026	−0.18
Junior high school	0.093*	1.70	0.089*	1.61	0.057	0.42	−0.271	−1.57
Senior high school and over	0.097	1.35	0.119*	1.63	−0.252	−1.16	0.005	0.02
Male	−0.134***	−3.46	−0.134***	−3.39	−0.042	−0.43	0.048	0.41
Self-reported health status (Very good)								
Good	0.094	1.57	0.076	1.26	0.341	1.47	−0.298	−2.16
Fair	0.569***	9.37	0.552***	9.03	0.549**	2.36	−0.225	−1.53
Poor	1.2567***	17.75	1.158***	16.22	1.223***	5.13	−0.118	−0.60

(continued)

Table 7.1 (continued)

	(1) Outpatient + Inpatient		(2) Outpatient		(3) Inpatient		(4) Health examination	
	Coef	z-value	Coef	z-value	Coef	z-value	Coef	z-value
Hypertension	0.359***	6.84	0.323***	6.06	0.336***	3.14	0.217	1.34
Diabetes	0.326***	2.24	0.246*	1.67	0.353	1.47	−0.001	0.00
Household income (Yuan)	0.000*	1.63	0.000	1.53	0.000	0.21	0.000	1.08
Regions (Jiangsu)								
Liaoning	−0.236**	−2.42	−0.249***	−2.58	−0.004	−0.02	−0.222	−0.70
Heilongjiang	−0.270***	−2.83	−0.286***	−3.03	0.084	0.43	−0.047	−0.17
Shandong	−0.197*	−1.94	−0.219**	−2.19	0.103	0.54	0.137	0.48
Henan	0.155*	1.69	0.137	1.52	0.175	0.98	−0.249	−0.79
Hubei	0.078	0.85	0.050	0.56	0.237	1.37	0.477*	1.86
Hernan	−0.032	−0.32	−0.046	−0.48	0.150	0.78	0.421	1.56
Guangxi	0.029	0.31	−0.001	−0.01	0.177	0.95	0.332	1.23
Guizhou	−0.099	−1.04	−0.116	−1.24	0.106	0.56	−0.888*	−1.95
Smoking	−0.011	−0.27	0.006	0.13	−0.157	−1.38	−0.086	−0.68
Drinking (No drinking)								
Less 2 times monthly	0.123**	2.07	0.134**	2.24	−0.159	−0.82	0.045	0.26
1–2 times weekly	0.097	1.59	0.093	1.52	0.041	0.25	0.207	1.28
3–4 times weekly	0.182**	2.35	0.167**	2.13	0.162	0.80	−0.442	−1.23
Everyday	−0.112*	−1.85	−0.115*	−1.88	−0.006	−0.03	−0.075	−0.42
Don't know	−0.052	−0.27	−0.071	−0.36	−0.005	−0.01	−4.871	0.00

(continued)

Table 7.1 (continued)

	(1) Outpatient + Inpatient		(2) Outpatient		(3) Inpatient		(4) Health examination	
	Coef	z-value	Coef	z-value	Coef	z-value	Coef	z-value
Health exercise	0.036	0.47	0.054	0.70	−0.080	−0.36	0.395**	2.19
Drink water inside the home	0.002	0.06	0.005	0.13	−0.002	−0.02	0.037	0.30
Toilet inside the home	−0.125**	−2.46	−0.134***	−2.61	0.112	0.98	0.077	0.61
No waste nearby the home	−0.015	−0.43	−0.024	−0.68	0.103	1.17	−0.015	−0.13
Constants	−2.241***	−19.86	−2.222***	−19.72	−3.515***	−10.90	−3.039***	−9.25
Observations	14,886		14,886		14,886		14,886	
Groups	531		531		531		531	
Log likelihood	−4268.851		−4133.230		−518.035		−473.751	
Wald chi2(37)	1146.770		1016.050		156.790		79.550	
Likelihood-ratio test of rho = 0 chibar2(01)	72.550		61.280		22.250		50.050	
Prob >= chibar2	0.000		0.000		0.000		0.000	

Source Calculated based on the data from CHNS of 2000, 2004, 2006
Notes ***$p < 0.01$, **$p < 0.05$, *$p < 0.10$

probability of visiting a hospital for outpatient services and having a health examination is higher in the NRCMS enrollment group than in the non-enrollment group. However, the NRCMS had no positive effect on using inpatient services.

Second, after controlling for the other factors, compared to 2000, the probability of visiting a hospital for outpatient services and having a health examination is higher in the NRCMS enrollment group in both 2004 and 2006. These results show that compared with the period when the NRCMS had not been established, both the enrollment and non-enrollment groups were significantly likely to utilize healthcare services during the NRCMS implementation period, that is 2004 and 2006.

Third, predisposing factors affect the probability of utilizing healthcare services. For example, the well-educated and older groups are more likely to utilize outpatient services, while individuals aged 30–39 years are more likely to go for a health examination. However, the coefficients of the individual attribute factors are insignificant in the probability estimations of inpatient visits.

Fourth, considering the health care need factors, individuals with poor health status and chronic diseases (e.g., hypertension, diabetes) are more likely to visit a hospital for outpatient or inpatient health care. Moreover, the groups that reported their health status as good are less likely to go for a health examination compared with the groups that report their health status as very good. These results can be explained by the fact that the group who report their health status as very good may be more health-conscious and aware of disease prevention.

Fifth, regarding the enabling factors, except for the effects of the NRCMS described above, the coefficients of geographic regions are significant in Models 1 and 2. These results show that the status of healthcare service supply, which differs by region, significantly affects the rural residents' utilization of health care services.

Finally, as pointed out in previous studies, the results show that lifestyle factors affect the utilization of healthcare services. For example, the frequency of alcohol consumption affects the probability of utilizing healthcare services. However, the relationship between them is non-linear. The group of individuals living in poor hygiene status, such as lacking a toilet at home, is less likely to utilize healthcare services.

7.3.2 Effects of the NRCMS on the Utilization of Healthcare Services: Evidence Based on the DID Method

Tables 7.2 summarizes the results using the DID method. First, the coefficients of the DID items in Models 1–3 were insignificant. They indicate that the utilization of healthcare services (both outpatient and inpatient) between the NRCMS enrollment and non-enrollment groups does not differ. In other words, keeping the other factors constant, the NRCMS did not affect ill persons' probabilities of visiting hospitals (either outpatient or inpatient) in the short term, after the implementation of the NRCMS (2004 or 2006).

Table 7.2 The impact of NRCMS on utilization of healthcare service (Total samples)

	(1) Outpatient + Inpatient				(2) Outpatient			
	DID (2000 vs.2004)		DID (2000 vs. 2006)		DID (2000 vs. 2004)		DID (2000 vs. 2006)	
	dy/dx	z-value	dy/dx	z-value	dy/dx	z-value	dy/dx	z-value
Treatment	0.042**	2.42	0.003	0.32	0.038**	2.25	0.006	0.56
Year	0.058***	8.35	0.053***	6.15	0.055***	8.10	0.051***	6.15
DID	−0.007	−0.41	0.019	1.45	−0.004	−0.23	0.016	1.26
Age category (Age 30–39)								
Age20–29	0.011	0.69	0.018	1.08	−0.002	−0.15	0.008	0.53
Age40–49	0.004	0.42	0.001	0.06	0.004	0.36	−0.002	−0.14
Age50–59	0.003	0.31	0.002	0.20	0.002	0.19	0.000	−0.04
Age60–69	0.032***	2.66	0.016	1.27	0.027**	2.30	0.010	0.83
Age70–79	0.041***	2.74	0.037**	2.41	0.034**	2.38	0.031**	2.16
Age 70 and over	0.048***	2.67	0.068***	3.57	0.053***	3.00	0.063***	3.46
Education category (No education)								
Primary school	0.013	1.39	0.002	0.26	0.016*	1.83	0.000	0.00
Junior high school	0.020**	1.98	0.003	0.32	0.023**	2.27	0.001	0.08
Senior high school and over	0.010	0.71	0.002	0.13	0.016	1.17	0.002	0.12
Male	−0.016**	−2.38	−0.019***	−2.92	−0.015**	−2.33	−0.019***	−2.95
Self-reported health status (Very good)								
Good	0.010	0.93	0.004	0.37	0.006***	0.60	0.001	0.10
Fair	0.073***	6.12	0.062***	4.93	0.067***	5.84	0.056***	4.68
Poor	0.253***	11.26	0.225***	10.09	0.224***	10.47	0.183***	8.82

(continued)

Table 7.2 (continued)

	(1) Outpatient + Inpatient				(2) Outpatient			
	DID (2000 vs.2004)		DID (2000 vs. 2006)		DID (2000 vs. 2004)		DID (2000 vs. 2006)	
	dy/dx	z-value	dy/dx	z-value	dy/dx	z-value	dy/dx	z-value
Hypertension	0.030***	2.56	0.058***	4.84	0.026**	2.29	0.044***	3.88
Diabetes	0.016	0.54	0.054*	1.65	0.003	0.11	0.049	1.57
Household income (Yuan)	0.000**	2.20	0.000	0.23	0.000**	2.23	0.000	0.23
Regions (Jiangsu)								
Liaoning	−0.022	−1.53	−0.035***	−2.80	−0.017	−1.24	−0.033***	−2.78
Heilongjiang	−0.037***	−2.95	0.000**	−2.16	−0.035***	−2.87	−0.026**	−2.19
Shandong	−0.017	−1.30	−0.029**	−2.29	−0.015	−1.12	−0.027**	−2.24
Henan	0.034**	2.13	0.028*	1.95	0.031**	2.01	0.027**	1.96
Hubei	0.020	1.32	0.001	0.07	0.020	1.38	0.001	0.09
Hernan	−0.008	−0.56	0.007	0.49	−0.010	−0.78	0.006	0.45
Guangxi	0.006	0.41	0.040***	2.57	0.005	0.32	0.038**	2.49
Guizhou	−0.022	−1.54	−0.006	−0.43	−0.019	−1.35	−0.010	−0.68
Smoking	0.005	0.70	−0.010	−1.34	0.006	0.86	−0.009	−1.27
Drinking (No drinking)								
Less 2 times monthly	−0.005	−0.46	0.036***	2.91	−0.003	−0.30	0.038***	3.12
1–2 times weekly	0.010	0.88	0.018	1.46	0.008	0.76	0.017	1.48
3–4 times weekly	0.004	0.31	0.029*	1.76	0.008	0.57	0.028*	1.73

(continued)

Table 7.2 (continued)

	(1) Outpatient + Inpatient				(2) Outpatient			
	DID (2000 vs.2004)		DID (2000 vs. 2006)		DID (2000 vs. 2004)		DID (2000 vs. 2006)	
	dy/dx	z-value	dy/dx	z-value	dy/dx	z-value	dy/dx	z-value
Everyday	−0.022**	−2.23	−0.005	−0.45	−0.021**	−2.21	−0.002	−0.21
Don't know	−0.029	−0.87	0.007	0.20	−0.024	−0.74	0.002	0.05
Health exercise	−0.004	−0.31	0.013	0.99	−0.003	−0.21	0.012	0.92
Drink water inside the home	0.009	1.35	0.008	1.21	0.007	1.02	0.008	1.18
Toilet inside the home	−0.008	−0.93	−0.026***	−3.26	−0.008	−0.92	−0.027***	−3.55
No waste nearby the home	0.002	0.34	0.009	1.38	0.001	0.21	0.006	1.01
Observations	7,813		7,753		7,813		7,753	
Log likelihood	−2069.397		−2090.289		−1990.674		−2000.472	
LR chi2(37)	1146.770		630.870		500.350		555.760	
Pseudo R2	0.117		0.131		0.112		0.122	
Prob >= chibar2	0.000		0.000		0.000		0.000	
	(3) Inpatient				(4) Health examination			
	DID (2000 vs. 2004)		DID (2000 vs. 2006)		DID (2000 vs. 2004)		DID (2000 vs. 2006)	
	dy/dx	z-value	dy/dx	z-value	dy/dx	z-value	dy/dx	z-value
Treatment	0.002	0.71	−0.002	−0.71	−0.001	−0.40	−0.004	−1.36
Year	0.002*	1.75	0.001	0.68	0.001	0.89	0.002	1.23
DID	−0.002	−0.84	0.002	0.68	0.007	1.25	0.017***	2.68

(continued)

Table 7.2 (continued)

	(3) Inpatient				(4) Health examination			
	DID (2000 vs. 2004)		DID (2000 vs. 2006)		DID (2000 vs. 2004)		DID (2000 vs. 2006)	
	dy/dx	z-value	dy/dx	z-value	dy/dx	z-value	dy/dx	z-value
Age category (Age 30–39)								
Age20–29	0.016**	2.53	0.014**	2.07	−0.001	−0.83	−0.001	−0.68
Age40–49	0.001	0.22	0.003	0.88	−0.003	−2.14	−0.002	−1.25
Age50–59	0.001	0.61	0.003	0.99	−0.001	−0.46	−0.002	−1.57
Age60–69	0.005	1.50	0.007	1.60	−0.002	−1.73	−0.001	−1.03
Age70–79	0.005	1.36	0.006	1.25	−0.001	−0.93	−0.002	−1.33
Age 70 and over	−0.002	−0.81	0.004	0.79	0.000	0.13	0.000	0.00
Education category (Not enrollment)								
Primary school	−0.002	−1.30	0.002	0.80	0.001	0.61	−0.001	−0.54
Junior high school	−0.001	−0.54	0.002	0.85	0.001	0.58	−0.003*	−1.93
Senior high school and over	−0.002	−1.31	0.000	0.06	0.004	1.13	−0.001	−0.47
Male	−0.001	−0.60	0.000	−0.14	0.001	1.21	0.000	0.40
Self-reported health status (Very good)								
Good	0.004	1.42	0.004	1.19	−0.001	−0.64	−0.004***	−2.85
Fair	0.008**	1.78	0.008*	1.62	0.000	0.09	−0.003**	−2.17
Poor	0.041***	3.12	0.058***	3.69	0.001	0.43	−0.002	−1.14
Hypertension	0.002	1.25	0.058***	3.03	−0.001	−0.45	0.001	0.63

(continued)

Table 7.2 (continued)

	(3) Inpatient				(4) Health examination			
	DID (2000 vs. 2004)		DID (2000 vs. 2006)		DID (2000 vs. 2004)		DID (2000 vs. 2006)	
	dy/dx	z-value	dy/dx	z-value	dy/dx	z-value	dy/dx	z-value
Diabetes	0.007	1.24	0.000	0.09	0.002	0.21	0.001	0.56
Household income (Yuan)	0.000	0.17	0.000	0.11	0.000	0.22	0.000	0.01
Regions (Jiangsu)								
Liaoning	−0.003	−1.47	−0.001	−0.25	−0.001	−0.82	0.000	−0.04
Heilongjiang	−0.001	−0.62	0.000	−0.06		−0.44	0.000	0.17
Shandong	−0.002	−0.81	−0.001	−0.32	0.000	−0.19	0.000	0.02
Henan	0.001	0.44	0.000	0.11	−0.002	−1.30	0.000	0.65
Hubei	0.000	−0.22	0.000	−0.07	−0.001	−0.33	0.006*	1.66
Hernan	0.001	0.43	0.000	0.13	0.000	0.24	0.015***	2.64
Guangxi	0.000	0.17	0.001	0.42	−0.001	−0.78	0.006	1.58
Guizhou	−0.002	−0.91	0.003	0.81	−0.001	−0.87	−0.002	−0.78
Smoking	−0.001	−0.41	−0.001	−0.55	0.000	0.03	−0.002*	−1.61
Drinking (No drinking)								
Less 2 times monthly	−0.001	−0.69	−0.001	−0.40	−0.002	−0.70	0.001	0.29
1–2 times weekly	0.000	0.24	0.000	0.11	0.000	−0.08	0.005*	2.20
3–4 times weekly	0.000	0.12	0.002	0.47	0.000	0.08	−0.001	−0.24
Everyday	−0.001	−0.31	−0.001	−0.69	0.001	0.54	−0.002	−1.18

(continued)

Table 7.2 (continued)

	(3) Inpatient				(4) Health examination			
	DID (2000 vs. 2004)		DID (2000 vs. 2006)		DID (2000 vs. 2004)		DID (2000 vs. 2006)	
	dy/dx	z-value	dy/dx	z-value	dy/dx	z-value	dy/dx	z-value
Don't know	0.000	−0.22	0.000	0.12	0.002	0.34	0.000	−0.89
Health exercise	−0.001	−0.27	0.001	0.27	0.003	1.11	0.003	1.35
Drink water inside the home	0.002	1.40	0.000	0.16	0.001	1.21	−0.001	−0.86
Toilet inside the home	0.000	−0.13	0.001	0.78	0.001	0.89	0.000	0.10
No waste nearby the home	0.001	0.53	0.002	1.19	0.000	0.13	−0.002*	−1.81
Observations	7,813		7,753		5,534		6,362	
Log likelihood	−232.092		−280.203		−137.620		−249.950	
LR chi2(37)	74.720		93.540		41.770		103.590	
Pseudo R2	0.139		0.143		0.132		0.172	
Prob >= chibar2	0.000		0.000		0.094		0.000	

Source Calculated based on the data from CHNS of 2000, 2004, 2006

Notes

(1) ***$p < 0.01$, **$p < 0.05$, *$p < 0.10$

(2) Marginal coefficients (dy/dx) are shown in the table

Second, the coefficients of the DID items in Model 4 are positively significant at a 1% level. This shows that compared with the non-enrollment group, the NRCMS enrollment group had a higher tendency to go for a health examination. These results indicate that enrolling in the NRCMS might promote disease prevention behavior.

7.3.3 *Effects of the NRCMS on the Utilization of Healthcare Services by Age Group*

Regarding the heterogeneous group, health status differs by age group, for example, both morbidity and mobility are higher in the older group than in the younger group. Therefore, it can be surmised that the utilization of healthcare services differs by age group. Using two sub-samples and the DID method, the impact of the NRCMS on the utilization of healthcare services is estimated by two groups: age 16–59 (the working age group) and age 60 and above (the elderly group).

Table 7.3 displays the results by age group. The main findings are as follows. First, the DID items in Models 1–2 are insignificant in both age groups. They indicate that the utilization of healthcare services (both outpatient and inpatient) between the NRCMS enrollment and non-enrollment groups does not differ. Therefore, it can be said that NRCMS did not affect healthcare utilization in either group.

Second, regarding the 2000 and 2006 samples, the coefficients of the DID items in Model 3 are positively significant at a 1% level in the 16–59 age group, but insignificant in the 60 and above age group. These results show that in the working age group (16–59), the NRCMS may have a positive effect on disease prevention behavior. However, in the elderly group ($\geq$60 years), the NRCMS does not affect the utilization of healthcare services.

7.3.4 *Estimations of Short-Term and Long-Term Effects*

Regarding to the effects of the NRCMS in short- and long-terms, we also performed estimations using the two waves of longitudinal data from the CHNS of 2000 and 2011. Table 7.4 summarizes the results.

The coefficients of the DID items in Models 1–3 are not statistically significant; moreover, the coefficients of the DID items in Model 4 (health examination) are negatively and statistically significant. This indicates that the utilization of healthcare services (both outpatient and inpatient, outpatient, inpatient) between the NRCMS enrollment group and the non-enrollment group did not differ and that the NRCMS enrollment group is less likely to utilize inpatient services and undergo a health examination than the NRCMS non-enrollment group. The results of Models 1–3 are consistent with those in Table 7.2.

Table 7.3 The Impact of NCMS on utilization of healthcare service by age group

	Age 60 and over		Age 16–59	
	Coef	z-value	Coef	z-value
2000 versus 2004				
(1) Outpatient + Inpatient				
Treatment	0.013	0.19	0.044**	2.52
Year	0.102***	4.33	0.050***	6.96
DID	0.052	0.65	−0.011	−0.69
(2) Outpatient				
Treatment	0.016	0.25	0.037**	2.20
Year	0.092***	4.07	0.048***	6.97
DID	0.039	0.53	−0.004	−0.24
(3) Health examination				
Treatment	0.000	−0.01	−0.001	−0.26
Year	0.000	−0.22	0.000	0.37
DID	0.763	0.01	0.004	0.88
2000 versus 2006				
(1) Outpatient + Inpatient				
Treatment	0.003	0.10	0.003	0.34
Year	0.094***	4.81	0.036***	4.15
DID	0.017	0.46	0.021*	1.62
(2) Outpatient				
Treatment	0.002	0.06	0.006	0.61
Year	0.086***	4.59	0.036***	4.25
DID	0.017	0.50	0.017	1.34
(3) Health examination				
Treatment	−0.055	−0.01	−0.002	−1.03
Year	0.001**	2.18	0.000	0.09
DID	0.441	0.01	0.017***	2.68

Source Calculated based on the data from CHNS of 2000, 2004, 2006

Notes

(1) $^{***}p < 0.01$, $^{**}p < 0.05$, $^{*}p < 0.10$

(2) Marginal coefficients (dy/dx) are shown in the table

(3) Age, education, sex, self-reported health status, Hypertension, Diabetes, household income, regions, smoking, drinking, drink water, toilet, and waste status variables have been estimated, but these results are not listed in the table

Table 7.4 The Impact of NCMS on utilization of healthcare service in a long-term

	(1) Outpatient + Inpatient		(2) Outpatient		(3) Inpatient		(4) Health examination	
	dy/dx	z-value	dy/dx	z-value	dy/dx	z-value	dy/dx	z-value
Treatment	0.169	0.68	0.197	0.79	−3.045	−0.02	0.534	1.15
Year	0.261**	2.39	0.381***	3.54	0.658***	2.58	1.203***	5.41
DID	−0.229	−0.88	−0.246	−0.95	2.651	0.02	−0.818	−1.70

Source Calculated based on the data from CHNS of 2000 and 2011
Notes
(1) ***$p < 0.01$, **$p < 0.05$.
(2) Marginal coefficients (dy/dx) are shown in the table
(3) Age, education, sex, self-reported health status, Hypertension, Diabetes, household income, regions, smoking, drinking, drink water, toilet, and waste status variables have been estimated, but these results are not listed in the table

However, the results of Model 4 differ from the results in Table 7.2 and are not consistent with Wagstaff et al. (2009), who reported that the NRCMS increases the probability of going for a health examination. This can be mainly attributed to the following. First, the analysis periods in these studies differed. In Wagstaff et al. (2009) and Table 7.2, the analyzed period is from 2000 to 2004 or 2006 whereas in Table 7.4, the analyzed period is from 2000 to 2011. In the early implementation period of the NRCMS, some local rural regions (counties) provided a free health examination per year for the members of the NRCMS who did not utilize any healthcare services in that year, to promote long term NRCMS membership. However, following the increase in the NRCMS enrollment rate, the provision of free health examination services has been reduced. Second, a NRCMS participant can only receive a free health examination per year if the healthy participant has not utilized the healthcare services, either outpatient or inpatient, which causes the reimbursement account to be zero. When a participant health status worsens so that he has to visit the hospital or clinic, the probability of receiving a free health examination may decrease. Third, a NRCMS participant can receive medical expense reimbursement when he is ill. Following the rise in reimbursement accounts, the effort to undergo health examinations for the early detection of an illness may decrease.

7.4 Conclusions

The Chinese government implemented the NRCMS in 2003. It was expected that public medical insurance would improve the unequal utilization of healthcare services in China. We investigated whether the NRCMS affect the utilization of healthcare services in rural China. Using a longitudinal data from four waves (2000, 2004, 2006, and 2011) of the CHNS and econometric methods (RE probit regression model and the DID method), this study performed an empirical analysis to investigate the impact of the NRCMS on the utilization of healthcare services. The major conclusions are as follows.

First, predisposing factors, enabling factors, healthcare need factors, and lifestyle factors affect the utilization of healthcare services. These results are consistent with those of Anderson (1995).

Second, the results obtained from using the DID method indicate that the NRCMS did not affect the utilization of healthcare services (outpatient and inpatient) for an ill person.

Third, the NRCMS did not affect the utilization of healthcare services (outpatient and inpatient) in either of the examined age group. The NRCMS positively affects disease prevention behavior (visiting the hospital for a health examination) in the working age group in the short term (from 2000 to 2004, or from 2000 to 2006). However, this was not the case in the elderly group.

Fourth, from a long-term perspective (from 2000 to 2011), the NRCMS did not affect the utilization of healthcare services (outpatient or inpatient). Further, the positive effect on health examination dissipated.

Regarding policy implications, the results show that the NRCMS insignificantly improved the utilization of health care services and that it might increase the probability of undergoing a health examination in the short term. The results further show that from a long-term perspective, the positive effect of the NRCMS on preventive medical care dissipated, which suggests that there might be an inequality in the utilization of healthcare services in China even after the implementation of the NRCMS in rural China. The NRCMS did not affect the utilization of healthcare services mainly because of the system design, which requires large share of OOP expenses on medical care. According to the NRCMS, patients (mostly inpatients) have to pay the total medical care expenses and then apply to the local government for reimbursement. Patients can receive such reimbursement (less than 50%) only after the local government checks their applications (Ma, 2015). The high proportions of OOP (more than 50%) in outpatient and inpatient medical care expenses in the NRCMS might have resulted in the poor effects of the NRCMS (or the absence of positive effects) on the utilization of healthcare services. In contrast, the Urban Employee Basic Medical Insurance (UEBMI) for employees in urban areas (majority of them with urban *hukou*), urban workers only pay 30% of the medical care expenses when utilizing inpatient services. Therefore, the differences in the system design in public medical insurance between rural and urban areas, which is related to the inequality in the utilization of health care services in China, should be noted. To resolve the problem, the reimbursement proportions by the government should increase; meaning that the government should pay more for the NRCMS and integrate the different public medical insurances in rural and urban areas to establish a realistic universal medical insurance nationwide.

This research has some limitations. For example, factors such as time preference, disease status, and distance from home to the hospital may affect an individual's utilization of healthcare services. In future, a detailed survey should be conducted to obtain additional information for better empirical analysis.

Notes

1. For empirical studies on the effects of public medical care insurance reforms on the utilization of healthcare services, please see Currie and Gruber (1996a, b, 1997), Decker and Rember (2004), Currie et al. (2008), Card et al. (2008), and Finkelstein and McKnight (2008). These studies use micro-data based on social experiments by RAND to estimate the effects of Medicare and Medicaid performed in the U.S. For empirical studies on developing countries, please see Jowett et al. (2004) and Sepehri et al. (2006) for Vietnam, Panopoulu and Velez (2001), Trujillo et al. (2005) for Columbia, and Gakidou et al. (2006) for Mexico.
2. Li and Zhao (2006), You and Kobayashi (2011), and Li and Zhang (2013) used Anderson's behavior model to conduct empirical studies on the utilization of healthcare services. They however did not focus on the effects of public medical insurance.
3. Predisposing factors included socio-demographic factors such as education, age, gender, and marital status.
4. In this study, income includes household income from agriculture, aquaculture, fruit and non-agricultural industry sectors, and transfer income.
5. Living environment variables included water (drinking water at home or outside home), toilets (in home or outside home), and waste status (whether or not there is waste near the house).

Appendix

See Table 7.5.

Table 7.5 Statistics description of variables (mean values)

	Variables	Total samples	Enrollment	Non-enrollment
Waves	Years			
	y2000	0.460	0.114	0.529
	y2004	0.269	0.181	0.286
	y2006	0.271	0.705	0.185
Predisposing	Age category			
factors	Age 20–29	0.025	0.022	0.026
	Age 30–39	0.117	0.85	0.125
	Age 40–49	0.211	0.192	0.216
	Age 50–59	0.228	0.272	0.216
	Age 60–69	0.221	0.232	0.218
	Age 70–79	0.121	0.125	0.120
	Age 70 and over	0.077	0.072	0.079
	Education category			
	Not enrollment	0.174	0.191	0.170
	Primary school	0.355	0.353	0.355
	Junior high school	0.371	0.356	0.374
	Senior high school	0.080	0.083	0.080
	Vocational school	0.014	0.012	0.014
	College and over	0.006	0.005	0.007
	Male	0.418	0.453	0.411
Need factors	Self-reported health Status			
	Very good	0.137	0.128	0.139
	Good	0.474	0.455	0.479
	Fair	0.319	0.330	0.317
	Poor	0.070	0.087	0.065
	Hypertension	0.054	0.077	0.049
	Diabetes	0.006	0.007	0.005
Enabling factors	Household income (Yuan)	1,073	1,661	945
	Regions			
	Liaoning	0.087	0.104	0.083
	Heilongjiang	0.112	0.098	0.114
	Jiangsu	0.090	0.259	0.056
	Shandong	0.090	0.152	0.077
	Henan	0.133	0.056	0.149
	Hubei	0.114	0.114	0.114
	Hernan	0.088	0.060	0.093

(continued)

Table 7.5 (continued)

	Variables	Total samples	Enrollment	Non-enrollment
	Guangxi	0.146	0.067	0.162
	Guizhou	0.140	0.090	0.152
Lifestyle factors	Smoking	0.270	0.279	0.267
	Drinking			
	Not drinking	0.683	0.661	0.688
	Less one time monthly	0.024	0.024	0.024
	1–2 times monthly	0.056	0.066	0.054
	1–2 times weekly	0.082	0.081	0.082
	3–4 times weekly	0.043	0.043	0.044
	Everyday	0.104	0.118	0.100
	Don't know	0.008	0.007	0.008
	Health exercise	0.051	0.041	0.054
	Drink water inside the home	0.377	0.461	0.361
	Toilet inside the home	0.166	0.162	0.166
	No waste nearby the home	0.567	0.660	0.548
	Observations	14,556	2,415	12,141

Source Calculated based on the data from CHNS of 2000, 2004, 2006

References

Andersen, R., & Newman, J. F. (1973). Social and individual determinants of medical care utilization in the United States. *Milbank Quarterly, 51*(1), 95–124.

Andersen, R. (1995). Revisiting the behavioral model and access to medical care: Does it matter? *Journal of Health and Social Behavior, 36*(1), 1–10.

Card, D., Dobkin, C., & Maestas, N. (2008). The impact of nearly universal insurance coverage on health care utilization and health: Evidence from Medicare. *American Economic Review, 98*(5), 2242–2258.

Cheng, L., Liu, H., Zhang, Y., Shen, K., & Zeng, Y. (2015). The impact of health insurance of health outcomes and spending of the elderly: Evidence from China's New Cooperative Medical Scheme. *Health Economics, 24*(6), 672–691.

Currie, J., & Gruber, J. (1996a). Health insurance eligibility, utilization of medical care and child health. *Quarterly Journal of Economics, 111*(2), 431–466.

Currie, J., & Gruber, J. (1996b). Saving babies: The efficacy and cost of recent changes in the Medicaid eligibility of pregnant women. *Journal of Political Economy, 104*(6), 1263–1296.

Currie, J., & Gruber, J. (1997). The technology of birth: Health insurance, medical interventions and infant health. Working Paper 5985. National Bureau Economic Research.

Currie, J., Decker, S., & Lin, W. (2008). Has public health insurance for older children reduced disparities in access to care and health outcomes? *Journal of Health Economics, 27*(6), 1567–1581.

Decker, S. L., & Remler, D. K. (2004). How much might universal health insurance reduce socioeconomic disparities in health? A comparison of the US and Canada. *Applied Health Economics and Health Policy, 3*(4), 205–216.

Finkelstein, A., & McKnight, R. (2008). What did Medicare do? The initial impact of Medicare on Mortality and out of pocket medical spending. *Journal of Public Economics, 92*(7), 1644–1668.

Gakidou, E., Lozano, R., Gonzalez-Pier, E., Abbott-Klafter, J., Barofsky, J. T., Bryson-Cahn, C., Feehan, D. M., Lee, D. K., Hernandez-Llamas, H., & Murray, C. J. (2006). Assessing the effect of the 2001–06 Mexican health reform: An interim report card. *The Lancet, 368*(9550), 1920–1935.

Grossman, M. (1972). On the concept of health capital and the demand for health. *Journal of Political Economy, 80*(2), 223–255.

Jowett, M., Deolalikar, A., & Martinsson, P. (2004). Health insurance and treatment seeking behavior: Evidence from a low-income country. *Health Economics, 13*(9), 845–857.

Lei, X., & Lin, W. (2009). The New Cooperative Medical Scheme in rural China: Does more coverage mean more service and better health? *Health Economics, 18*(2), 25–46.

Li, X., & Zhang, W. (2013). The impacts of health insurance on health care utilization among the older people in China. *Social Science & Medicine, 85*, 59–65.

Li, Y., Wu, Q., Liu, C., Kang, Z., Xie, X., Yin, H., Jiao, M., Liu, G., Hao, Y., & Ning, N. (2014). Catastrophic health expenditure and rural household impoverishment in China: What role does the New Cooperative Health Insurance Scheme play? *PLoS ONE, 9*(4), 1–9.

Liu, G., & Zhao, Z. (2006). Urban employee health insurance reform and the impact on out-of-pocket payment in China. *International Journal of Health Planning and Management, 21*(3), 211–228.

Liu, Y., Hsiao, W. C. L., Li, Q., Liu, X., & Ren, M. (1995). Transformation of China's rural health insurance financing. *Social Science & Medicine, 41*(8), 1085–1093.

Lu, C., Liu, Y., & Shen, J. (2012). Does China's Rural Cooperative Medical System achieve its goals? Evidence from the China Health Surveillance Baseline Survey in 2001. *Contemporary Economic Policy, 30*(1), 93–112.

Ma, X. (2015). *Public medical insurance reform in China*. Kyoto University Press. (in Japanese).

Panopoulu, G., & Velez, C. (2001). *Subsidized health insurance, proxy means testing and the demand for health care among the poor in Colombia, Colombia Poverty Report* (Vol. II). World Bank.

Sepehri, A., Sarma, S., & Simpson, W. (2006). Does non-profit health insurance reduce financial burden? Evidence from the Vietnam Living Standards Survey Panel. *Health Economics, 15*(6), 603–616.

Shi, W., Chongsuvivatwong, V., Geater, V., Zhang, J., Zhang, H., & Brombal, D. (2010). The influence of the Rural Health Security Schemes on health utilization and household impoverishment in rural China: Data from a household survey of western and central China. *International Journal for Equity in Health, 9*(7), 1–11.

Song, X. (2006). *Reform: Enterprise, labor and social security*. Social Science Literature Press. (in Chinese).

Song, X. (2009). Retrospect and prospect of China's medical insurance system in the 60 Years since the founding of the People's Republic of China. *Chinese Journal of Health Policy, 2*(19), 6–14. (in Chinese).

Trujillo, A. J., Portillo, J. E., & Vernon, A. (2005). The impact of subsidized health insurance for the poor: Evaluating the Colombian experience using propensity score matching. *International Journal of Health Care Finance and Economics, 5*(3), 211–239.

Wagstaff, A., & Lindelow, M. (2008). Can insurance increase financial risk? The curious case of health insurance in China. *Journal of Health Economics, 27*(4), 990–1005.

Wagstaff, A., Lindelow, M., Gao, J., Xu, L., & Qian, J. (2009). Extending health insurance to the rural population: An impact evaluation of China's New Cooperative Medical Scheme. *Journal of Health Economics, 28*(1), 1–19.

You, X., & Kobayashi, Y. (2011). Determinants of out-of-pocket health expenditure in China. *Application Health Economic Health Policy, 9*(1), 39–49.

Chapter 8
Medical Insurance and Out-Of-Pocket Expenses on Medical Care

Abstract This study tries to answer two questions: (i) Does public medical insurance affect out-of- pocket (OOP) expenses on medical care? (i) Does public medical insurance affect the probability of catastrophic medical expenses (CME)? Using longitudinal data from the China Health and Nutrition Surveys of 2000, 2004, and 2006, an empirical analysis was conducted to explore how public medical insurance influences OOP expenses and the probability of CME. The results reveal that the impact of public medical insurance on OOP expenses and the probability of CME are not statistically significant in urban and rural areas. Other factors such as age, education, health status, and lifestyle affect OOP expenses and the probability of CME, and the effects of these factors are greater in rural areas than in urban areas.

Keywords Medical insurance · Out-of-pocket expense · Medical care · Catastrophic medical expense · China

8.1 Introduction

In China, the Cooperative Medical Scheme (CMS) managed by people's commune was implemented in rural areas during the planned economy period. Under the market-oriented reform period in rural areas, the dismantling of the people's commune in rural areas led to a collapse in the CMS. The rate of implementation of the CMS dropped significantly from 90% in the planned economy period to 10% in 1993 (Liu et al., 1995; Wagstaff & Lindelow, 2008; Wagstaff et al., 2009; Cheng et al., 2015). Since the 1990s, public medical insurance for rural and urban residents has been reformed, the government introduced the principle of a competitive market in the healthcare service sector, and medical care expenses increased dramatically. The problem of medical care inequality caused by income inequality has become severe. Most people in rural areas have succumbed to poverty in the course of dealing with illnesses. It has been said that "it is difficult to obtain healthcare services, and the medical care expenses are high (*Kanbingnan Kanbinggui*)." To address these problems, in 2003, the Chinese government implemented the New Rural Cooperative Medical Insurance Scheme (NRCMS), which covers all rural residents. Participation in NRCMS is voluntary, and its financial fund is composed

X. Ma, *Public Medical Insurance Reforms in China*,
https://doi.org/10.1007/978-981-16-7790-8_8

of three parts: (i) participants' insurance contribution, (ii) village subsidy, and (iii) government subsidy. However, owing to the miniscule size of the insurance fund, the majority of medical care expenses are paid by rural residents themselves. Therefore, even when enrolled in the NRCMS, the probability of utilizing healthcare services might be small when ill, and the probability of falling prey to poverty due to serious illness might still be high.

In contrast, in urban areas, under the planned economy period, the labor insurance medical system covered all employees in corporates, and the publicly funded medical systems covered all civil servants in government offices and government-related organizations, both of which are close to the qualities of free medical care system. Insured workers were not required to pay medical insurance premiums, and the out-of-pocket expenses on medical care (Hereinafter referred to as "OOP expenses") was almost "zero," which caused problems of over-examination and over-consumption of medicines. To address these problems, the government started to reform public medical insurances in the 1990s. Specifically, on December 14, 1998, the State Council promulgated the "*State Council Decision on the Construction of the Basic Medical Insurance System for Urban Employees*". The Urban Employee Basic Medical Insurance (UEBMI) covering urban employees was introduced and enforced in all corporates (state-owned enterprises, collectively owned enterprises, foreign-owned enterprises, privately owned enterprises, etc.) and non-corporate sectors (government organizations, social organizations, etc.). As the proportion of OOP expenses in total medical care expenses is almost 30% in UEBMI, it can be assumed that the risk of poverty is higher in the low-income group than in the high-income group, even in urban areas.

To evaluate the influence of the reform of public medical insurance in China, empirical research is required to investigate the effect of medical insurance on OOP expenses. Using longitudinal data from the China Health and Nutrition Study (CHNS) of 2000, 2004, and 2006 (CHNS 2000, 2004, 2006), this study tries to answer two questions as follows: (i) Does public medical insurance affect OOP expenses? (i) Does public medical insurance affect the probability of catastrophic medical expenses (CME)?[1] Considering the differences in medical insurance establishment between the NRCMS and UBEMI, we also compare the effects of medical insurance between rural and urban residents.

The remainder of this chapter is organized as follows: Sect. 8.2 summarizes the results of the literature review. Section 8.3 introduces the methodology, including the decomposition model and the data used. Section 8.4 summarizes the results of the descriptive statistics on the enrollment of public medical insurance and OOP expense. Section 8.5 introduces and explains the results of the econometric analysis. Section 8.6 summarizes the major findings and concludes the study.

8.2 Literature Review

Numerous empirical studies on the impact of medical insurance on OOP expenses have been conducted, and due to space limitations, only empirical studies for China are summarized in Appendix Table 8.6.[2]

The results of the empirical studies on rural residents in China are mixed. For example, using data from the 2003 National Health Service Survey and probit regression model and instrument variable (IV) method (Probit_IV), generalized linear model and IV, and logistic regression model and fixed-effects (FE) model, Wagstaff et al. (2009) found that the NRCMS has no significant effect on OOP expenses. Shi et al. (2010) conducted a logistic regression analysis using survey data of residents in three rural provinces (Hebei, Shaanxi, and Inner Mongolia) in 2008, and found that the NRCMS dummy was not significant for the length of inpatient, and the NRCMS had no influence on reducing poverty due to serious illness. Using longitudinal survey data from the Chinese Longitudinal Healthy Longevity Survey (CLHLS) of 2005 and 2008 and the propensity score matching (PSM) method, Cheng et al. (2015) found that the NRCMS has no significant effect on reducing OOP expenses. Using data from the China Health Surveillance Baseline of 2001 and PSM and the IV method, Lu et al. (2012) found that the effect of NRCMS on the probability of CME is not statistically significant. Using data from longitudinal surveys conducted in Shandong and Ningxia in 2006 and 2008, and the difference in difference method, Jing et al. (2013) found that NRCMS does not reduce the probability of CME. Using CHNS in 2004 and Heckman two-step method, You and Kobayashi (2011) found that NRCMS did not significantly affect OOP expenses. However, using a survey data of women in rural Shandong province from December 2008 to March 2009 and a logistic regression model, Xiao et al. (2010) reported that OOP expenses tends to be lower for the NRCMS enrollment group than for the counterpart.

Some empirical studies have analyzed the issue focusing on urban residents or the whole population, including urban and rural residents in China. For instance, using longitudinal survey data from the CLHLS of 2002 and 2005, and Heckman two-step method and the two-part model, Huang and Gan (2010) found that OOP expenses tend to be lower for the UEBMI participant group than the counterpart. Wagstaff and Lindelow (2008) used three types of datasets—(i) CHNS of 1991, 1993, 1997, 2000; (ii) Gansu Survey of Children and Families of 2000 and 2003; (iii) World Bank China Health VIII Project Baseline Survey, and the logistic regression model, IV method, and FE models, and found that total medical care expenses tend to be higher, but the probability of CME is lower for the medical insurance participant group than for the non-participant group. Using the data from the CLHLS of 2005 and the Heckman two-step method and the two-part model, Liu et al. (2011) reported that OOP expenses tends to be lower for public medical insurance participants than non-participants. However, using the China Health and Retirement Longitudinal Study of 2008 and the two-part model, Li and Zhang (2013) found that the impact of public medical insurance on OOP expenses is not statistically significant.

Although previous studies investigated the impact of public medical insurance on OOP expense and probability of CME in China, some issues require further discussion. The main contributions of this study are as follows. First, the scope of analysis here is nationwide, including rural and urban residents, which is similar to the work of You and Kobayashi (2011), Liu et al. (2011), and Li and Zhang (2013); however, previous studies used one-point survey data, and the change in the impact of medical insurance on the OOP expenses and probability of CME over the years is not clear. This study investigates the changes in medical insurance effects over time using a longitudinal data from the CHNS of 2000, 2004, and 2006.

Second, there may be a heterogeneity problem in the results. For example, the higher the degree of risk aversion, the higher the probability of participating in medical insurance, and the higher the OOP expenses. However, most of the previous studies did not consider individual heterogeneity problem. This study uses a random effects (RE) model to address the problem based on a longitudinal survey data.

Finally, Wagstaff et al. (2009) addressed the heterogeneity problem, but the analysis period was from 1991 to 2000. Further, the influences of the NRCMS, implemented since 2003 across all rural areas, was not analyzed. In contrast, this study uses a longitudinal data from 2000 to 2006 to conduct an empirical study on the effects of public medical insurance, including the NRCMS.

8.3 Methodology and Data

8.3.1 Model

To address the sample selection bias, this study uses the Heckman two-step method (Heckman, 1979) and the two-part model (Duan et al., 1984). The Heckman two-step method is expressed as Eqs. (8.1)–(8.5) and the two-part model is expressed by the Eqs. (8.6)–(8.10).

[Heckman two-step method].

Selection function:

$$y_{1i}^{*} = a_1 + \beta_1 X_i + \varepsilon_{1i} \tag{8.1}$$

$$y_{1i}^{*} = \begin{cases} 1 \text{ if } y_{1i}^{*} > 0 \\ 0 \text{ if } y_{1i}^{*} \leq 0 \end{cases} \tag{8.2}$$

OOP expense function:

$$OOP_{1j} = b_1 + \gamma_1 H_{1j} + u_{1j} \tag{8.3}$$

$$\varepsilon_1 \sim N(0, 1),\ u_1 \sim N(0, \sigma_1^2),\ \text{cov}(\varepsilon_1, u_1) \neq 0 \tag{8.4}$$

$$OOP_{1i} = b_1 + \gamma_1 H_{1i} + \rho\sigma_1 \emptyset(\beta_1 X_i)/\Phi(\beta_1 X_i) + u_{1i} \tag{8.5}$$

[Two-part model].
Selection function:

$$y^*_{2i} = a_2 + \beta_2 X_{2i} + \varepsilon_{2i} \tag{8.6}$$

$$y^*_{2i} = \begin{cases} 1 \text{ if } y^*_{2i} > 0 \\ 0 \text{ if } y^*_{2i} \leq 0 \end{cases} \tag{8.7}$$

OOP expense function:

$$OOP_{2j} = b_2 + \gamma_2 H_{2j} + u_{2j} \tag{8.8}$$

$$\varepsilon_2 \sim N(0, 1),\ u_2 \sim N\left(0, \sigma_2^2\right),\ \text{cov}(\varepsilon_2, u_2) = 0 \tag{8.9}$$

$$E\left(OOP^*_{2i}|y_2 = 1, X_2\right) = \Phi(\beta_2 X_{2i}) \exp(\gamma_2 H_{2i}) + \sigma_2^2/2 \tag{8.10}$$

where subscript i and j is individual, OOP is the logarithmic value of OOP expenses on medical care, y^* is the probability of healthcare service utilization, X and H are factors that influence the probability of healthcare service utilization and OOP expenses, a and b are constant terms, and ε and u are error terms.

A random-effects (RE) model was used to address the heterogeneity problem. The reasons for using the RE model are as follows. First, although a FE model can be used, it fails to measure variables that do not change with time, such as educational background, age, living environment, and region. Therefore, this study uses a RE model to examine the effects of these factors. Second, it is well known that when the wave of a longitudinal survey is short and the number of samples is large, only a small difference is seen between the measurement results of the RE and FE models. In fact, we used these two models to perform the estimations, and the results of the two models were almost the same. Thus, we reported results based on the RE model in this study. The RE model is expressed by Eq. (8.11).

$$OOP/CME_{jt} = b_t + \gamma H_{jt} + v_j + \varepsilon_{jt} \tag{8.11}$$

In the results based on Eqs. (8.5), (8.10), and (8.11), when the coefficient of the public medical insurance dummy variable is negative and statistically significant, it is shown that the OOP expenses and the probability of CME are less among the public medical insurance participant group than in the non-participant group.

8.3.2 Data and Variable Setting

Three-point longitudinal data from CHNS 2000, 2004, and 2006 were used for the analysis. These surveys were conducted at the University of North Carolina in the United States. The subjects of the survey included both urban and rural residents. The scope of these surveys covered the nine representative provinces of China (Jiangsu, Liaoning, Heilongjiang, Shandong, Henan, Hubei, Hunan, Guangxi, and Guizhou). In terms of the survey method, based on the register used in the national census, data was sampled using a multi-step random sampling method, a surveyor visiting survey, and a detention survey. The sample size (individual vote) was 16,150 in 2000, 9,856 in 2004, and 9,788 in 2006. The CHNS includes information on medical insurance enrollment status, OOP expenses on medical care, health status, utilization of healthcare services, income, and individual attributes. It is, thus, the most appropriate data for empirical analysis in this study.

The question items "How much did you pay for medical care when you were ill this past year?" and "What is the percentage of medical care expenses you paid yourself?" were used to identify the dependent variable setting. We calculated the OOP expenses as "total medical care expenses multiplied by percentage of OOP expenses". The logarithmic value was used as the dependent variable in the OOP expense function.

Second, we divided the OOP expenses by the household income to calculate the ratio of OOP expenses to the total household income.[3] We defined CME as a situation where the ratio is 40% or more. The binary variable of CME (1 = 40% or more, 0 = less than 40%) was used in the CME probability function.

Third, the binary variable (1 = outpatient/inpatient services used within 4 weeks, 0 = otherwise) was used in the probability functions of healthcare service utilization (selection function of two-step estimation).

Based on Anderson model of healthcare service utilization (Andersen, 1995; Andersen & Newman, 1973), the independent variables were constructed using five factor groups (see Appendix Table 8.7).

First, we used age,[4] education,[5] and sex as indicators of predisposing factors. It is assumed that older and well-educated groups are more likely to use medical care services. A male dummy was used to control for the difference between men and women.

Second, regarding the factors related to the possibility of using healthcare services (enabling variables), the medical insurance system and income were used as indicators of medical care demand side factors, and regional medical supply was used as an indicator of medical care supply side factors. The public medical insurance system participation dummy, household income per capita, and regional dummies (Jiangsu, Liaoning, Heilongjiang, Shandong, Henan, Hubei, Hunan, Guangxi, and Guizhou) were used in this study. Household income includes household income from agriculture, aquaculture, fruit, and non-agricultural industry sectors, and transfer income. The household income per capita was calculated by dividing household income by the number of family members in the household.

Third, regarding the medical care demand factor (health care need factor), self-reported health status (very good, good, fair, poor), and chronic disease (hypertension, diabetes) dummy variables were constructed. It is assumed that the group with poor health status, hypertension, and diabetes tend to need more healthcare services, and the OOP expenses may be higher.

Fourth, smoking behavior,[6] drinking behavior,[7] health exercise,[8] and living environment[9] dummy variables are constructed as the indicators of lifestyle factors.

Fifth, the OOP expenses and the probability of CME may differ by age, and age dummy variables were constructed.

The analyzed objects were both urban and rural residents aged 18 years and older. Missing values for each variable were excluded. The number of samples used in the analysis was 24,784 (public medical insurance participant group 7,026, non-participant group 17,758). To secure the analyzed sample (particularly, the few samples that responded to OOP expenses) we used the unbalanced longitudinal data in this study.

8.4 Descriptive Statistic Results

Table 8.1 summarizes the proportion of participation in medical insurance by insurance type. The types of medical insurance are divided into seven types: (1) publicly funded medical system, (2) UEBMI, (3) NRCMS, (4) commercial insurance, (5) family insurance, (6) general insurance, and (7) other insurance. First, for the change in the proportion of participants by medical insurance type, (1) the percentage of

Table 8.1 Proportion of participants in medical insurances in China. Unit: %

	2000			2004			2006		
	Nation	Urban	Rural	Nation	Urban	Rural	Nation	Urban	Rural
PFMS	6.9	9.7	4.6	7.5	15.8	1.4	2.8	5.3	1.0
UEBMI	3.6	5.5	2.3	4.1	8.8	0.6	16.2	35.6	2.3
NRCMS	4.8	5.4	4.5	7.5	3.1	10.7	27.7	9.0	41.1
Commercial	1.6	1.1	1.5	2.5	3.5	1.7	0.7	0.9	0.5
Family	0.2	0.6	0.1	0.5	0.9	0.1			
General	0.4	0.2	0.2	4.8	10.4	0.6			
Others	2.1	2.4	2.0	0.5	1.3	0.1	0.7	1.7	0.1
Non-insurance	80.4	75.0	84.8	72.6	56.2	84.8	51.9	47.5	55.0

Source Calculated based on the data from CHNS 2000, 2004 and 2006

Notes (1) PFMS: publicly funded medical system; UEBMI: urban employee basic medical insurance; NRCMS: new rural cooperative medical scheme; Commercial: commercial insurance; Family: family insurance; general: general insurance; Others: other insurance; Non-insurance: individuals who have not participated in any type of medical insurance. (2) There are not questionnaire items of family insurance and general insurance in CHNS 2006

non-participants decreased from 80.4% in 2000 to 72.6% in 2004 and 51.9% in 2006. The percentage of people who joined medical insurance increased over the years, but it can be observed that the percentage of individuals who are not covered by any one medical insurance was still higher until 2006. (2) The percentage of the publicly funded medical system participants decreased from 6.9% in 2000 and 7.5% in 2004 to 2.8% in 2006, while the percentage of UEBMI participants increased from 3.6% in 2000 to 4.1% in 2004 to 16.2% in 2006. After the implementation of the UEBMI in 1998, the reform of publicly funded medical insurance was delayed, but in recent years, it can be observed that the integration of UEBMI and publicly funded medical system is progressing. (3) The percentage of NRCMS participants increased significantly from 4.8% in 2000 to 7.5% in 2004 to 27.7% in 2006 owing to the implementation of NRCMS in 2003.

Second, to compare the proportion of participants by medical insurance scheme type between urban and rural areas, the results suggest that they differ. For example, in 2006, the percentage of those who joined the UEBMI was 35.6% in urban areas, which is higher than that in rural areas (2.3%), while the percentage of those who joined the NRCMS was 41.1% in rural areas, which is higher than that in urban areas (9.0%). It is observed that the enrollment rates of medical insurance differ between urban and rural areas.

Figure 8.1 shows the kernel density distribution of the logarithm value of the OOP expenses by the public medical insurance participant group and non-participant group. In urban areas, compared to the non-participant group, the OOP expenses is slightly higher for the non-participant group, while in rural areas, it is slightly higher for the participant group.

The descriptive statistical results reveal that the proportion of participants by medical insurance type differs between urban and rural areas, and the OOP expenses by participant and non-participant groups also differ between urban and rural areas. However, these are the results when other factors are not controlled. The results of the multivariable analysis are reported below.

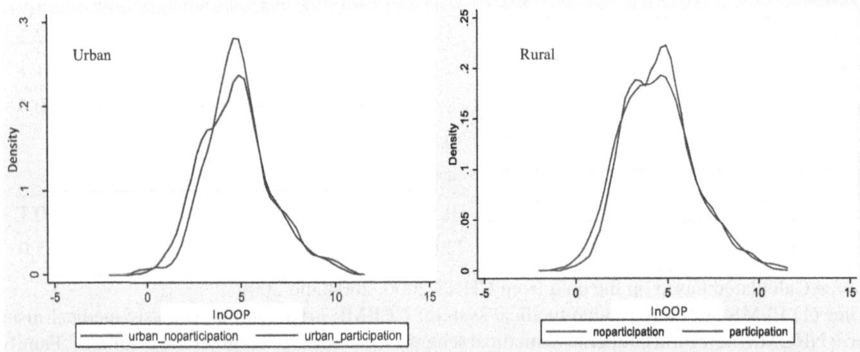

Fig. 8.1 Kernel distribution of logarithm value of OOP expenses on medical care by participant or non-participant groups. *Source* Calculated based on the data from CHNS2000, 2004 and 2006

8.5 Econometric Analysis Results

8.5.1 Results of OOP Expenses on Medical Care

Table 8.2 (nationwide, including urban and rural areas), Table 8.3 (urban areas), and Table 8.4 (rural areas) summarize the results of determinants of OOP expenses on medical care. The Heckman two-step method (Model1), two-part model (Model 2), and random-effects model (Model 3) were used in analysis. The coefficient of the inverse Mills ratio in Model 1 of Table 8.2 is 3.632, and it is statistically significant at the 1% level; it is not statistically significant in Model1 of Table 8.3; it is 5.869 and significant in Model 1 of Table 8.4. This suggests that the estimation results may be underestimated when the sample selection bias is not considered in the analysis of nationwide and rural areas. The main findings on the determinants of OOP expenses are as follows.

First, regarding the impact of public medical insurance, for the nationwide estimations, the results that addressed the sample selection bias (Model 1, Model 2), and the results that addressed the individual heterogeneity problem (Model 3) reveal that the impact of public medical insurance on the OOP expenses is not statistically significant. This indicates that public medical insurance does not have the effect of reducing OOP expenses. In addition, the results for urban and rural areas reveal that the impact of public medical insurance on the OOP expenses is not statistically significant for both urban and rural areas. It is shown that public medical insurance did not contribute to reducing the individual or household burden of medical care expenses in rural or urban areas.

Second, in terms of other factors,

(1) the OOP expense is 7.0–32.0% higher in urban areas than in rural areas.

(2) Regarding the effect of age, since the probability of developing a serious illness is relatively high in the elderly group, it is assumed that the OOP expense is higher in the elderly group. The results indicate that in urban areas, the OOP expense is 60.4–83.6% (the group aged 70–79 years) and 56.0–86.9% (the group aged 80 years and over) higher in the elderly group than in the group aged 30–39 years; in rural areas, the OOP expense is 1.13 times (the group aged 70–79 years) and 1.51 times (the group aged 80 years and over) higher in the elderly group than in the group aged 30–39 years. The difference in the OOP expenses between young and older groups was larger in rural areas than in urban areas.

(3) In urban areas, the OOP expense is 57.5% higher in senior high school graduate groups than in groups who did not attend school. In rural areas, the OOP expense is 9.1–46.8% higher in the junior high school graduate group than in the group that did not attend school. In both urban and rural areas, the OOP expense is higher in the middle-level educated group than in the low-level educated group.

Table 8.2 Public medical insurances and out-of-pocket expenses on medical care (nationwide)

	(1) Heckman				(2) Two-part				(3) Random effects	
	Second step		First step		Second step (Possion)		First step (logit)			
	Coef	z-value	Coef	z-value	Coef	z-value	Coef	z-value	Coef	z-value
Medical insurance	0.359	1.27	0.114***	4.06	0.010	0.33	0.219***	4.13	0.062	0.55
Urban	0.315***	3.23	0.075**	2.35	0.070***	2.68	0.138**	2.26	0.320***	3.27
Age (age 30–39)										
Age 20–29	0.214	0.70	0.154**	2.05	−0.054	−0.67	0.309**	2.00	−0.201	−0.69
Age 40–49	0.140	0.72	0.001	0.01	0.038	0.72	0.008	0.08	0.175	0.89
Age 50–59	−0.022	−0.12	0.022	0.46	−0.011	−0.22	0.052	0.54	−0.038	−0.20
Age 60–69	0.430**	2.06	0.137***	2.82	0.010	0.20	0.279***	2.87	0.060	0.31
Age 70–79	0.895***	3.41	0.277***	5.12	0.031	0.55	0.518***	4.91	0.157	0.76
Age 80+	1.078***	3.52	0.367***	6.11	0.025	0.42	0.681***	5.91	0.127	0.56
Education (not enrollment)										
Primary school	0.063	0.47	0.086**	2.31	−0.033	−0.97	0.171**	2.49	−0.155	−1.22
Junior high	0.287*	1.89	0.053	1.27	0.042	1.04	0.107	1.36	0.201	1.33
Senior high	0.138	0.66	0.048	0.91	0.023	0.42	0.096	0.95	0.096	0.46
Vocational school	−0.062**	−1.97	−0.151**	−2.21	−0.029	−0.37	−0.296**	−2.20	−0.134	−0.45
College and higher	0.210	0.74	0.121*	1.77	0.004	0.05	0.226*	1.72	0.013	0.05
Male	−0.127	−1.00	−0.151***	−4.05	0.035	1.21	−0.209**	−3.81	0.177	1.63
Health status (very good)										
Good	0.704***	2.94	0.141***	3.05	0.054	0.87	0.330***	3.23	0.230	1.06
Fair	2.369***	5.16	0.605***	13.05	0.119**	1.97	1.244***	12.36	0.513*	2.38

(continued)

Table 8.2 (continued)

	(1) Heckman				(2) Two-part				(3) Random effects	
	Second step		First step		Second step (Possion)		First step (logit)			
	Coef	z-value	Coef	z-value	Coef	z-value	Coef	z-value	Coef	z-value
Not good	5.200***	6.18	1.300***	24.01	0.320***	5.07	2.436***	22.11	1.502***	6.62
Hypertension	1.042***	4.77	0.327***	9.19	0.040	1.31	0.583***	9.31	0.196*	1.68
Diabetes	1.098***	3.73	0.362***	4.78	0.042	0.74	0.619***	4.82	0.233	1.03
Income	0.000***	1.81	0.000***	2.24	0.000	0.56	0.000**	2.28	0.000	0.78
Province (Jiangsu)										
Liaoning	−0.371	−1.48	−0.275***	−5.39	0.070	1.40	−0.527***	−5.37	0.375*	1.95
Heilongjiang	−0.199	−0.70	−0.328***	−5.93	0.132**	2.39	−0.609***	−5.62	0.670***	3.14
Shandong	−0.433*	−1.93	−0.185***	−3.64	0.005	0.10	−0.316***	−3.25	0.044	0.22
Hernan	0.196	1.05	0.102**	2.11	−0.039	−0.84	0.191**	2.11	−0.147	−0.86
Hubei	0.202	1.15	0.058	1.21	0.003	0.07	0.100	1.11	0.038	0.22
Hunan	0.084	0.44	−0.054	−1.10	0.063	1.29	−0.109	−1.16	0.317*	1.72
Guangxi	−0.337*	−1.93	0.037	0.75	−0.094**	−1.99	0.070	0.76	−0.403**	−2.30
Guizhou	−1.309***	−5.83	−0.208***	−3.92	−0.176***	−3.33	−0.367***	−3.66	−0.754***	−3.97
Smoking	−0.254*	−2.13	−0.006	−0.20	−0.056*	−1.72	−0.018	−0.29	−0.242*	−2.02
Drinking (no drinking)										
Less than once a month	0.228	0.81	0.095	1.32	−0.012	−0.16	0.157	1.12	−0.057	−0.21
1–2 times a month	−0.322	−1.54	0.071	1.35	−0.123**	−2.08	0.128	1.26	−0.520**	−2.53

(continued)

Table 8.2 (continued)

	(1) Heckman				(2) Two-part				(3) Random effects	
	Second step		First step		Second step (Possion)		First step (logit)			
	Coef	z-value	Coef	z-value	Coef	z-value	Coef	z-value	Coef	z-value
1–2 times a week	−0.217	−1.19	0.026	0.56	−0.057	−1.13	0.045	0.49	−0.290	−1.59
3–4 times a week	0.327	1.33	0.170***	2.87	−0.033	−0.55	0.313***	2.73	−0.165	−0.74
Every day	−0.263	−1.55	−0.065	−1.45	−0.015	−0.33	−0.138	−1.58	−0.084	−0.51
Don't know	– 0.074	-0.14	0.087	0.66	– 0.089	-0.61	0.164	0.64	– 0.423	-0.79
Heath exercise			0.040	0.96			0.081	1.01		
Indoor drinking water			−0.006	−0.20			−0.012	−0.20		
Indoor toilets			−0.145***	−4.43			−0.255***	−4.10		
No stool around the living room			−0.045	−1.51			−0.101*	−1.79		
Co-residence			0.005	0.17			0.006	0.11		
Year (2000)										
2004	−0.894	−2.85	0.420***	11.73	−0.079*	−1.90	0.914***	12.38	−0.357	−2.30
2006	−0.600	−2.10	0.363***	10.02	−0.108***	−2.59	0.800***	10.69	−0.493	−3.16
Constants	−4.799	−2.43	−2.096***	−25.31	1.420	17.09	−3.962***	−23.48	4.106	13.49
Inverse Mills ratio	3.632***	4.57								
Observations	24,784				24,784		1,675		1,675	
Groups									449	
Sensoring	23,109									

(continued)

Table 8.2 (continued)

	(1) Heckman				(2) Two-part				(3) Random effects	
	Second step		First step		Second step (Possion)		First step (logit)			
	Coef	z-value	Coef	z-value	Coef	z-value	Coef	z-value	Coef	z-value
Non-sensoring	1,675									
R-sq: within									0.1012	
Between									0.2151	
Overall									0.1473	
Breusch-Pagan test									$chi^2(1) = 26.42$	
									$Prob > chi^2 = 0.0000$	

Source Calculated based on the data from CHNS2000, 2004 and 2006
Note $^{***}p < 0.01$, $^{**}p < 0.05$, $^{*}p < 0.10$.

Table 8.3 Public medical insurances and out-of-pocket expenses on medical care (urban areas)

	(1) Heckman				(2) Two-part				(3) Random effects	
	Second step		First step		Second step (Possion)		First step (logit)			
	Coef	z-value	Coef	z-value	Coef	z-value	Coef	z-value	Coef	z-value
Medical insurance	0.202	1.16	0.122***	2.93	0.025	0.57	0.228***	2.90	0.074	0.46
Age (age 30–39)										
Age 20–29	−0.168	−0.38	0.235*	1.90	−0.073	−0.59	0.465*	1.88	−0.355	−0.83
Age 40–49	0.593*	1.83	−0.021	−0.27	0.143	1.56	−0.057	−0.35	0.615*	1.93
Age 50–59	0.300	0.94	−0.036	−0.47	0.082	0.92	−0.105	−0.67	0.345	1.11
Age 60–69	0.281	0.89	0.128*	1.61	0.045	0.51	0.225	1.42	0.158	0.51
Age 70–79	0.836**	2.34	0.299***	3.53	0.132	1.47	0.546***	3.32	0.603*	1.92
Age 80+	0.869**	2.16	0.385***	4.19	0.129	1.36	0.685***	3.88	0.560*	1.67
Education (not enrollment)										
Primary school	0.036	0.17	0.094	1.42	−0.012	−0.21	0.183	1.53	−0.047	−0.23
Junior high	0.214	0.90	−0.010	−0.14	0.050	0.77	−0.015	−0.12	0.222	0.94
Senior high	0.550*	1.90	0.031	0.39	0.111	1.39	0.061	0.41	0.575**	1.99
Vocational school	−0.255	−0.66	−0.201***	−2.27	−0.014	−0.14	−0.405**	−2.40	−0.048	−0.14
College and higher	0.220	0.67	0.111	1.27	0.037	0.41	0.196	1.19	0.157	0.48
Male	−0.070	−0.41	−0.099***	−2.30	0.001	0.02	−0.186***	−2.26	0.026	0.17
Health status (very good)										
Good	0.321	0.84	0.208***	2.80	0.027	0.27	0.457***	2.80	0.144	0.42
Fair	1.044*	1.71	0.672***	9.01	0.097	0.96	1.354***	8.39	0.464	1.37
Not good	2.561**	2.48	1.381***	15.79	0.278***	2.63	2.559***	14.43	1.398***	3.88

(continued)

Table 8.3 (continued)

	(1) Heckman				(2) Two-part				(3) Random effects	
	Second step		First step		Second step (Possion)		First step (logit)			
	Coef	z-value	Coef	z-value	Coef	z-value	Coef	z-value	Coef	z-value
Hypertension	0.362	1.48	0.288***	5.78	0.027	0.60	0.509***	5.79	0.097	0.60
Diabetes	0.384	1.07	0.391***	4.33	0.018	0.25	0.675***	4.39	0.077	0.29
Income	0.000	−0.20	0.000*	1.83	0.000	−0.41	0.000*	1.85	0.000	−0.60
Province (Jiangsu)										
Liaoning	0.074	0.21	−0.033***	−4.65	0.073	0.98	−0.623***	−4.63	0.327	1.14
Heilongjiang	0.223	0.45	−0.472***	−5.07	0.118	1.16	−0.895***	−4.84	0.593	1.48
Shandong	−0.066	−0.23	−0.189***	−2.56	0.019	0.26	−0.330**	−2.38	0.059	0.21
Hernan	−0.236	−0.84	0.020	0.26	−0.060	−0.76	0.047	0.33	−0.238	−0.79
Hubei	0.139	0.56	0.038	0.54	0.025	0.37	0.046	0.35	0.043	0.16
Hunan	0.161	0.59	−0.111*	−1.60	0.060	0.86	−0.198	−1.51	0.221	0.81
Guangxi	−0.281	−1.08	0.024	0.33	−0.052	−0.71	0.041	0.30	−0.235	−0.82
Guizhou	−0.985**	−2.33	−0.351***	−3.86	−0.133	−1.42	−0.633***	−3.67	−0.722**	−2.08
Smoking	−0.206	−1.07	0.006	0.11	−0.049	−0.90	0.007	0.08	−0.250	−1.31
Drinking (no drinking)										
Less than once a month	−0.060	−0.16	0.037	0.35	−0.018	−0.17	0.052	0.26	−0.079	−0.21
1–2 times a month	−0.395	−1.21	0.057	0.69	−0.098	−1.02	0.124	0.77	−0.399	−1.24
1–2 times a week	−0.662**	−2.13	−0.053	−0.70	−0.133	−1.47	−0.111	−0.73	−0.611**	−2.00

(continued)

Table 8.3 (continued)

	(1) Heckman				(2) Two-part				(3) Random effects	
	Second step		First step		Second step (Possion)		First step (logit)			
	Coef	z-value	Coef	z-value	Coef	z-value	Coef	z-value	Coef	z-value
3–4 times a week	−0.040	−0.10	0.161*	1.70	−0.041	−0.36	0.324**	1.76	−0.198	−0.51
Every day	−0.317	−1.31	0.009	0.13	−0.066	−0.95	0.015	0.11	−0.308	−1.27
Don't know	−0.016	−0.02	0.273	1.43	−0.058	−0.25	0.481	1.30	−0.418	−0.55
Heath exercise			0.029	0.57			0.058	0.60		
Indoor drinking water			−0.050	−0.86			−0.058	−0.54		
Indoor toilets			−0.129**	−2.46			−0.223**	−2.45		
No stool around the living room			−0.165**	−2.34			−0.331**	−2.55		
Co-residence			0.014	0.32			0.025	0.31		
Year (2000)										
2004	0.287	0.80	0.326***	5.62	−0.007	−0.10	0.720***	6.10	0.009	0.04
2006	0.069	0.20	0.303***	5.30	−0.050	−0.72	0.672***	5.75	−0.197	−0.80
Constants	1.300	0.59	−1.828***	−12.72	1.379***	10.17	−3.420***	−11.92	3.983***	8.35
Inverse Mills ratio	1.116	1.22								
Observations	10,041				10,041		641		641	
Groups									236	
Sensoring	9,400									

(continued)

Table 8.3 (continued)

	(1) Heckman				(2) Two-part				(3) Random effects	
	Second step		First step		Second step (Possion)		First step (logit)			
	Coef	z-value	Coef	z-value	Coef	z-value	Coef	z-value	Coef	z-value
Non-sensoring	641									
R-sq: within									0.122	
between									0.225	
overall									0.162	
Breusch-Pagan test									$chi^2(1) = 10.12$	
									Prob > $chi^2 = 0.0015$	

Source Calculated based on the data from CHNS2000, 2004 and 2006
Note ***$p < 0.01$, **$p < 0.05$, *$p < 0.10$.

Table 8.4 Public medical insurances and out-of-pocket expenses on medical care (rural areas)

	(1) Heckman				(2) Two-part				(3) Random effects	
	Second step		First step		Second step (Possion)		First step (logit)			
	Coef	z-value	Coef	z-value	Coef	z-value	Coef	z-value	Coef	z-value
Medical insurance	0.611	1.22	0.132***	3.37	−0.002	−0.05	0.260***	3.47	0.007	0.04
Age (age 30–39)										
Age 20–29	0.418	0.97	0.105	1.10	−0.023	−0.21	0.216	1.09	−0.140	−0.34
Age 40–49	0.110	0.43	0.038	0.63	−0.017	−0.25	0.092	0.74	−0.075	−0.30
Age 50–59	0.193	0.73	0.092	1.52	−0.053	−0.80	0.212*	1.73	−0.241	−0.97
Age 60–69	0.827***	2.60	0.178***	2.83	−0.006	−0.10	0.379***	3.01	−0.039	−0.15
Age 70–79	1.138***	2.81	0.282***	3.89	−0.038	−0.51	0.539***	3.81	−0.177	−0.62
Age 80+	1.506***	3.09	0.371***	4.51	−0.038	−0.45	0.718***	4.58	−0.176	−0.55
Education (not enrollment)			0.073	1.58						
Primary school	0.054	0.30			−0.055	−1.25	0.152*	1.77	−0.242	−1.45
Junior high	0.468**	2.17	0.091*	1.71	0.025	0.47	0.192*	1.91	0.113	0.56
Senior high	−0.202	−0.66	0.055	0.74	−0.079	−0.95	0.125	0.86	−0.341	−1.11
Vocational school	0.645	1.05	0.091	0.63	0.030	0.19	0.242	0.86	0.161	0.26
College and higher	1.664**	2.18	0.243	1.23	0.137	0.73	0.502	1.30	0.580	0.79
Male	−0.304	−1.51	−0.134***	−3.52	0.067*	1.71	−0.239***	−3.21	0.308**	2.06
Health status (very good)										
Good	0.895***	2.91	0.101*	1.69	0.080	1.00	0.247**	1.88	0.340	1.20
Fair	3.485***	5.04	0.574***	9.61	0.148*	1.89	1.191***	9.21	0.629**	2.23
Not good	7.492***	5.64	1.265***	18.18	0.365***	4.46	2.385***	16.88	1.648***	5.51

(continued)

Table 8.4 (continued)

	(1) Heckman				(2) Two-part				(3) Random effects	
	Second step		First step		Second step (Possion)		First step (logit)			
	Coef	z-value	Coef	z-value	Coef	z-value	Coef	z-value	Coef	z-value
Hypertension	1.718***	4.69	0.354***	6.84	0.053	1.24	0.640***	7.06	0.241	1.45
Diabetes	1.678***	3.39	0.333**	2.33	0.084	0.84	0.581**	2.40	0.458	1.10
Income	0.000***	2.80	0.000	1.16	0.000*	1.69	0.000	1.20	0.000**	1.98
Province (Jiangsu)										
Liaoning	−0.469	−1.40	−0.215***	−2.88	0.087	1.25	−0.423***	−2.90	0.422	1.55
Heilongjiang	−0.302	−0.88	−0.231***	−3.19	0.135*	1.93	−0.421***	−2.96	0.650**	2.37
Shandong	−0.861**	−2.37	−0.190***	−2.62	−0.001	− 0.02	−0.324**	−2.30	0.019	0.06
Hernan	0.768***	2.61	0.168***	2.60	−0.020	−0.33	0.315**	2.54	−0.077	−0.34
Hubei	0.454*	1.75	0.089	1.36	−0.001	−0.01	0.171	1.37	0.007	0.03
Hunan	0.163	0.60	−0.010	−0.14	0.064	0.92	−0.039	−0.28	0.294	1.09
Guangxi	−0.168	−0.67	0.070	1.01	−0.117*	−1.82	0.133	1.01	−0.488**	−2.03
Guizhou	−1.165**	−4.47	−0.112*	−1.61	−0.138***	−2.78	−0.184	−1.40	−0.771***	−3.11
Smoking	−0.299*	−1.92	−0.010	−0.24	−0.061	−1.46	−0.029	−0.36	−0.269*	−1.71
Drinking (no drinking)										
Less than once a month	0.809*	1.84	0.155	1.54	0.004	0.03	0.270	1.37	0.010	0.02
1–2 times a month	−0.172	−0.61	0.086	1.27	−0.142*	−1.87	0.142	1.08	−0.583**	−2.17
1–2 times a week	0.225	0.94	0.080	1.34	−0.030	−0.49	0.152	1.30	−0.139	−0.61

(continued)

Table 8.4 (continued)

	(1) Heckman				(2) Two-part				(3) Random effects	
	Second step		First step		Second step (Possion)		First step (logit)			
	Coef	z-value	Coef	z-value	Coef	z-value	Coef	z-value	Coef	z-value
3–4 times a week	−0.668**	−2.04	0.176**	2.32	−0.032	−0.44	0.313**	2.12	−0.152	−0.55
Every day	−0.427*	−1.64	−0.117***	−1.98	0.032	0.54	−0.255**	−2.15	0.133	0.58
Don't know	−0.650	−0.87	−0.068	−0.36	−0.107	−0.54	−0.078	−0.22	−0.492	−0.65
Heath exercise			0.067	0.89			0.142	0.94		
Indoor drinking water			0.009	0.26			0.008	0.12		
Indoor toilets			−0.133***	−2.86			−0.228**	−2.55		
No stool around the living room			−0.030	−0.90			−0.073	−1.15		
Co-residence			−0.006	−0.15			−0.019	−0.25		
Year (2000)										
2004	−1.617***	−3.02	0.472***	10.19	−0.138***	−2.60	1.032***	10.72	−0.617***	−3.03
2006	−1.127**	−2.47	0.386***	7.95	−0.157***	−2.85	0.858***	8.56	−0.702***	−3.33
Constants	−1.546***	−3.17	−2.191***	−20.17	1.458***	13.28	−4.183***	−18.85	4.334***	10.61
Inverse Mills ratio	5.869***	4.51								
Observations	14,743				14,743	1,034			1,034	
Groups									285	
Sensoring	13,709									
Non-sensoring	1,034									

(continued)

Table 8.4 (continued)

	(1) Heckman				(2) Two-part				(3) Random effects	
	Second step		First step		Second step (Possion)		First step (logit)			
	Coef	z-value	Coef	z-value	Coef	z-value	Coef	z-value	Coef	z-value
R-sq: within									0.116	
between									0.195	
overall									0.147	
Breusch-Pagan test									chi2(1) = 24.18	
									Prob > chi2 = 0.0002	

Source Calculated based on the data from CHNS2000, 2004 and 2006
Note ***$p < 0.01$, **$p < 0.05$, *$p < 0.10$.

(4) The OOP expense is lower in the group who stated their health status as "fair" and "not good" than in the group who stated "very good." The OOP expense tends to be higher in groups with poor subjective health status. In addition, the OOP expense is higher in both groups with chronic diseases such as hypertension and diabetes. To compare urban areas and rural areas, the OOP expense in the group who stated their health status as "not good" is higher than the group that stated it as "very good." It is 27.8–256.1% higher in urban areas, and 36.5–749.2% higher in rural areas, which suggest that the influence of subjective health status on OOP expense is higher for rural residents than for urban residents. In urban areas, the influence of chronic diseases (hypertension and diabetes) on the OOP expenses is not statistically significant, while in rural areas, this amount is higher in both groups having hypertension or diabetes. These results indicated that the influence of health status on OOP expense is greater in rural areas than in rural areas.

(5) The results for the nationwide sample indicate that the OOP expense is higher for high-income group. In urban areas, the impact of household income on the OOP expenses is not statistically significant, while in rural areas, the OOP expense is higher for high-income groups than others. The results reveal that the impact of liquidity constraints on medical care expenses is greater in rural areas than in urban areas.

(6) Regional disparities exist in the OOP expenses. In general, when the other factors are held constant, the OOP expense is 13.2–67.0% higher in Heilongjiang province, and 36.7–130.9% lower in Guizhou Province as compared to the level in Jiangsu province. In urban areas, it is 72.2–98.5% lower in Guizhou province. In rural areas, the level is higher in Heilongjiang (13.5–65.0%), Henan (76.8%), and Hubei, but 86.1% lower in Shandong. This suggests that the regional disparity in the OOP expense is more pronounced in rural areas than in urban areas.

(7) In terms of the influence of lifestyle, the OOP expense is 5.6–25.4% higher in the smoking group than in the non-smoking group for the nationwide sample. The main reason is that the smoking group has a relatively lower risk aversion to health risks than the non-smoking group; therefore, when a smoker has the same illness, the probability of visiting a hospital may be lower, and the OOP expenses will be lower. Compared to the non-drinking group, the OOP expense is 12.3–52.0% higher for the group drinking once or twice a month. Comparing urban and rural areas, in urban areas, the effects of smoking dummies were not significant, but in rural areas, the OOP expense is 26.9–29.9% higher in the smoking group than in the non-smoking group. In addition, compared to the non-drinking group, in urban areas the OOP expense is 61.1–66.2% lower for the group drinking once or twice a week; in rural areas, the OOP expense is 66.8% lower for the group drinking once or twice a week, and 14.2%–58.3%

lower for the group drinking once or twice a month. Lifestyle-related choices affect the OOP expenses in both urban and rural areas.

(8) For the change in OOP expenses by period, compared with 2000, the OOP expense was 7.9% lower in 2004 and 10.8% lower in 2006. In urban areas, the difference in the OOP expenses among different periods is small, but in rural areas, the amount tends to decrease over the years, which indicates that as the coverage of the NRCMS increases, the amount of OOP expense tends to decrease in rural areas.

8.5.2 Results on the Probability of Catastrophic Medical Expenses

Table 8.5 summarizes the results of the probability of CME for the nationwide sample (Model 1), urban areas (Model 2), and rural areas (Model 3). The random-effects logit model was used to address the individual heterogeneity problem. The main findings are as follows.

First, the results from Models 1 to 3 indicate that the influence of public medical insurance on the probability of CME is not statistically significant. This reveals that the implementation of public medical insurance might not resolve the problem of poverty due to high expenses for medical care during illness.

Second, regarding other factors,

(1) the probability of CME in urban areas is higher than that in rural areas.

(2) In urban areas, the difference in educational background and probability of CME is not remarkable, but in rural areas, compared to the low-level educated group (no-enrolled group), the probability of CME in the middle-level educated group (senior high school, vocational schools) is lower.

(3) The difference among subjective health status type and its effect on the probability of CME is small in urban areas, but in rural areas, compared to the group who answered "very good," the probability of CME is higher in the case of groups who answered "fair" and "not good." The difference between poor and good health status groups in the context of the probability of CME is greater in rural areas than in urban areas.

(4) In both urban and rural areas, the higher the household income, the lower the probability of CME. This suggests that the association between household income and poverty due to high medical care expenses is significant.

(5) Regional disparity exists. For example, in rural areas, when the other factors are held constant, the probability of CME in Liaoning is higher than that in Jiangsu, while it is lower in Guizhou.

(6) Regarding the influence of lifestyle, smoking, and drinking conditions do not have a significant effect on the probability of CME in urban areas, while in

Table 8.5 Public medical insurance and probability of catastrophic medical expenses

	(1) Nationwide		(2) Urban		(3) Rural	
	Coef	z-value	Coef	z-value	Coef	z-value
Medical insurance	−0.025	−0.14	−0.076	−0.26	−0.002	−0.01
Urban	0.507***	3.22				
Age (age 30–39)						
Age 20–29	−0.220	−0.46	−0.639	−0.76	−0.121	−0.17
Age 40–49	0.294	0.98	0.827	1.51	0.011	0.02
Age 50–59	−0.043	−0.14	0.774	1.45	−0.401	−0.89
Age 60–69	−0.318	−1.04	−0.261	−0.49	−0.489	−1.08
Age 70–79	−0.384	−1.19	0.056	0.10	−0.695	−1.40
Age 80+	−0.395	−1.11	−0.021	−0.03	−0.687	−1.24
Education (not enrollment)						
Primary school	−0.248	−1.21	−0.265	−0.67	−0.260	−0.93
Junior high	−0.120	−0.48	−0.374	−0.79	−0.169	−0.49
Senior high	−0.088	−0.26	0.444	0.81	−1.090*	−1.81
Vocational school	−0.727	−1.60	−0.726	−1.09	−1.586*	−1.62
College and higher	−0.500	−1.20	−0.634	−1.04	0.833	0.79
Male	0.366**	2.13	−0.052	−0.17	0.813***	3.28
Health status (very good)						
Good	−0.074	−0.21	−0.118*	−1.77	0.783	1.48
Fair	0.419	1.25	−0.740	−1.19	1.450***	2.74
Not good	1.548***	4.39	0.553	0.83	2.606***	4.69
Hypertension	0.260	1.40	0.116	0.36	0.337	1.27
Diabetes	− 0.117	−0.32	−0.507	−0.95	0.317	0.53
Income	0.000***	−8.01	−0.001***	−5.48	0.000***	−4.66
Province (Jiangsu)						
Liaoning	0.665**	2.29	0.719	1.32	0.913**	2.06
Heilongjiang	0.107	0.31	0.290	0.39	0.092	0.19
Shandong	0.438	1.39	0.292	0.46	0.504	1.08
Hernan	−0.027	−0.10	0.309	0.52	−0.078	−0.20
Hubei	0.095	0.35	0.637	1.19	−0.212	−0.51
Hunan	0.351	1.15	0.290	0.51	0.646	1.32
Guangxi	−0.475	−1.55	−0.146	−0.24	−0.619	−1.33
Guizhou	−0.731**	−2.22	−0.334	−0.49	−0.912**	−1.98
Smoking	−0.452**	−2.32	−0.242	−0.66	−0.636**	−2.41
Drinking (no drinking)						

(continued)

Table 8.5 (continued)

	(1) Nationwide		(2) Urban		(3) Rural	
	Coef	z-value	Coef	z-value	Coef	z-value
Less than once a month	0.140	0.32	−0.070	−0.10	0.442	0.69
1–2 times a month	−0.872**	−2.06		−1.16	−1.364**	−2.13
1–2 times a week	−0.241	−0.81	−0.459	−0.74	−0.275	−0.72
3–4 times a week	0.023	0.07	−0.516	−0.71	0.014	0.03
Every day	−0.065	−0.24	−0.235	−0.51	−0.128	−0.32
Don't know	−0.118	−0.13	0.283	0.17	−0.443	−0.35
Year (2000)						
2004	−1.163***	−4.66	−0.602	−1.22	−1.940***	−5.18
2006	−1.155***	−4.63	−0.431	−0.91	−2.702***	−5.37
Constants	0.033	0.07	0.709	0.83	- 0.081	- 0.12
Observations	1,478		578		900	
Groups	428		225		266	
Log likelihood	−657.950		−259.965		−373.313	
Pseudo R^2	0.1896					
Likelihood-ratio test of rho = 0	chibar2(01) = 1.05		chibar2(01) = 5.05		chibar2(01) = 0.53	
Prob ≥ chibar2	0.153		0.012		0.232	

Source Calculated based on the data from CHNS 2000, 2004 and 2006
Notes (1) ***p < 0.01, **p < 0.05, *p < 0.10. (2) Logit regression and random effects model (Logit-RE) were used

rural areas, the probability of CME is lower in the smoking group than in the non-smoking group. In addition, the probability of CME among the group drinking once or twice a month was lower than that in the non-drinking group.

(7) In urban areas, there is little difference between age groups in the probability of CME, but in rural areas, it tends to decrease over the years.

8.6 Conclusions

Using longitudinal data from the China Health and Nutrition Survey of 2000, 2004, and 2006, this study conducted an empirical analysis to explore how public medical insurance influences the OOP expenses on medical care and the probability of CME. The sample selection bias and individual heterogeneity problem were considered in these analyses, and the situation between urban and rural areas was compared. The main conclusions are as follows.

First, the impacts of public medical insurance on the OOP expenses are not statistically significant in either urban or rural areas. It has been shown that public medical insurance has no positive effect on reducing the OOP expenses in both urban and rural areas.

Second, the impact of public medical insurance on the probability of CME is not statistically significant in both urban and rural areas. This suggests that the effect of public medical insurance on solving the problem of poverty due to significant OOP expenses is not significant.

Finally, other factors like age, educational background, health status, community, and lifestyle affect the OOP expenses and the probability of CME. The effects of these factors are greater in rural areas than in urban areas.

The results of these analyses are considered to have the following policy implications. First, the results indicate that in both urban and rural areas, the effect of public medical insurance on reducing OOP expenses, and the problem succumbing to poverty due to high OOP medical care expenses is not significant. This reveals that the reform of the public medical insurance targeted to reduce medical care inequality caused by income inequality since the late 1990s has not been successful. To deal with the poverty problem caused by serious illness, continuing the reform of public medical insurance as well as improving other social security systems has become an important issue for the Chinese government. It may also be necessary to establish a special medical aid system for those suffering from serious illnesses. In addition, the analysis results showed that if other factors were constant, both the OOP expenses and the probability of CME is higher for the older group than for the other groups. China has experienced population aging; therefore, it is important to implement a poverty reduction policy targeting elderly patients[10] in the future. For example, a public medical insurance for the elderly, as implemented in developed countries such as Japan and the U.S., could prove beneficial.

Notes

1. Catastrophic medical expenditure (CME) is a situation in which life becomes difficult due to high medical care expenses. The criteria differ from those in previous studies. For the definition of CME in this chapter, please refer to Sect. 8.3.
2. For the empirical studies of other countries, Currie and Gruber (1996a, 1996b, 1997), Decker and Rember (2004), Currie et al. (2008), Card et al. (2008), and Finkelstein and McKnight (2008) used the difference in difference (DID) method to investigate the impact of public medical care insurance (e.g., Medicare, Medicaid) on the OOP expenses for medical care in the U.S. For the other developing countries, the empirical studies for Vietnam (Jowett et al., 2004; Sepehri et al., 2006), Columbia (Panopoulu & Velez, 2001; Trujilo et al., 2005), and Mexico (Gakidou et al., 2006) were conducted. Most studies found that public medical insurance reduced the OOP expenses in the participant group.

3. Based on the consumption smoothing hypothesis (Deanton, 1992; Deanton & Paxson, 1994; Townsend, 1994), it is stated that most households in developing countries address the risk of income decrease and poverty through intra-household risk sharing. Considering the intra-household, this study calculated the ratio of CME using individual OOP expenses on medical care and per capita household income.
4. The age dummy variables in increments of 10 years were set to control for the differences in the usage of healthcare services by age.
5. Five variables were set as not enrollment, elementary school, junior high school, senior high school/vocational school, and university graduate dummy variables.
6. The smoking dummy variable was set as "1 = have smoked and are currently smoking, 0 = otherwise."
7. Regarding drinking behavior, based on the drinking status (frequency of drinking) in the questionnaire item, seven kinds of dummy variables: no drinking, drinking less than once a month, drinking 1–2 times a month, drinking 1–2 times a week, drinking 3–4 times a week, and drinking alcohol every day, and "I don't know" were constructed.
8. The health exercise dummy variable is constructed as "1 = when participating in martial arts, gymnastics, athletics, soccer, tennis, and other sports (such as Tai Chi) and 0 = otherwise."
9. Three dummy variables—living in a room with indoor drinking water (1 = room with indoor drinking water facilities, 0 = otherwise), indoor toilets (1 = toilet is in room, 0 = otherwise), and stool status around the living room (1 = when there is no stool around the living room, 0 = otherwise) were used as the indicators of living environment.
10. Medicare is implemented in the U.S. for public medical insurance for the elderly, and the latter-stage elderly medical care system is implemented in Japan.

Appendix

See Tables 8.6 and 8.7.

Table 8.6 Summary of previous studies

Author	Published year	Data	Areas	Model	Result
Wagstaff et al.	2009	National Health Service Survey of 2003	Rural	IV, GLM (IV), FE logit	OOP (×)
Xiao et al.	2010	Survey data of 2008–2009	Rural	Logit	OOP (−)
Shi et al.	2010	Survey data of 2008	Rural	Logit	CME (×)
Lu et al.	2012	China Health Surveillance Baseline of 2001	Rural	PSM, IV	OOP (×)
Jing et al.	2013	Survey data of 2006 and 2008	Rural	DID	CME (×)
Cheng et al.	2014	Chinese Longitudinal Healthy Longevity Survey of 2005 and 2008	Rural	PSM	OOP (×)
Li et al.	2014	National Health Service Survey of 2008	Rural	Logit	OOP (×)
Huang and Gan	2010	Chinese Longitudinal Healthy Longevity Survey of 2002 and 2005	Urban	Heckman two-step model, Two-part model	OOP (–)
Wagstaff and Lindelow	2008	(i) 1991, 1993, 1997, 2000 China Health and Nutrition Survey of 1991,1993,1997 and 2000; (ii) Gansu Survey of Children and Family of 2000 and 2003; (iii) World Bank China Health VIII Project Baseline Survey	Nationwide	Logit, IV, FE	OOP (+), CME (–)
You and Kobayashi	2011	China Health and Nutrition Survey of 2004	Nationwide	Heckman two-step	OOP (×)
Liu et al.	2011	Chinese Longitudinal Healthy Longevity Survey of 2005	Nationwide	Heckman two-step, Two-part	OOP (–)

(continued)

Table 8.6 (continued)

Author	Published year	Data	Areas	Model	Result
Li and Zhang	2013	China Health and Retirement Longitudinal Study of 2008	Nationwide	Two-part	OOP (×)

Source Created by the author
Notes (1) (×): not statistically significant; (−) significant negative effect; (+) significant positive effect. (2) Logit: logistic regression model; FE: fixed effects model; FE: random effects model; IV: instrument variable method; PSM: propensity score matching model; DID: difference in difference method; OOP: out-of-pocket expenses on medical care; CME: catastrophic medical expenditure

Table 8.7 Descriptive statistics of variables

	Total		Participant		Non-participant	
	Mean	SD	Mean	SD	Mean	SD
OOP expense	724	3145	862	4283	667	2583
CME	0.256	0.437	0.239	0.427	0.264	0.441
Medical insurance	0.283	0.451				
Urban	0.413	0.492	0.535	0.499	0.363	0.481
Age category						
Age 20–29	0.048	0.213	0.027	0.162	0.055	0.228
Age 30–39	0.147	0.354	0.097	0.295	0.144	0.351
Age 40–49	0.199	0.399	0.181	0.385	0.209	0.407
Age 50–59	0.216	0.411	0.240	0.427	0.216	0.412
Age 60–69	0.184	0.387	0.221	0.415	0.179	0.383
Age 70–79	0.116	0.320	0.142	0.349	0.110	0.313
Age 80+	0.080	0.275	0.092	0.286	0.077	0.266
Education						
Not enrollment	0.146	0.353	0.123	0.328	0.155	0.362
Primary school	0.274	0.446	0.244	0.430	0.287	0.452
Junior high	0.340	0.474	0.302	0.459	0.354	0.478
Senior High	0.129	0.335	0.136	0.343	0.126	0.331
Vocational school	0.058	0.234	0.093	0.291	0.044	0.206
College and higher	0.053	0.225	0.102	0.302	0.034	0.183
Male	0.432	0.495	0.477	0.499	0.414	0.493
Health status						
Very good	0.141	0.348	0.139	0.346	0.142	0.349
Good	0.474	0.499	0.459	0.498	0.479	0.500
Fair	0.317	0.465	0.330	0.470	0.312	0.463
Not good	0.068	0.252	0.072	0.258	0.067	0.249

(continued)

Table 8.7 (continued)

	Total		Participant		Non-participant	
	Mean	SD	Mean	SD	Mean	SD
Hypertension	0.073	0.261	0.113	0.316	0.058	0.234
Diabetes	0.012	0.107	0.022	0.146	0.008	0.087
Income	1239	2632	1704	3418	1041	2177
Province						
Jiangsu	0.109	0.312	0.130	0.336	0.103	0.304
Liaoning	0.100	0.300	0.100	0.300	0.104	0.305
Heilongjiang	0.110	0.313	0.246	0.431	0.057	0.232
Shandong	0.107	0.309	0.135	0.341	0.094	0.292
Hernan	0.115	0.319	0.061	0.239	0.140	0.347
Hubei	0.106	0.307	0.102	0.302	0.110	0.313
Hunan	0.109	0.312	0.088	0.283	0.121	0.326
Guangxi	0.127	0.333	0.070	0.256	0.148	0.355
Guizhou	0.117	0.322	0.068	0.254	0.123	0.329
Smoking	0.260	0.439	0.266	0.442	0.259	0.438
Drinking						
No drinking	0.676	0.468	0.639	0.480	0.693	0.461
Less than once a month	0.027	0.161	0.033	0.180	0.024	0.152
1–2 times a month	0.057	0.233	0.064	0.245	0.054	0.227
1–2 times a week	0.085	0.278	0.095	0.293	0.080	0.271
3–4 times a week	0.044	0.206	0.046	0.211	0.043	0.204
Every day	0.103	0.303	0.114	0.318	0.097	0.297
Don't know	0.008	0.091	0.009	0.088	0.009	0.092
Heath exercise	0.090	0.286	0.127	0.333	0.073	0.261
Indoor drinking water	0.575	0.494	0.694	0.461	0.525	0.499
Indoor toilets	0.396	0.489	0.518	0.500	0.348	0.476
No stool around the living room	0.719	0.450	0.816	0.388	0.679	0.467
Year						
2000	0.411	0.492	0.244	0.429	0.468	0.499
2004	0.295	0.456	0.255	0.436	0.318	0.466
2006	0.294	0.455	0.501	0.500	0.214	0.410
Observation	24,784		7,026		17,758	

Source Calculated based on the data from CHNS2000, 2004 and 2006
Note OOP: out-of-pocket; CME: catastrophic medical expenditure

References

Andersen, R. (1995). Revisiting the behavioral model and access to medical care: Does it matter? *Journal of Health and Social Behavior, 36*(1), 1–10.

Andersen, R., & Newman, J.F. (1973). Social and individual determinants of medical care utilization in the United States. *Milbank Quarterly, 51*(1), 95–124.

Card, D., Dobkin, C., & Maestas, N. (2008). The impact of nearly universal insurance coverage on health care utilization and health: Evidence from Medicare. *American Economic Review, 98*(5), 2242–2258.

Cheng, L., Liu, H., Zhang, Y., Shen, K., & Zeng, Y. (2015). The impact of health insurance of health outcomes and spending of the elderly: Evidence from China's New Cooperative Medical Scheme. *Health Economics, 24*(6), 672–691.

Currie, J., & Gruber, J. (1996). Health insurance eligibility, utilization of medical care and child health. *Quarterly Journal of Economics, 111*(2), 431–466.

Currie, J., & Gruber, J. (1996). Saving babies: The efficacy and cost of recent changes in the Medicaid eligibility of pregnant women. *Journal of Political Economy, 104*(6), 1263–1296.

Currie, J., & Gruber, J. (1997). The technology of birth: Health insurance, medical interventions and infant health. Working Paper 5985, *National Bureau Economic Research*, Cambridge, MA.

Currie, J., Decker, S., & Lin, W. (2008). Has public health insurance for older children reduced disparities in access to care and health outcomes? *Journal of Health Economics, 27*(6), 1567–1581.

Decker, S. L., & Remler, D. K. (2004). How much might universal health insurance reduce socioeconomic disparities in health? A comparison of the US and Canada. *Applied Health Economics and Health Policy, 3*(4), 205–216.

Deanton, A. (1992). Saving and income smoothing in Cote d'Ivoire. *Journal of African Economics, 1*(1), 1–24.

Deanton, A., & Paxson, C. (1994). Intertemporal choice and inequality. *Journal of Political Economy, 102*, 436–467.

Duan, N., Manning, W. G., Jr., Morris, C. N., & Newhouse, J. P. (1984). Choosing between the sample-selection model and the multi-part model. *Journal of Business & Economic Statistics, 2*(3), 283–289.

Finkelstein, A., & McKnight, R. (2008). What did Medicare do? The initial impact of Medicare on mortality and out of pocket medical spending. *Journal of Public Economics, 92*(7), 1644–1668.

Gakidou, E., Lozano, R., Gonzalez-Pier, E., Abbott-Klafter, J., Barofsky, J. T., Bryson-Cahn, C., Feehan, D. M., Lee, D. K., Hernandez-Llamas, H., & Murray, C. J. (2006). Assessing the effect of the 2001–06 Mexican health reform: An interim report card. *The Lancet, 368*(9550), 1920–1935.

Heckman, J. J. (1979). Sample selection bias as a specification error. *Econometrica, 47*(1), 153–161.

Huang, F., & Gan, L. (2010). Over demand and efficient demand: An empirical study on health and medical insurance of urban elderly. *Economic Research Journal, 6*, 105–119. (in Chinese).

Jing, S., Yin, A., Shi, L., & Liu, J. (2013). Whether New Cooperative Medical Schemes reduce the economic burden of chronic disease in rural China. *PLoS One, 8*(1), 1–6.

Jowett, M., Deolalikar, A., & Martinsson, P. (2004). Health insurance and treatment seeking behavior: Evidence from a low-income country. *Health Economics, 13*(9), 845–857.

Li, X., & Zhang, W. (2013). The impacts of health insurance on health care utilization among the older people in China. *Social Science & Medicine, 85*, 59–65.

Liu, G., Cai, C., & Li, L. (2011). An empirical study on medical insurance and demand of health service of elderly in China. *Economic Research Journal, 3*, 95–107.

Liu, Y., Hsiao, W., Li, Q., Liu, X., & Ren, M. (1995). Transformation of China's rural health insurance financing. *Social Science & Medicine, 41*(8), 1085–1093.

Lu, C., Liu, Y., & Shen, J. (2012). Does China's Rural Cooperative Medical System achieve its goals? Evidence from the China Health Surveillance Baseline Survey in 2001. *Contemporary Economic Policy, 30*(1), 93–112.

Panopoulu, G., & Velez, C. (2001). Subsidized health insurance, proxy means testing and the demand for health care among the poor in Colombia. *Colombia Poverty Report Volume II*. Washington DC, World Bank.

Sepehri, A., Sarma, S., & Simpson, W. (2006). Does non-profit health insurance reduce financial burden? Evidence from the Vietnam Living Standards Survey Panel. *Health Economics, 15*(6), 603–616.

Shi, W., Chongsuvivatwong, V., Geater, A., Zhang, J., Zhang, H., & Brombal, D. (2010). The Influence of the Rural Health Security Schemes on health utilization and household impoverishment in rural China: Data from a household survey of western and central China. *International Journal for Equity in Health, 9*(7), 1–11.

Townsend, R. (1994). Risk and insurance in village India. *Econometrica, 62*(3), 539–591.

Trujillo, A. J., Portillo, J. E., & Vernon, A. (2005). The impact of subsidized health insurance for the Poor: Evaluating the Colombian experience using propensity score matching. *International Journal of Health Care Finance and Economics, 5*(3), 211–239.

Wagstaff, A., & Lindelow, M. (2008). Can insurance increase financial risk? The curious case of health insurance in China. *Journal of Health Economics, 27*, 990–1005.

Wagstaff, A., Lindelow, M., Gao, J., Xu, L., & Qian, J. (2009). Extending health insurance to the rural population: An impact evaluation of China's New Cooperative Medical Scheme. *Journal of Health Economics, 28*, 1–19.

Xiao, S., Yan, H., Shen, D., & Y.S., Hemminki, E., Wang, D., & Long, Q. (2010). Utilization of delivery care among rural women in China: Does the health insurance make a difference? A cross-sectional study. *BMC Public Health, 10*, 1–7.

You, X., & Kobayashi, Y. (2011). Determinants of out-of-pocket health expenditure in China. *Applied Health Economics and Health Policy, 9*(1), 39–49.

Chapter 9
Medical Insurances and Financial Portfolio Choice

Abstract Using three-wave longitudinal data, this study estimates the influence of public medical insurances on financial portfolio choice of individuals aged 45 years and older. Three new findings emerge. First, public medical insurance positively affects the probability of holding risky financial assets, but when addressed the heterogeneity problem, the effect of public medical insurances on the probability of holding and share of risky financial assets is not significant, which suggests the unobservable individual heterogeneity might affect risky financial market participation. Second, the influence of public medical insurance differs by risky financial asset type. It is greater for higher-risk (stocks) than for lower-risk (bonds) financial assets. Third, the influences of public medical insurance differ by age and *hukou* group, the positive effects are higher for older and urban resident group than middle-aged and rural resident group.

Keywords Public medical insurance · Financial portfolio · Risky financial asset · Risky financial market participation · China

9.1 Introduction

Over the past decades, household savings and investment in the financial market have influenced national economic growth. Consequently, empirical studies on household financial market participation, household financial asset allocation, and the determinants of individuals' or households' financial behavior have attracted attention worldwide. Individual attributes may affect individuals' or households' participation in risky financial markets. These include the following: age, education, political background, marital status (Angrisani et al., 2018; Campbell, 2006; Cooper & Zhu, 2017; Ge et al., 2021; Grinblatt et al., 2011; Zhou & Xiao, 2018; Zhou et al., 2017), household characteristics (Betermier et al., 2017; Ge et al., 2021; Zhou et al., 2017), income factors such as household income and housing (Chen & Ji, 2017; Chetty et al., 2017; Cooper & Zhu, 2017; Ge et al., 2021), social capital (Brown et al., 2008; Fafchamps & Gubert, 2007; Ge et al., 2021; Hong et al., 2004), financial literacy (Balloch et al., 2015; Zou & Deng, 2019), and institutional factors (Cooper & Zhu, 2017). However, most previous studies focus on developed countries, and

X. Ma, *Public Medical Insurance Reforms in China*,
https://doi.org/10.1007/978-981-16-7790-8_9

the evidence for developing countries or emerging economies is scarce—where the financial market is not developed, and the awareness of participation in the financial market is lower (Zhou et al., 2017).

In addition, public medical insurance has been implemented in most countries worldwide, including developed and developing countries. The implementation of public medical insurance may affect risky financial market participation through a set of channels: For example, the public medical insurance may reduce the risk of high payment of out-of-pocket (OOP) expenses on medical care during illness (income increased effect), and improve health (health improved effect). This may reduce precautionary savings and increase the probability of risky financial market participation or holding more risky financial assets. Conversely, when an individual or a household is not covered by public medical insurance, the probability of risky financial market participation may become higher than the counterpart by the precautionary saving motivation. They may have a higher incentive to obtain high capital gains from risky financial investment to correspond to future income uncertainty. Therefore, the influence of public medical insurance on risky financial market participation is uncertain and should be explored through empirical studies. However, studies on this issue are scarce.

The original contributions of this study are summarized as follows. First, few studies have directly investigated the association between public medical insurance and risky financial market participation (Angrisani et al., 2018; Zhou et al., 2017). This study addresses this neglected area. Second, Zhou et al. (2017) only focus on urban residents in China, while this study investigates both urban and rural residents aged 45 years and older, most of whom are influenced by social insurance. Third, public medical insurance schemes differ by household registration system (rural and urban *hukou*), and the influence of medical insurance may differ by age group. This study performs estimations by group. Fourth, we use three-wave national longitudinal data from 2011 to 2015 and fixed effects (FE)/random effects (RE) models, including lagged items, to address the endogeneity problems to provide robust evidence.

The following three new findings emerge. First, public medical insurance positively affects the probability of holding risky financial assets, but when addressed the heterogeneity problem, the effect of public medical insurances on the probability of holding and share of risky financial assets is not significant, which suggests the unobservable individual heterogeneity might affect risky financial market participation. Second, the influence of public medical insurance differs by risky financial asset type. It is greater for higher-risk (stocks) than for lower-risk (bonds) financial assets. Third, the influences of public medical insurance differ by age and *hukou* group, the positive effects are higher for older and urban resident group than middle-aged and rural resident group.

The remainder of this chapter is organized as follows. Section 9.2 summarizes the results of the published empirical studies on these issues. Section 9.3 introduces the methodology of the study, including the models, data, and variables used. Section 9.4 reports and discusses the basic results and the results of the robustness checks. Finally, Sect. 9.5 concludes the chapter.

9.2 Literature Review

From an economics theory perspective, based on the life cycle permanent income model, Lehand (1968) advocated the precautionary saving model. Subsequently, Sandmo (1970) and Dreze and Modigliani (1972) developed it into a multi-period model of precautionary saving. This model proposes that precautionary saving may ease life cycle consumption and reduce uncertainty: higher risk and uncertainty in the future may cause more savings (wealth accumulation), which may affect household portfolios (Blanchard & Mankiw, 1988; Browning & Lusardi, 1996; Hall, 1978).

Based on these models, it is assumed that public medical insurance may affect risky financial market participation behavior. Using data from the 2002 Chinese Household Income Project Survey, Zhou et al. (2017) found that medical insurance coverage significantly influences Chinese urban households' preference for holding financial assets, particularly for risky financial assets (both the probability of holding risky financial assets and their share). Using a longitudinal data from the Health and Retirement Study and an FE model, Angrisani et al. (2018) found that in the United States, before Medicare eligibility, households in poor health status, who face a higher risk of medical expenses, are less likely to hold stocks than their healthier counterparts. However, this gap is mostly eliminated by Medicare.

Although direct empirical studies are scarce, some studies are related to this issue. Firstly, considering the health improvement effect, the results on the association between health status (health risk) and precautionary saving are mixed. For example, using data from the Household Retirement Survey and a RE model, Rosen and Wu (2004) found that poor health status reduces the probability of holding risky assets and their share in household assets. As medical insurance may improve health status by increasing the utilization of health care service, it is expected that medical insurance may increase the probability of risky financial market participation. Using a unique longitudinal dataset (U.S. New Beneficiary Survey 1982 and 1991) and a FE model, Fan and Zhao (2009) found that the health effect on the share of risky financial assets is significant. Using a U.S. dataset, Coile and Milligan (2006) showed a negative effect of chronic health shocks on the probability of holding financial risky assets. However, Love and Smith (2010) reported that there is no significant association between health and financial portfolio allocation when addressing the heterogeneity problem. Berkowitz and Qiu (2006) found that once omitted variable biases are addressed, health events affect portfolio choices indirectly by reducing financial wealth. Coile and Milligan (2006) found no effect of chronic health shocks on the share of risky financial assets in the U.S. Cardak and Wilkins (2009) reported that the relationship between health status and holding risky financial assets becomes non-significant once risk and time preference variables are controlled. Edwards (2008) showed that individuals with a higher risk of payment for higher medical care expenses tend to increase the share of lower-risk portfolios and reduce savings.

Then, household income may positively affect risky financial market participation. For example, using the 2009 Survey of Household Finances and Attitudes, Wei et al. (2019) found that rich people tend to own high-yield assets like stocks in China.

Using a longitudinal data from the China Family Panel Studies of 2014–2018, Ge et al. (2021) reported that wealth positively affects household risky financial market participation. As medical insurance may reduce OOP medical care expenses, it can be assumed that the public medical insurance may increase the probability of risky financial market participation through the income increased effect.

Based on the precautionary saving and uncertainty hypotheses, and previous studies mentioned above, it can be assumed that public medical insurance might influence participation in risky financial market through two channels—income increased effect and health improved effect. However, empirical studies in China focusing on this issue are scarce, and this study can fill this gap.

9.3 Methodology and Data

9.3.1 Models

As the basic model, the logit regression model is utilized to investigate the probability of holding risky financial assets, and the Tobit regression model is used to analyze the share of risky financial assets, which are expressed by Eq. (9.1):

$$RFA_i = a + \beta_{PMI} PMI_i + \beta_X X_i + \varepsilon_i \tag{9.1}$$

where RFA is the dependent variable (probability of holding risky financial assets or share of risky financial assets), i represents the individual, PMI denotes the public medical insurance, X represents factors (i.e., demographics, income, social capital, other social insurance etc.) that affect risky financial market participation, β is the estimated coefficient, and ε is a random error item.

Two types of econometric problems can be considered in the results based on Eq. (9.2). First, heterogeneity problems may occur in the estimated results. We use FE/RE models to address this problem. The individual heterogeneity (v_i) will decrease in the FE or RE models as follows:

$$RFA_{it} = a + \beta_{PMI} PMI_{it} + \beta_X X_{it} + v_i + \varepsilon_{it} \tag{9.2}$$

Second, reverse causality problem may be maintained. For example, participation in risky financial markets may obtain capital gains, which may increase the incentives to participate in pubic medical insurance, such as preferring longevity much more. The lagged items of the variables were used to address the problem. We used the lagged variables model (LV). For example, the medical insurance status in the prior survey year (e.g., public medical insurance scheme enrollment in 2011) was used to investigate their influence on risky financial market participation in the current survey year (e.g., probability of holding risky financial assets in 2013 or share of risky financial assets in 2013). The LV model is expressed as follows:

$$RFA_{it} = a + \beta_{PMI} PMI_{it\_1} + \beta_X X_{it} + v_i + \varepsilon_{it} \tag{9.3}$$

9.3.2 Data and Variable Setting

The analysis in this study uses three-wave (2011, 2013, and 2015) longitudinal data from the China Health and Retirement Longitudinal Study (CHARLS2011, 2013 and 2015). CHARLS was conducted from 2011 to 2015 by Peking University at two-year intervals and covers representative regions in China. Participants were individuals aged 45 years and above. The baseline national wave of CHARLS conducted in 2011 includes approximately 10,000 households and 17,708 individuals in 150 counties/districts and 450 villages/resident committees. The first and second follow-up survey waves were recorded for 2014 and 2016. CHARLS includes data on urban and rural *hukou* residents. They provide information about the situation of household assets, including risky financial assets (e.g., stocks and bonds), total financial assets, and other factors such as demographic factors (e.g., sex, education, *hukou,* and marital status) and income factors (e.g., household income, owning housing), which can be used in this analysis. The CHARLS covers 29 provinces or metropolitan areas, which is a survey with the largest coverage of regions in China.

The analytic objects were individuals aged 45 years and older. Abnormal value samples, no answer samples, and samples with missing values were deleted.

The dependent variable setting for the probability function of holding risky financial assets is a binary variable equal to 1 when an individual owns risky financial assets, including both stocks and bonds. In the Tobit regression model, the dependent variable is the share of risky financial assets, which is the proportion of risky assets to total household financial assets. Total household financial assets comprise risky financial assets (e.g., stocks and bonds) and non-risky financial assets (e.g., savings and cash). We use the household total values and the number of family members to calculate the per capita risky financial assets. When the volume of risky financial assets is greater than 0, it is defined that the individual is in a household holding risky financial assets.

The independent variables were constructed as follows. First, the key independent is a binary variable of enrollment of public medical insurance, which is equal to 1when has enrolled public medical insurance, equal to 0 when not enrollment. Based on the questionnaire items of the CHARLS, the public medical insurances consist of the Urban Employee Basic Medical Insurance Programme (UEBMI), the New Rural Cooperative Medical Insurance Scheme (NRCMS), and the Urban Residents Basic Medical Insurance Programme (URBMI).

Second, the variables of age, age squared, sex (1 = female, 0 = male), educational attainment (junior high school and lower, senior high school, college, and higher), marital status (1 = married, 0 = otherwise), urban *hukou,* and health status (number of diseases[1], having inpatient experience in survey year, instrumental activities of daily living [IADL] [2], basic activities of daily living [BADL] [3]) were constructed as demographic factors.

Third, four kinds of variables—(i) household income per capita (first–fifth income quintiles), (ii) debt, (iii) owning housing, and (iv) non-work (retirement) dummy variables—were constructed as the indices of income factors.

Fourth, we used the number of family members and social participation[4] to control for the influences of social interactions and social capital. It is found that social capital affect individuals' well-being (Ma & Oshio, 2020), which may affect the participation in risky financial market. It is expected that social interaction and social capital may be more for the group with more family members or that participating in social activities.

Fifth, regional dummy variables (east, central, west, and northeast) were constructed to control the influence of regional disparities in the financial market. The year dummy variables are used to control for the influence of the business cycle and change in the macroeconomic environment by period.

Appendix Table 9.9 summarizes the descriptive statistics of variables for the total sample, the holding risky finacial assets group, and the non-holding group. Differences remain in the mean values of the variables between the two groups. Thus, these variables should be considered in empirical analysis. When we do not control for other factors, the shares of risky financial assets are lower for the group of participation in social insurance than those for the non-participation group.

9.4 Results

9.4.1 Basic Results of Probability of Holding Risky Financial Asset

The results of the association between public medical insurance and the probability of holding risky financial assets are reported in Tables 9.1 and 9.2 using different econometric models.

First, four models (Models1–4) were used in the logit regression analyses (Table 9.1). Model1 used the public medical insurance, public pension and regional and year dummies as dependent variables. Model 2 added the demographic variables, Model 3 added the income factors, and Model 4 added the social capital variables except the variables used in the prior model.

The results indicate that the public medical insurance positively affects the probability of holding risky financial assets. However, the results differed when different variables were used. For example, when demographic factors were added, the positive effect of public medical insurance increased, the value of the coefficients of medical insurance increased from 0.650 to 0.740. When income factors or social capital factors are added, the changes in the size of public medical insurance are small. This suggests that the effect of public medical insurance on participation in

Table 9.1 Public medical insurance and probability of holding risky financial assets

	(1) Logit		(2) Logit		(3) Logit		(4) Logit	
	Coef	z-value	Coef	z-value	Coef	z-value	Coef	z-value
Medical insurance	0.650***	3.04	0.740***	3.40	0.616***	2.82	0.589***	2.63
Age			−0.013	−0.26	−0.023	−0.45	−0.027	−0.53
Age_sq			0.000	−0.07	0.000	−0.05	0.000	0.01
Female			0.280***	3.57	0.158*	1.94	0.143*	1.73
Education (Junior high)								
Senior high school			0.760***	8.33	0.625***	6.72	0.581***	6.14
College and higher			1.254***	9.34	1.023***	7.44	0.984***	7.03
Married			0.504***	3.63	0.459***	3.26	0.485***	3.37
Urban hukou			1.982***	22.64	1.672***	16.32	1.652***	15.82
Disease number			−0.082	−0.95	−0.071	−0.80	−0.056	−0.62
Inpatient			0.174	1.48	0.117	0.98	0.134	1.12
IADL			−0.024	−0.57	−0.026	−0.62	−0.003	−0.08
BADL			−0.245***	−4.66	−0.128***	−4.06	−0.129***	−4.01
Income (First quintile)								
Second quintile					−0.386**	−2.08	−0.401**	−2.14
Third quintile					−0.617***	−3.52	−0.632***	−3.54
Fourth quintile					−0.383**	−2.49	−0.395**	−2.55
Fifth quintile					0.411***	2.97	0.356**	2.53
Debt					0.000	1.32	0.000	1.12
Housing owned					0.210	1.60	0.205	1.54

(continued)

Table 9.1 (continued)

	(1) Logit		(2) Logit		(3) Logit		(4) Logit	
	Coef	z-value	Coef	z-value	Coef	z-value	Coef	z-value
Non-work					0.371***	3.93	0.364***	3.79
Social participation							0.378***	4.51
Family number							−0.020	−0.67
Pension	0.800***	7.30	0.302***	2.82	0.333***	3.01	0.328***	2.90
Regions (East)								
Central	−0.442***	−3.68	−0.627***	−5.06	−0.635	−5.05	−0.628	−4.95
West	0.107	1.33	0.092	1.11	0.080	0.94	0.078	0.91
Northeast	−0.375	−1.31	−0.418	−1.43	−0.493	−1.67	−0.459	−1.56
Years (2011)								
2013	−0.425***	−3.75	0.058	0.52	−0.033	−0.28	−0.085	−0.72
2015	−0.539***	−4.37	0.040	0.32	−0.040	−0.31	−0.078	−0.59
Constants	−4.496***	−20.33	−5.075***	−3.35	−4.420	−2.84	−4.320***	−2.72
Observations	31,814		31,814		31,814		31,814	
Log likelihood	−21,741		−3095		−2986		−2986	
Adj R-squared	0.039		0.172		0.189		0.189	

Source Calculated based on the data from CHARLS2011, 2013 and 2015
Note ***$p < 0.01$, **$p < 0.05$, *$p < 0.1$

Table 9.2 Public medical insurance and probability of holding risky financial assets considering the endogeneity problems

	(1) FE Logit		(2) RE Logit		(3) LV Logit		(4) LV_RE Logit	
	Coef	z-value	Coef	z-value	Coef	z-value	Coef	z-value
Medical insurance	−0.012	−0.02	0.613**	2.05	0.617**	2.03	0.866**	2.11
Age	0.080	0.28	−0.056	−0.70	−0.055	−0.79	−0.101	−1.03
Age_sq	−0.001	−0.38	0.000	0.35	0.000	0.54	0.001	0.83
Female			0.246*	1.81	0.205*	1.86	0.280*	1.77
Education (Junior high)								
Senior high school			1.023***	5.89	0.509***	4.00	0.793***	3.95
College and higher			1.867***	6.57	0.907***	4.57	1.513***	4.34
Married	0.118	0.16	0.785***	3.44	0.418**	2.16	0.528**	1.98
Urban hukou	−0.024	−0.05	2.210***	12.89	1.370***	10.30	1.713***	8.64
Disease number	−0.869**	−2.31	−0.121	−0.85	−0.011	−0.09	−0.003	−0.02
Inpatient	0.011	0.04	0.121	0.71	0.224	1.54	0.263	1.32
IADL	0.151*	1.90	0.033	0.59	0.039	0.73	0.064	0.93
BADL	−0.138*	−1.82	−0.165***	−3.64	−0.144***	−3.46	−0.180***	−3.24
Income (First quintile)								
Second quintile	−0.839***	−2.87	−0.456**	−1.97	0.031	0.13	−0.055	−0.19
Third quintile	−0.381	−1.18	−0.740***	−3.23	−0.019	−0.08	−0.085	−0.29
Fourth quintile	−0.181	−0.60	−0.359*	−1.76	0.189	0.88	0.193	0.73
Fifth quintile	0.032	0.10	0.533	2.77	0.963***	4.91	1.124***	4.54
Debt	0.000	−1.37	0.000***	1.21	0.000	1.09	0.000	1.27
Housing owned	0.622*	1.73	0.407**	2.01	0.233	1.33	0.485*	1.92

(continued)

Table 9.2 (continued)

	(1) FE Logit		(2) RE Logit		(3) LV Logit		(4) LV_RE Logit	
	Coef	z-value	Coef	z-value	Coef	z-value	Coef	z-value
Non-work	−0.299	−1.08	0.307**	2.10	0.375***	3.00	0.426**	2.43
Social participation	0.711***	3.66	0.595***	4.90	0.305***	2.75	0.435***	2.89
Family number	0.103	1.30	−0.002	−0.04	0.055	1.49	0.080*	1.63
Pension	0.115	0.54	0.348**	2.22	0.292**	2.16	0.365**	1.98
Regions (East)								
Central			−0.710***	−3.49	−0.713***	−4.07	−0.848	−3.44
West			0.140	0.97	0.162	1.44	0.201***	1.22
Northeast			−0.813*	−1.67	−0.953*	−1.84	−1.189*	−1.76
Years (2011)								
2013			−0.010	−0.06				
2015	0.386	1.47	0.028	0.15	−0.162	−1.16	−0.217	−1.18
Constants	0.348	0.85	−6.919***	−2.79	−4.184*	−1.93	−6.919***	−1.88
Observations	31,814		31,814		17,676		17,676	
Groups	15,987		15,987				12,037	
Log likelihood	−2710		−2714		−1684		−1633	
Hausman test	chi2(20) = 83.53							
	Prob > chi2 = 0.000							
Breusch and Pagan Lagrangian multiplier test			chibar2(01) = 2267.03					
			Prob > chibar2 = 0.000					

(continued)

Table 9.2 (continued)

	(1) FE Logit		(2) RE Logit		(3) LV Logit		(4) LV_RE Logit	
	Coef	z-value	Coef	z-value	Coef	z-value	Coef	z-value
LR test of rho = 0			chibar2(01) = 365.55				chibar2(01) = 100.56	
			Prob > = chibar2 = 0.000				Prob > = chibar2 = 0.000	
Adj R-squared					0.169			

Source Calculated based on the data from CHARLS2011, 2013 and 2015
Note
(1) ***$p < 0.01$, **$p < 0.05$, *$p < 0.1$
(2) FE: fixed-effects model; RE: random-effects model; LV: t_1 period of lagged item of social insurance variables are used; LV_RE: LV and RE model; Logit: logistic regression model

risky financial markets differs by demographic group (e.g., urban residents vs. rural residents; middle-aged group vs. elderly group).

Second, regarding the individual heterogeneity problem, we performed the analysis using RE or FE models (Models 5 and 6 in Table 9.2). The results from the RE model are similar to those in Models1–4, while the results of the FE model indicate that the influence of public medical insurance on the probability of holding risky financial assets is not-significant. This reveals that unobservable individual heterogeneity might affect risky financial market participation.

Third, considering the reverse causality, we used the LV model to employ the estimations (Models 7 and 8 in Table 9.2). The public medical insurance positively affects the probability of holding risky financial assets. The results are similar to those in Models 1–5. The positive effect of public medical insurance was confirmed once more.

9.4.2 Basic Results of Share of Risky Financial Asset

The results of the association between public medical insurance and the share of risky financial assets in the total household assets are presented in Tables 9.3 and 9.4. The main findings are as follows.

First, the results from Model1 in Table 9.3 indicate that public medical insurance, positively affects the share of risky household financial assets. When demographic factors and other factors are added (Models 2–5 in Table 9.3), public medical insurance still positively affects the share of household risky financial assets, and the size of the coefficients is almost unchanged.

Second, regarding the heterogeneity problem, we performed the analysis using RE or FE models (Models 6–7 in Table 9.4). The results from the RE model indicate that public medical insurance may increase the share of risky financial assets, while the results of the FE model indicate that the influence of public medical insurance on the share of risky financial assets is not significant. The results reveal that unobservable individual factors (e.g., personality, ability, risk preference) might affect the share of risky financial assets.

Third, considering reverse causality problem, the results using the LV model (Models 8–9 in Table 9.4) indicate that the influence of public medical insurance on the share of risky financial assets is not significant.

9.4.3 Calculations by Type of Risky Financial Assets

Regarding the differences by type of risky financial assets, we performed the estimations by two types—stocks and bonds; the capital gain risk is higher for stocks than for bonds. The results are summarized in Tables 9.5 and 9.6.

Table 9.3 Public medical insurance and share of risky financial assets

	(1) Tobit		(2) Tobit		(3) Tobit		(4) Tobit		(5) OLS	
	Coef	z-value	Coef	z-value	Coef	z-value	Coef	z-value	Coef	z-value
Medical insurance	0.004*	1.92	0.005***	2.62	0.005**	2.52	0.004**	2.31	0.004**	2.31
Age			0.001*	1.81	0.001**	2.56	0.001**	2.59	0.001**	2.59
Age_sq			−0.000**	−2.01	−0.000***	−2.79	−0.000***	−2.84	−0.000***	−2.84
Female			0.003***	3.08	0.002**	2.30	0.002*	1.83	0.002*	1.83
Education (Junior high)										
Senior high school			0.014***	9.11	0.012***	8.24	0.012***	7.75	0.012***	7.74
College and higher			0.045***	12.38	0.043***	11.69	0.041***	11.23	0.041***	11.22
Married			0.001	0.43	0.001	0.41	0.001	0.65	0.001	0.65
Urban hukou			0.021***	17.99	0.017***	13.52	0.017***	13.16	0.017***	13.15
Disease number			−0.001	−1.44	−0.002	−1.57	−0.001	−1.3	−0.001	−1.30
Inpatient			0.004***	3.20	0.004***	2.84	0.004***	3.02	0.004***	3.02
IADL			0.000	−0.25	0.000	−0.63	0.000	−0.43	0.000	−0.43
BADL			−0.001**	−2.25	−0.001**	−2.13	−0.001**	−2.03	−0.001**	−2.03
Income (First quintile)										
Second quintile					−0.001	−0.51	−0.001	−0.64	−0.001	−0.64
Third quintile					−0.002*	−1.84	−0.002*	−1.73	−0.002*	−1.73
Fourth quintile					−0.001	−0.87	−0.001	−0.83	−0.001	−0.83
Fifth quintile					0.006***	3.87	0.005***	3.39	0.005***	3.39
Debt					0.000***	6.89	0.000***	7.07	0.000***	7.07
Housing owned					0.002	1.20	0.002	1.24	0.002	1.24

(continued)

Table 9.3 (continued)

	(1) Tobit		(2) Tobit		(3) Tobit		(4) Tobit		(5) OLS	
	Coef	z-value	Coef	z-value	Coef	z-value	Coef	z-value	Coef	z-value
Non-work					0.004***	3.84	0.004***	3.84	0.004***	3.84
Social participation							0.002**	2.03	0.002**	2.02
Family number							0.000	−1.54	0.000	−1.54
Pension	0.005***	3.87	0.002	1.53	0.002	1.57	0.002	1.57	0.002	1.57
Regions (East)										
Central	−0.001	−0.63	−0.002	−1.36	−0.002	−1.54	−0.002	−1.68	−0.002*	−1.68
West	0.002**	2.42	0.002**	2.36	0.002**	2.28	0.002	2.06	0.002**	2.06
Northeast	−0.002	−0.77	−0.003	−1.25	−0.004	−1.50	−0.004	−1.52	−0.004	−1.52
Years (2011)										
2013	−0.004***	−3.32	−0.002	−1.38	−0.002*	−1.64	−0.003*	−1.87	−0.003*	−1.87
2015	−0.004***	−2.98	−0.002	−1.22	−0.002	−1.55	−0.003*	−1.82	−0.003*	−1.82
Constants	0.003	1.55	−0.028*	−1.84	−0.041***	−2.64	−0.041***	−2.59	−0.041***	−2.59
Obs	27,075		27,075		27,075		27,075		27,075	
Log likelihood	34,675		35,069		34,978		33,863			
Pseudo R2	0.000		0.013		0.014		0.014			
Adj R-squared									0.034	

Source Calculated based on the data from CHARLS2011, 2013 and 2015

Note

(1) ***$p < 0.01$, **$p < 0.05$, *$p < 0.1$

(2) Tobit: Tobit regression model; OLS: ordinary least squares regression

Table 9.4 Public medical insurance and share of risky financial assets considering the endogeneity problems

	(1) FE		(2) RE		(3) LV_ Tobit		(4) LV_RE Tobit	
	Coef	z-value	Coef	z-value	Coef	z-value	Coef	z-value
Medical insurance	0.003	1.22	0.004**	2.23	0.002	0.86	0.002	0.82
Age	0.004**	2.06	0.001**	2.25	0.001	1.42	0.001	1.30
Age_sq	−0.000*	−1.61	−0.000*	−2.45	0.000	−1.47	0.000	−1.36
Female			0.002*	1.84	0.002*	1.62	0.002*	1.62
Education (Junior high)								
Senior high school			0.015***	7.91	0.010***	4.95	0.010***	4.94
College and higher			0.043***	9.91	0.043***	8.32	0.042***	7.72
Married	−0.008	−1.24	0.000	0.10	0.003	1.22	0.002	1.13
Urban hukou	0.001	0.25	0.017***	11.66	0.013***	7.51	0.012***	7.04
Disease number	−0.008***	−3.29	−0.002**	−2.04	−0.002	−1.09	−0.002	−1.27
Inpatient	0.000	0.16	0.003	2.09	0.005***	3.27	0.006***	3.40
IADL	0.000	−0.21	0.000	−0.32	0.000	−0.27	0.000	−0.01
BADL	0.000	−0.41	−0.000*	−1.60	−0.000*	−1.67	−0.000*	−1.83
Income (First quintile)								
Second quintile	−0.001	−0.89	−0.001	−0.99	0.001	0.69	0.001	0.61
Third quintile	0.000	−0.02	−0.002	−1.24	0.001	0.72	0.001	0.81
Fourth quintile	0.001	0.68	0.000	0.00	0.004**	2.03	0.004**	2.14
Fifth quintile	0.003	1.34	0.005***	3.14	0.009***	4.96	0.009***	4.81
Debt	0.000	0.71	0.000***	6.65	0.000***	10.08	0.000***	9.78
Housing owned	0.002	0.81	0.002	1.40	0.001	0.56	0.001	0.81
Non-work	0.000	0.16	0.003***	2.95	0.004***	2.83	0.004***	2.84
Social participation	0.000	0.35	0.001*	1.66	0.002	1.37	0.002	1.40
Family number	0.000	0.41	0.000	−1.38	0.000	−0.13	0.000	−0.16
Pension	−0.002	−1.11	0.001	0.68	0.002	1.18	0.002	1.24
Regions (East)								
Central			−0.003***	−1.74	−0.002	−1.3	−0.002	−1.41
West			0.001	1.07	0.004***	2.83	0.003***	2.58

(continued)

Table 9.4 (continued)

	(1) FE		(2) RE		(3) LV_ Tobit		(4) LV_RE Tobit	
	Coef	z-value	Coef	z-value	Coef	z-value	Coef	z-value
Northeast			−0.004	−1.29	−0.007*	−1.86	−0.007*	−1.81
Years (2011)								
2013	−0.001	−0.59	−0.001	−1.23				
2015	−0.002	−0.68	−0.001	−0.88	−0.001	−0.79	−0.001	−0.87
Constants	−0.129***	−2.08	−0.040**	−2.16	−0.041**	−1.75	−0.037	−1.56
Observations	27,075		27,075		14,098		14,098	
Groups	15,112		15,112					
Hausman test	chi2(20) = 69.32 Prob > chi2 = 0.000							
Breusch and Pagan Lagrangian multiplier test			chibar2(01) = 1284.43 Prob > chibar2 = 0.000					
Adj R-squared					0.0365			
LR test of sigma_u = 0							chibar2(01) = 282.08 Prob > = chibar2 = 0.000	

Source Calculated based on the data from CHARLS2011, 2013 and 2015
Note
(1) ***$p < 0.01$, **$p < 0.05$, *$p < 0.1$
(2) FE: fixed-effects model; RE: random-effects model; LV: t_1 period of lagged item of social insurance variables are used; LV_RE: LV and RE model; Tobit: Tobit regression model

First, regarding the association between public medical insurance and the probability of holding stocks or bonds, the results in Table 9.5 indicate that the positive influence of public medical insurance is more significant for stocks than for bonds.

Second, considering the relationship between public medical insurance and share of risky financial assets, the results in Table 9.6 also show that the positive influence of public medical insurance is more significant for stocks than for bonds. The results indicate that the positive influence of public medical insurance is greater for higher-risk financial assets (stock) than for lower-risk ones (bonds).

Table 9.5 Summary of results of public medical insurance and probability of holding stocks and bonds

	(1) Stocks		(2) Bonds	
	Coef	z-value	Coef	z-value
Model1: Logit	0.800***	2.76	0.079	0.25
Model2: FE Logit	0.988	1.37	−1.564	−1.34
Model3: RE Logit	1.100**	2.46	0.030	0.09
Model4: LV_Logit	0.408	1.27	1.161	1.62
Model5: LV_RE Logit	0.680	1.28	1.161	1.62

Source Calculated based on the data from CHARLS2011, 2013, and 2015
Note
(1) ***$p < 0.01$, **$p < 0.05$
(2) Logit: logistic regression model; FE: fixed-effects model; RE: random-effects model; LV: t_1 period of lagged item of social insurance variables are used; LV_RE: LV and RE model. The coefficients of public medical insurance are presented
(3) Only results of public medical insurance are expressed. The other controlled variables including demographic factors (age, age squared, sex, education, married, urban hukou, disease, inpatient, LADL, BADL), income factors (income, debt, owing housing, non-work), social capital (social participation, number of family member), pensions, regions (east, central, west, and northeast) and year dummy variables have been estimated, but the results are not listed in the table

Table 9.6 Summary of results of public medical insurance and share of stocks and bonds in total household assets

	(1) Stocks		(2) Bonds	
	Coef	z-value	Coef	z-value
Model1: Tobit	0.004**	2.21	0.001	0.79
Model2: FE	0.004**	2.15	−0.001	−0.84
Model3: RE Tobit	0.004***	2.58	0.001	0.67
Model3: LV_Tobit	0.001	0.56	0.001	0.81
Model4: LV_RE Tobit	0.001	0.55	0.001	0.81

Source Calculated based on the data from CHARLS2011, 2013, and 2015
Note
(1) ***$p < 0.01$, **$p < 0.05$
(2) Tobit: Tobit regression model; FE: fixed-effects model; RE: random-effects model; LV: t_1 period of lagged item of social insurance variables are used; LV_RE: LV and RE model. The coefficients of public medical insurance are presented
(3) Only results of public medical insurance are expressed. The other controlled variables including demographic factors (age, age squared, sex, education, married, urban hukou, disease, inpatient, LADL, BADL), income factors (income, debt, owing housing, non-work), social capital (social participation, number of family member), pensions, regions (east, central, west, and northeast) and year dummy variables have been estimated, but the results are not listed in the table

9.4.4 Considering Heterogeneity by Group: Differences by Age and Hukou Groups

Regarding the group heterogeneity, we employed the estimations by age and *hukou* groups using the RE model with the lagged item (LV_RE model), and the results are presented in Table 9.7 (by age) and Table 9.8 (by *hukou*).

First, regarding the public medical insurance effect by age group (see Table 9.7), we performed the estimations by the middle-age group (aged 45–59 years) and the older group (aged $\geq$ 60 years). The results indicate that public medical insurance positively affects the probability of holding risky financial assets for the group aged $\geq$ 60 years, while its effect is not significant for the group aged 45–59 years.

Table 9.7 Summary of results of public medical insurance and risky financial assets by age group

	(a) Holding		(b) Share	
	Coef	z-value	Coef	z-value
Age 45–59	0.461	0.95	0.002	0.56
Age 60 and over	1.781**	2.09	0.003	0.75

Source Calculated based on the data from CHARLS2011, 2013, 2015
Note
(1) **$p < 0.05$
(2) LV_random-effects model is used. Two estimations using samples aged 45–59 and aged 60 and over are performed separately
(3) Only the coefficients of public medical insurance are presented. The other controlled variables including demographic factors (sex, education, married, urban hukou, disease, inpatient, LADL, BADL), income factors (income, debt, owing housing, non-work), social capital (social participation, number of family member), pensions, regions (east, central, west, and northeast) and year dummy variables have been estimated, but the results are not listed in the table

Table 9.8 Summary of results of public medical insurance and risky financial assets by *hukou* group

	(a) Holding		(b) Share	
	Coef	z-value	Coef	z-value
Urban	1.317**	2.07	0.009	0.94
Rural	0.552	0.92	0.000	0.16

Source Calculated based on the data from CHARLS2011, 2013, 2015
Note
(1) **$p < 0.05$
(2) LV_random-effects model is used. Two estimations using samples of rural residents and urban residents are performed separately.
(3) Only the coefficients of public medical insurance are presented. The other controlled variables including demographic factors (age, age squared, sex, education, married, disease, inpatient, LADL, BADL), income factors (income, debt, owing housing, non-work), social capital (social participation, number of family member), pensions, regions (east, central, west, and northeast) and year dummy variables have been estimated, but the results are not listed in the table

Second, considering the heterogenous influence by *hukou* type, the results in Table 9.8 show that the influence of public medical insurance is only significant for urban residents, while it is not significant for rural residents.

The reasons for these results can be considered as follows. Contrary to other countries, China's public medical insurance schemes have been fragmented by *hukou* (e.g., rural and urban *hukou*) since the planned economy period. The public scheme for medical insurance for urban employees was established in the 1950s based on *Labor Contract Law*, which was reformed to the UEBMI in the 1990; Since 2007, Chinese government has enforced to establish the URBMI which covers all urban *hukou* residents who did not join the UEBMI. In rural areas, the Cooperative Medical Scheme (CMS), which was managed by people's communities in rural areas but unsupported by the central government, was introduced in the 1950s. The NRCMS was introduced in 2003 to replace CMS with more subsidies from central and local governments. However, the proportion of OOP expenses of medical care is higher, and the covered types of diseases are less for NRCMS than for UEBMI (Ma & Oshio, 2020). As there is a large difference in the systems of public medical insurance by urban and rural *hukou* residents, the results show that the influence of public medical insurance differs by *hukou* group.

9.5 Conclusions

Using three-wave longitudinal data from the CHARLS and LV_RE/FE models, this study estimated the influence of public medical insurance on risky financial market participation of middle-aged and older groups (aged 45 years and older).

Three new findings emerged. First, public medical insurance positively affects the probability of holding risky financial assets, while the influence of medical insurance on the share of risky financial assets is not significant. This indicates that the influence of public medical insurance is greater for the probability of participation in risky financial markets but not for the volumes of holding risky financial assets. However, when addressed the heterogeneity problem, the positive effect disappeared, which suggests that some unobservable factors may affect the behavior of participating in risky financial markets.

Second, the influence of public medical insurance differs by type of risky financial assets: public medical insurance positively affects the probability of holding stocks and the share of stocks to total financial assets, while it is not significant for bonds. The influence of public medical insurance is greater for higher-risk financial assets (stocks) than for lower-risk financial assets (bonds).

Third, the influences of social insurance differ by age and *hukou* group. The effect of public medical insurance is significantly positive for the group aged 60 years and older. Public medical insurance only influences the risky financial assets for urban residents, while it is not significant for rural residents.

The establishment of public medical insurance may promote the development of the financial market. It is expected that more individual participation in the financial market may accelerate innovation in firms and improve the transparency of the securities market. Therefore, we should evaluate the effects of the establishment of public medical insurance from multiple perspectives. However, the effects of public medical insurance differ between urban and rural residents. This may be because the level of public medical security is lower for rural (than urban) residents. For example, the share of OOP expenses is higher for rural resident.[5] The problem of inequality in social security should be addressed. It can be expected that when the actual universal medical insurance is established in the whole of China—implying that the levels of social security for rural residents become equal to those for urban residents—the consumption and probability of participation in the financial market may increase. This may improve investment in venture firms and accelerate economic growth.

This study had some limitations. The enrollment rate of public medical insurance is higher during the analyzed period from 2011 to 2015, which may affect the robustness of results. In additions, we investigated the association between public medical insurance and participation in risky financial markets by using LV_ RE or FE models. However, the causality relationship should be examined furthermore in the future. Moreover, estimations should include younger generations based on an appropriate survey data.

Notes

1. Based on the item "Have you been diagnosed with diseases by a doctor?" in the questionnaire, seven types of diagnosed diseases were included: (a) hypertension or dyslipidemia; (b) diabetes or high blood sugar; (c) heart attack or stroke; (d) cancer or malignant tumor; (e) emotional, nervous, psychiatric problems or memory-related diseases; (f) stomach or other digestive diseases; and (g) other diseases. We calculated the number of diseases in each individual.
2. The variable of IADL was constructed as follows. CHARLS asked the respondents whether they had any difficulty in performing each of the following activities: (a) doing household chores; (b) preparing hot meals; (c) shopping for groceries; (d) taking the right portion of medication on time; and (e) managing money for IADL. Respondents' responses were scored as follows: *I do not have any difficulty* = 4; *I have difficulty but can still do it* = 3; *I have difficulty and need help* = 2; *I cannot do it* = 1. The scores were summed and defined as IADL scores (5–20).

3. The variable of BADL was constructed as follows. CHARLS asked the respondents whether they had any difficulty in performing each of the following activities: (a) dressing; (b) bathing; (c) eating; (d) getting into or out of bed; (e) using the toilet; and (f) controlling urination and defecation for BADL. The respondents' responses were scored as follows: *I do not have any difficulty* = 4; *I have difficulty but can still do it* = 3; *I have difficulty and need help* = 2; *I cannot do it* = 1. The scores were summed and defined as BADL scores (6–24).
4. For the dummy variable of social participation, CHARLS asked respondents, "Have you done any of these activities in the last month?," listing seven types of social activities: (a) interacting with friends; (b) playing Mah-jongg, chess, cards, or going to a community club; (c) providing help to family, friends, or neighbors who do not live with you and did not pay for your help; (d) going to a sport, social, or other club activity; (e) participating in a community-related organization; (f) doing volunteer or charity work; and (g) caring for a sick or disabled adult who does not live with you and does not pay for your help. Seven binary variables of each social participation (SP) activity were constructed by allocating "1" to the answer *yes* and "0" otherwise. A binary variable of overall SP was constructed by allocating "1" to those participating in at least one type of social participation activity and "0" to others.
5. For the detailed information on differences of out-of-pocket of expenses on medical care between rural and urban residents, please refer Chap. 4 in this book.

Appendix

See Table 9.9.

Table 9.9 Descriptive statistics of variables

Variable items	Total	Insured	Non-insured	t-test	
		(a)	(b)	(a)–(b)	*p*-value
Holding risky financial assets	0.154	0.148	0.318	−0.170***	0.000
Holding storks	0.148	0.142	0.313	−0.171***	0.000
Holding bonds	0.137	0.130	0.314	−0.184***	0.000
Medical insurance	0.935				
Age	59.791	59.802	59.494	0.308**	0.031
Female	0.514	0.513	0.538	−0.025***	0.007
Education					
Junior and lower	0.876	0.876	0.869	0.007	0.254
Senior	0.101	0.101	0.110	−0.009	0.166

(continued)

Table 9.9 (continued)

Variable items	Total	Insured	Non-insured	t-test	
		(a)	(b)	(a)–(b)	*p*-value
College and higher	0.023	0.023	0.021	0.002	0.778
Married	0.865	0.868	0.790	0.078***	0.000
Urban *hukou*	0.217	0.213	0.330	−0.117***	0.000
Disease	0.714	0.720	0.563	0.157***	0.000
Inpatient	0.127	0.129	0.063	0.066***	0.000
IADL (0–7)	0.786	0.790	0.688	0.102***	0.006
BADL (0–10)	1.845	1.858	1.511	0.347***	0.000
Per capita income	9519	9526	9319	207	0.676
Debt	8401	8479	5837	2642	0.469
Owning housing	0.889	0.890	0.862	0.028***	0.000
Non-work	0.325	0.323	0.386	−0.063***	0.000
Social participation	0.497	0.499	0.425	0.074***	0.000
Number of Family members	3.398	3.403	3.249	0.154***	0.000
Regions					
East	0.191	0.194	0.167	0.027**	0.011
Central	0.212	0.209	0.248	−0.039***	0.000
West	0.567	0.567	0.560	0.007	0.531
Northeast	0.030	0.030	0.025	0.005	0.156
Survey year					
2011	0.312	0.301	0.593	−0.292***	0.000
2013	0.329	0.332	0.265	0.067***	0.000
2015	0.359	0.367	0.142	0.225***	0.000
Observations	31,814	19,489	12,325		

Source Calculated based on the data from CHARLS2011, 2013 and 2015
Note ***$p < 0.01$, **$p < 0.05$

References

Angrisani, M., Atella, V., & Brunetti, M. (2018). Public health insurance and household portfolio choices: Unravelling financial "side effects" of medicare. *Journal of Banking and Finance, 93*, 198–212.

Balloch, A., Nicolae, A., & Phillip, D. (2015). Stock market literacy, trust, and participation. *Review of Finance, 19*(5), 1925–1963.

Berkowitz, M. K., & Qiu, J. (2006). A further look at household portfolio choice and health status. *Journal of Banking & Finance, 30*, 1201–1217.

Betermier, S., Calvet, L. E., & Socini, P. (2017). Who are the value and growth investors? *Journal of Finance, 72*(1), 5–46.

Blanchard, O. J., & Mankiw, N. G. (1988). Consumption: Beyond certainty equivalence. *The American Economic Review, 78*(2), 173–177.

Brown, J. R., Ivkovie, Z., Smith, P. A., & Weisbenner, S. (2008). Neighbors matter: Causal community effects and stock market participation. *Journal of Finance, 63*(3), 1509–1531.

Browning, M., & Lusardi, A. (1996). Household saving: Micro theories and micro facts. *Journal of Economic Literature, 34*(4), 1797–1855.

Campbell, J. Y. (2006). Household finance. *Journal of Finance, 61*(4), 1553–1604.

Cardak, B. A., & Wilkins, R. (2009). The determinants of household risky asset holdings: Australian evidence on background risk and other factors. *Journal of Banking & Finance, 33*(5), 850–860.

Chen, X., & Ji, X. (2017). The effect of house price on stock market participation in China: Evidence from CHFS microdata. *Emerging Markets Finance and Trade, 53*(5), 1020–1044.

Chetty, R., Sandor, L., & Szeidl, A. (2017). The effect of housing on portfolio choice. *Journal of Finance, 72*(3), 1171–1212.

Coile, C., & Milligan, K. (2006). How household portfolios evolve after retirement: The effect of aging and health shocks. Working Paper 12391, NBER.

Cooper, R., & Zhu, G. (2017). Household finance in China. NBER Working Paper 23741.

Dreze, J. H., & Modigliani, F. (1972). Consumption decisions under uncertainty. *Journal of Economic Theory, 5*(3), 308–335.

Edwards, R. D. (2008). Health risk and portfolio choice. *Journal of Business and Economic Statistics, 26*, 472–485.

Fafchamps, M., & Gubert, F. (2007). Risk sharing and network formation. *American Economic Review, 97*(2), 75–79.

Fan, Y., & Zhao, R. (2009). Health status and portfolio choice: Causality or heterogeneity? *Journal of Banking & Finance, 33*, 1079–1088.

Ge, Y., Chen, H., Zou, L., & Zhou, Z. (2021). Political background and household financial asset allocation in China. *Emerging Markets Finance and Trade, 57*(4), 1232–1246.

Grinblatt, M., Keloharji, M., & Linnainmaa, J. (2011). IQ and stock market participation. *Review of Finance, 15*(4), 27–42.

Hall, R. E. (1978). Stochastic implications of the life cycle-permanent income hypothesis: Theory and evidence. *Journal of Political Economy, 86*(6), 971–987.

Hong, H., Kubik, J. D., & Stein, J. C. (2004). Social interaction and stock market participation. *Journal of Finance, 59*(1), 137–163.

Leland, H. E. (1968). Savings and uncertainty: The precautionary demand for savings. *The Quarterly Journal of Economics, 82*(3), 465–473.

Love, D. A., & Smith, P. A. (2010). Does health affect portfolio choice? *Health Economics, 19*, 1441–1460.

Ma, X., & Oshio, T. (2020). The impact of social insurance on health among middle-aged and older adults in rural China: A longitudinal study using a three-wave nationwide survey. *BMC Public Health, 20*, 1842.

Rosen, H. S., & Wu, S. (2004). Portfolio choice and health status. *Journal of Financial Economics, 72*, 457–484.

Sandmo, A. (1970). The effect of uncertainty on savings decisions. *The Review of Economic Studies, 37*(3), 353–360.

Wei, S., Wu, W., & Zhang, L. (2019). Portfolio choices, asset returns and wealth inequality: Evidence from China. *Emerging Markets Review, 38*, 423–437.

Zhou, J., & Xiao, T. (2018). Analyzing determinants of household financial decision-making: Household stock investment in China. *Emerging Markets Finance and Trade, 54*(15), 3385–3400.

Zhou, Q., Basu, K., & Yuan, Y. (2017). Does health insurance coverage influence household financial portfolios? A case study in urban China. *Frontiers of Economics in China, 12*(1), 94–112.

Zou, J., & Deng, X. (2019). Financial literacy, housing value and household financial market participation: Evidence from urban China. *China Economic Review, 55*, 52–66.

Chapter 10
Public Medical Insurances and Subjective Well-Being in Rural China

Abstract Using three-wave longitudinal data from the China Health and Retirement Longitudinal Study of 2011, 2013, and 2015, this study investigates the correlation between the New Rural Cooperative Medical Scheme (NRCMS) and subjective well-being (SWB) among the middle-aged and the elderly in rural China. The dynamic fixed effects model and lagged variable model were used to address heterogeneity and other endogeneity problems. The results suggest that the impact of the NRCMS on SWB is not significant, but the influences of the NRCMS differ by groups, its positive effect is greater for the group aged 70–79, high-income group and individuals in central regions than the other groups.

Keywords New Rural Cooperative Medical Scheme (NRCMS) · Subjective well-being · Rural China

10.1 Introduction

Public medical insurance is implemented in developed and developing countries to address the aging population problem. As a developing country with the largest population and a family-planning (one-child) policy implemented since 1979, China has faced a serious aging population problem. According to the National Population Census in China, the ratio of the population aged 65 and older to the total population has increased from 7.0% in 2000 to 13.5% in 2020 (NBS, 2020, 2021). The speed of becoming an aging population is so fast for China. Thus, establishing public medical insurance has become an important issue for the Chinese government. Simultaneously, in China, with the transition from a planned economy to a market-oriented economy, public medical system was reformed from government security system to social insurance.

However, public medical insurance was fragmented by the population registration system called *hukou* (e.g., rural *hukou* and urban *hukou*) in China (Ma, 2015; Qin et al., 2014). Concretely, during the planned economy period, for the urban *hukou* residents, the labor insurance, including medical insurance, which covered all employees in state-owned enterprises (SOEs) or collective-owned enterprises (COEs), and the publicly funded medical insurance, which covered all civil servants

X. Ma, *Public Medical Insurance Reforms in China*,
https://doi.org/10.1007/978-981-16-7790-8_10

in government offices or government-related organizations (*Shiye Danwei*), were introduced in the 1950s. Since the 1990s, the public medical insurance which covered all employees has been reform to the Urban Employee Basic Medical Insurance (UEBMI). Since 2007, Chinese government has enforced to establish the Urban Residents Basic Medical Insurance (URBMI) which covers all urban *hukou* residents who did not join the UEBMI. For the rural *hukou* residents, the Cooperative Medical System (CMS), a community mutual assistance system, was promoted along with disseminating the people's communes in rural areas—in the 1960s. However, with the dramatic reduction in the number of people's communes alongside the implementation of the Household Contract Responsibility System, the CMS enrollment rates decreased dramatically (from 90% in 1981 to 5% in the 1990s), indicating the majority of rural residents had to pay the total expenditures for medical care themselves (Cheng et al., 2015; Ma, 2015; Song, 2009). To address poverty caused by high out-of-pocket (OOP) expenses on medical care among rural residents, the Chinese government introduced a new public medical insurance program—the New Rural Cooperative Medical Scheme (NRCMS) in 2013. The NRCMS covers all rural residents. Although enrollment into the NRCMS is voluntary, participation in the scheme was promoted by the central and local governments. Since 2016, Chinese government has promoted the integration of URBMI and NRCMS.

From an economic perspective, because public medical insurance can reduce the OOP expenses and reduce the uncertainty of risk in the future, it is thought that public medical insurance may affect an individual's subjective well-being (SWB, such as life satisfaction, or happiness). However, because there is a set of problems in system designs and utilization, some empirical studies argue that public medical insurance reform might not improve the individuals' SWB (Park, 2018; Schatz et al., 2012). Did the NRCMS enforced by the Chinese government in the 2000s improve the SWB of rural residents in China? Although it is reported that there exists a positive association between public medical insurance and the SWB for developed countries and developing countries, including China (Gu et al., 2017; Tran et al., 2017; Xiao & Su, 2017; Yin et al., 2019), some issues are not considered in these previous studies, and they should be discussed.

The main contributions of this study can be considered as follows: First, because most empirical studies on the issue employ the estimation using data from a cross-sectional survey, it is thought that there may be a heterogeneity problem in these results. This study conducts an empirical study based on three-wave longitudinal survey data to address the endogeneity problem. To the best of our knowledge, this study is the first to employ a dynamic longitudinal data analysis method on the issue for China.

Second, although it is thought that the influence of public medical insurance on the SWB may differ by group (e.g., women vs. men, middle-age group vs. older-group, low-income group vs. high-income group), the heterogeneity of these groups is not considered in the previous studies. This study employs estimations by using subsamples and compares the influences of the NRCMS between different groups.

The results of this study can provide new evidence for policymakers to take public medical insurance reform to improve the individuals' SWB in the future.

Additionally, the experiences of the reform of Chinese public medical insurance policies may provide rich evidence for developing countries to establish or reform their medical insurance in the future.

The remainder of this chapter is structured as follows: Sect. 10.2 summarizes the channels on the influence of public medical insurance on the SWB and previous empirical studies on the issue. Section 10.3 describes the methods of analysis, including the introduction of the models and data. Section 10.4 describes and interprets the econometric results. The main conclusions, policy implications, and limitations are presented in the last part.

10.2 Literature Review

For the determinants of SWB, it is found that (i) the demographic factor, (ii) income factor based on the absolute income hypothesis (Leibenstein, 1950; Easterlin, 1974, 2001; Ferrer-i-Carbonell, 2005; Vendrik & Woltjer, 2007; Appleton & Song, 2008; Smyth et al., 2010; Jiang et al., 2011; Wang & VanderWeele, 2011; Ma & Piao, 2019a, 2019b) and the relative income hypothesis (Easterlin, 1974; Boskin & Sheshinski, 1978; Layard, 1980; Frank, 1985; Akerlof & Yellen, 1990; Luo, 2006, 2009; Brockmann et al., 2009; Wang & VanderWeele, 2011; Ma & Piao, 2019a, 2019b; Zhang & Churchill, 2020), and (iii) social capitals (Haller & Hanler, 2006; Han, 2015; Han et al., 2013; Helliwell et al., 2014; Hommerich & Tiefenbach, 2018; Leung et al., 2011; Neria et al., 2018) influence the SWB. Because this study focuses on the NRCMS, we will discuss why and how public medical insurance can influence individual SWB and summarize the empirical study results on this issue in the following section.

10.2.1 Channels of Associations Between Medical Insurance and SWB

Two channels can be considered concerning the mechanisms. First, public medical insurance may reduce the OOP medical care expenses, improving the SWB (income effect). For example, based on the NRCMS regulations, patients can obtain reimbursements to reduce the OOP expenses. Consequently, public medical insurance may increase income indirectly. As pointed out in the absolute income hypothesis, SWB is higher for the high-income group than for the low-income group. Therefore, it is assumed that SWB is higher for participants with public medical insurance than individuals without public medical insurance.

Second, public medical insurance can reduce the poverty risk and increase the probability of utilization of healthcare services when ill (uncertainty reduction effect).

Both effects (income and uncertainty reduction effects) may improve an individual's SWB. Thus, it is expected that enrollment in public medical insurance may improve SWB.

10.2.2 Empirical Studies on Associations Between Medical Insurance and SWB

Previous studies report that medical insurance may improve life satisfaction or happiness (Gu et al., 2017; Keng & Wu, 2014; Tran et al., 2017; Xiao & Su, 2017; Yin et al., 2019).

For example, Tran et al. (2017) used the data of 2010 survey conducted by the Centers for Disease Control and Prevention, Behavioral Risk Factor Surveillance System, and the instrument variables (IV) method and a probit regression model to estimate the Affordable Care Act on life satisfaction of the United States adults. They found that individuals without medical insurance coverage were less likely to be "very satisfied" or "satisfied" with life.

Xiao and Su (2017) used data from the Chinese General Social Survey to investigate the impact of basic medical insurance on well-being and found that participation in basic medical insurance could significantly enhance individuals' SWB.

Gu et al. (2017) used data from the China Health and Retirement Longitudinal Survey (CHARLS) of 2013 and an ordered probit regression model to estimate the effects of medical insurance on the life satisfaction of the elderly. They found that medical insurance could facilitate the improvement of the life satisfaction of the elderly, and its effect is greater for urban residents than for rural residents.

Yin et al. (2019) used a longitudinal data from CHARLS of 2011 and 2013 and found that NRCMS is beneficial to promoting the overall life satisfaction of the rural elderly.

Keng and Wu (2014) used data from the Survey on the Health and Living Status of the Middle-aged and Elderly from 1989 to 2003 and the difference in difference method to estimate the impact of Taiwan's National Health Insurance (NHI) on the SWB. They reported that NHI has a significant effect on happiness and life satisfaction in Taiwan.

Based on economics theories and previous empirical studies, this study focuses on the impact of the NRCMS on the SWB of rural *hukou* residents, we will compare the NRCMS effects by groups. These new findings may enrich the knowledge on this issue.

10.3 Methodology and Data

10.3.1 Model

For the estimation of life satisfaction, in previous studies, when the dependent variable is an ordered category variable, the ordered logit regression model or ordered probit regression model is used; when the dependent variable is a continuous variable, the Ordinary Least Squares regression (OLS) model is used. The estimated results based on these methods are almost consistent (Ferrer-i-Carbonell, 2005). When the dependent variable is a continuous variable, the results are easily understood.[1] Therefore, the life satisfaction score (completely satisfied = 5, very satisfied = 4, somewhat satisfied = 3, not very satisfied = 2, not at all satisfied = 1) is used as the dependent variable.[1]

The SWB function is expressed as Eq. (10.1):

$$SWB_i = a + \gamma NRCMS_i + \theta X_i + \varepsilon_i \tag{10.1}$$

In Eq. (10.1) i denotes individual, t denotes survey year (three waves: 2011, 2013, 2015), SWB is the index of SWB (here, the life satisfaction score from 1 to 5),$NRCMS$ expresses the NRCMS, X are factors (e.g., demographic, income, social capital factors) that may influence life satisfaction. a is a constant, γ, θ are the estimated coefficients. ε is an error item.

However, three types of endogeneity problems may be maintained in Eq. (10.1). First, because ε includes an item related to individual-specific and time-invariant factors v_i, when v_i is not considered, heterogeneity problems may occur in the estimated results. To address this problem, fixed effects (FE) and random effects (RE) models are used, as shown in Eq. (10.2). In the FE and RE models, v_i will drop out; thus, the heterogeneity problem can be addressed.

$$SWB_{it} = a + +\gamma NRCMS_{it} + \theta X_{it} + v_i + u_{it} \tag{10.2}$$

Second, as pointed out by Wooldridge (2002, 2005) and Contoyannis et al. (2004), there may remain an initial dependent problem in Eq. (10.2), which means that the SWB in time t_1 might affect the SWB in time t. To address this problem, a dynamic FE or RE model is used in this study. It is expressed by Eq. (10.3). In Eq. (10.3), SWB_{t_1} denotes the SWB in time t_1. The definitions of the others are similar in Eq. (10.2).

$$SWB_{it} = a + \rho SWB_{it\_1} + \gamma NRCMS_{it} + \theta X_{it} + v_i + u_{it} \tag{10.3}$$

Third, regarding the reverse causality problem, the lagged variable (LV) model is also used to take the robustness check, as shown in Eq. (10.4).

$$SWB_{it} = a + \gamma NRCMS_{it\_1} + \theta X_{it\_1} + u_{it} \tag{10.4}$$

The F-test, Breusch and Pagan Lagrangian multiplier test, and Hausman specification test are employed to compare the appropriateness of these models.

10.3.2 Data and Variable Setting

Three waves of longitudinal data from the CHARLS conducted by Peking University on representative regions in China in 2011, 2013, and 2015 (CHARLS 2011, 2013 and 2015) were used in this study. The survey objects were individuals aged 45 years and older. The baseline wave included approximately 10,000 households and 17,708 individuals in 150 counties/districts and 450 villages/resident committees. The CHARLS contained a rich set of individual and household-level information, such as life satisfaction, demographic factors, family structure, household income, health status, and other related information.

In this study, the individuals, who were aged 45 and older in the baseline survey and remained in at least one of two follow-up surveys, were focused on. The number of samples were 17,708 for 2011, 18,612 for 2013, and 21,097 for 2015. After further excluding the respondents who were missing key variables used in the statistical analysis, the total number of individuals used in this study was 29,715 (11,613 for 2011, 10,319 for 2013, and 7,783 for 2015). The unbalance panel dataset was used. The samples differed by using different variables and models.

The dependent variables are an ordered category variable and a continuous variable of life satisfaction, used as indices of the SWB. They are calculated as "completely satisfied = 5, very satisfied = 4, somewhat satisfied = 3, not very satisfied = 2, not at all satisfied = 1."

The independent variables are as follows. First, the key independent variable is the binary variable of enrollment of the NRCMS, which is equal to 1 when an individual is a NRCMS participant, equal to 0 when not participating in the public medical insurance.

Second, as shown in previous studies, demographic factors (e.g., age, sex, and education) influence an individual's SWB. Therefore, age, age squared, education level (junior high school and lower, senior high school, college, and higher), sex, married, urban *hukou*, and health status (disease, inpatient, instrumental activities of daily living [IADL], basic activity of daily living [BADL]) dummy variables were utilized.

Third, three types of variables were used as income factors. (1) According to the absolute and relative income hypothesis, household income per capita was utilized as the indicator of absolute income; The first to the fifth income quintile dummy variables were constructed.

(2) The household income gap (the difference between actual household income and the reference group household income) was used as the relative income indicator. According to Ma and Piao (2019a, 2019b), the income of the reference group is an imputed value calculated based on income functions.[2] The equivalent income was calculated using an equivalent coefficient.[3] In addition, household income from 2011 to 2015 was adjusted by the Chinese consumption price index (CPI) from 2011 to

2015, which were published by the National Bureau of Statistics. The CPI in 2011 provides the standard.

(3) Non-work dummy variable was equal to 1 when unemployed in the survey year and equal to 0 when otherwise.

Fourth, the social capital variables were conducted regarding the influence of social capital on an individual's SWB. (1) It is thought that social participation may increase contact with other people and enlarge the social capital. The social participation dummy variable was used.[4]

(2) In China, particularly in rural areas, the influence of Confucianism on lifestyle is still significant. For example, intra-household risk-sharing is common in Chinese society. It is thought that the greater the number of family members, the greater the social capital. The number of family members within a household was used in the study.

(3) Living arrangements may influence social capital. For example, it is assumed that comparing the elderly group with children living in other cities, the help and communications from children are more for the elderly with children living nearby. Dummy variables were constructed by living near children's houses and living with children in a house (co-residence with child).

Fifth, it was reported that public pensions positively affect the SWB (Abruquah et al., 2019; Fang & Sakellariou, 2016; Kollamparambil & Etinzock, 2019; Sasaki et al., 2018; Xiao & Su, 2017; Zhang et al., 2014). To control the influence of public pension, a binary variable of enrollment of the New Rural Social Pension Insurance Scheme (NRSPI) was used, which is equal to 1 when an individual is a NRSPI participant, equal to 0 when not participating in the NRSPI.

Sixth, regional blocks (East, Central, West, Northeast)[5] and survey year (2011, 2013, 2015) dummy variables were used to control the influence of regional disparity of economy, culture, lifestyle, and time trend changes.

The statistical descriptions of the dependent and independent variables are summarized in Appendix Table 10.7 by different groups (completely satisfied and very satisfied, somewhat satisfied, and not satisfied groups). The test results for the differences in mean values between the satisfied and not satisfied groups show that there remain significant differences in the majority variables between these two groups. It indicates that variables such as demographic factors, income factors, and social capital factors should be controlled in the analyses.

10.4 Results

10.4.1 Basic Results

The results of NRCMS, and other control variables are shown in Table 10.1. Four types of models—(1) the ordered logit regression model based on the pooling cross-section data [Model1], (2) lagged variable of time t-1 model (LV) [Model2], (3)

Table 10.1 Results of medical insurance and SWB

	(1) Ordered logit		(2) LV		(3) Dynamic RE		(4) Dynamic FE	
	Coef	z-value	Coef	z-value	Coef	z-value	Coef	z-value
SWBt_1					−0.178***	−19.55	0.470***	31.32
NRCMS	0.161***	3.50	0.184	2.96	0.045	1.95	0.033	0.89
Age	0.008	0.53	−0.010	−0.44	−0.011	−1.20		
Age_sq	0.000	1.36	0.000	1.78	0.000*	2.18		
Female	0.087***	3.22	0.061	1.76	0.004	0.26		
Education (Junior high and low)								
Senior high school	−0.063	−1.17	−0.068	−0.99	−0.010	−0.33		
College and higher	−0.153	−0.60	−0.450	−1.28	−0.150	−1.03		
Married	0.176***	4.10	0.179***	3.21	0.083***	3.63	0.067	0.72
Disease number	−0.163***	−5.34	−0.193***	−4.70	−0.047***	−2.71	0.084*	2.05
Inpatient	−0.117***	−2.83	−0.105*	−2.09	−0.016	−0.82	0.028	0.96
IADL	−0.071***	−6.94	−0.065***	−4.77	−0.028***	−5.41	−0.010	−1.10
BADL	−0.138***	−15.04	−0.132***	−11.40	−0.042***	−9.23	−0.006	−0.74
Income (1st quintile)								
Second quintile	0.033	0.88	0.022	0.46	−0.007	−0.39	−0.053*	−2.04
Third quintile	0.059	1.50	0.047	0.93	0.003	0.13	−0.014	−0.47
Fourth quintile	0.187***	4.52	0.165***	3.15	0.042*	2.01	0.008	0.24
Fifth quintile	0.316***	6.48	0.214***	3.53	0.063*	2.42	−0.025	−0.56
Relative income	0.011	1.80	0.018*	2.26	0.011*	2.05	0.006	0.70
Retire	0.124***	3.65	0.156***	3.62	0.036*	2.11	−0.051	−1.69

(continued)

Table 10.1 (continued)

	(1) Ordered logit		(2) LV		(3) Dynamic RE		(4) Dynamic FE	
	Coef	z-value	Coef	z-value	Coef	z-value	Coef	z-value
Social participation	0.080***	3.08	0.103***	3.07	0.026*	1.97	0.016	0.74
Number of family members	0.014	1.52	0.021	1.75	0.010*	2.18	0.015*	2.00
Living arrangement								
Housing near child	0.035	0.79	0.060	1.10	0.035	1.63	0.049	1.33
Co-residence with child	−0.066	−1.87	−0.088	−2.05	−0.036*	−2.15	−0.015	−0.56
NRSPI	0.092***	2.70	0.132***	2.79	0.039***	2.59	0.040	1.74
Regions	Yes		Yes		Yes		Yes	
Year	Yes		Yes		Yes		Yes	
Observations	23,649		14,027		12,534		12,534	
Groups					8,704		8,704	
R-sq. within					0.009		0.290	
between					0.205		0.132	
overall					0.150		0.045	
F-test that all u_i = 0							F(8703, 3809) = 2.03	
							Prob > F = 0.000	
Hausman specification test					2992.43(Prob > chibar2 = 0.000)			

(continued)

Table 10.1 (continued)

	(1) Ordered logit		(2) LV		(3) Dynamic RE		(4) Dynamic FE	
	Coef	z-value	Coef	z-value	Coef	z-value	Coef	z-value
Breusch and Pagan Largangian multiplier test for random effects					8.22(Prob > chibar2 = 0.0021)			
Log likelihood	−25,504.423		−15,281.6					
Pseudo R2	0.036		0.036					

Source Calculated based on the data from CHARLS2011, 2013 and 2015

Note

***$p < 0.01$, *$p < 0.1$

LV: lagged variable model; FE: fixed-effects model; RE: random-effects model.

dynamic random effects model (dynamic RE) [Model3], and (4) dynamic fixed effects model (dynamic FE) based on panel data [Modle4] were used in the estimations. The results based on the F-test and the Breusch and Pagan Lagrangian multiplier tests indicated that the dynamic FE model and dynamic RE model are more appropriate than the linearity regression model. Moreover, the results based on the Hausman specification test indicated that the dynamic FE model is more appropriate than the dynamic RE model. Concerning the heterogeneity problems, we will mainly discuss the results based on the LV model (Model 2) and the dynamic FE model (Model 4) and compare the results between different models.

First, the results from Model1, which is usually used in previous studies based on cross-sectional survey data, indicate that NRCMS positively affect the SWB. These results are consistent with those of the previous studies. However, the results from the longitudinal data analysis models show different results. For example, the results from Models 2–4 suggested that the influence of NRCMS on SWB is not statistically significant. The results suggest that although there is a positive relationship between NRCMS and SWB based on cross-sectional survey data, there may be bias in the results when some unobservable individual attributes are not controlled, or the reverse causality problem is not addressed. Thus, we employed the following estimations using the longitudinal data analysis method to address these problems.

Then other factors also affect the SWB. Based on the results from Model 2 and Model 4, (1) for the demographic factors, the healthy individual is likely to feel satisfied than an unhealthy one.

(2) The coefficients of the fourth and fifth quintiles of income are positive and statistically significant at the 0.1% level (Model 2). This suggests that the high-income group is likely to feel more satisfied than the low-income group, and the results support the absolute income hypothesis. The coefficients of relative income are positive and statistically significant at the 5% level (Model 2), suggesting that the group whose income is higher than the reference group may feel more satisfaction, and the relative income hypothesis is supported. The coefficients of non-work (0.011) are positive and statistically significant at the 0.1% level (Model 2). It indicates that an individual is likely to feel satisfied when retired. This study focuses on individuals aged 45 and over; the non-work (retirement, early retirement) group may prefer a longer leisure time. They can receive pension benefits, which may allow them to feel satisfied much more. However, the significance of these results was smaller for Model 4. This suggests that the influences of these factors may be related to individual heterogeneities, such as unobservable personality or other factors.

(3) Social capital positively affects an individual's SWB. Specifically, the results indicate that social participation positively affects the SWB (Model 2), and an individual with more family members is likely to feel satisfied (Model 4).

(4) Based on the results of Models 1–3, it is shown that when the income factors are controlled, the NRSPI positively affects the SWB (Model 2). This suggests that the NRSPI may improve rural individuals' SWB through other channels, such as reducing the uncertainty of risk in the elderly.

10.4.2 Results by Groups

With regards to the heterogeneities by group, the estimations are employed by using different subsamples. The results based on the dynamic FE model are summarized in Table 10.2 (by gender), Table 10.3 (by age groups), Table 10.4 (by migrants and rural residents), Table 10.5 (by household income groups), and Table 10.6 (by regional groups). The main results are as follows:

First, the influences of the NRCMS on SWB are not statistically significant for both men and women (Table 10.2). It suggests that the gender gap in the NRCMS effects on the SWB is smaller.

Second, the influence of the NRCMS on SWB differs by age group (Table 10.3). Specifically, the influences of the NRCMS are not statistically significant for the group aged 45–59, whereas there remains a positive correlation between the NRCMS and SWB for the group aged 70–79.

These results can be explained as follows. Regarding the effect of public medical insurance, according to the health capital model (Grossman, 1972), it is thought that the probability of becoming patient or unhealthy is higher for the group aged 70–79 than for the other younger groups (the groups aged 45–59 and 60–69). The NRCMS can reduce the OOP expenses and increase the utilization of healthcare services (Ma, 2015; Qin et al., 2014; Wagstaff et al., 2009). Therefore, it may improve the well-being of individuals, particularly for the elderly aged 70–79 who face a higher risk of illness.

Third, the influences of NRCMS on SWB are not significant for both migrants[6] and rural residents (Table 10.4).

Fourth, it is thought that the household liquidity constraints differ by the low-, medium-, and high-income groups; therefore, the influence of social insurance may differ by income groups. The results in Table 10.5 indicate that the results suggest that NRCMS only positively affects the SWB of the high-income group.

The results can be explained as follows: the influence of worrying about the uncertainty of illness risk in the future may be greater for the high-income group. Therefore, the positive effects of the NRCMS are greater for the high-income group.

Finally, China has a large regional disparity in the East, Central, and West regions. The economic development level (GDP per capita or income and expenditure per capita) is highest in the East region, lowest in the West regions. Therefore, it is assumed that the influence of social insurance on well-being may differ by region. The results in Table 10.6 indicate that there is a positive relationship between the NRCMS and SWB only for individuals in the Central region, whereas the influences of the NRCMS on SWB are not statistically significant for individuals in both East and West region. The reasons for this are as follows: According to the Chinese government' public medical insurance policy of "low benefit, large coverage" for the rural *hukou* residents, the healthcare service levels are low in rural areas, which cannot fill the needs of income security and healthcare service utilization of individuals in the well-developed rural areas (East region); therefore, the influences of NRCMS on SWB are not significant for individuals in the East region. In additions, the per capita

Table 10.2 Summaries of the results by gender

	(1) Men		(2) Women	
	Coef	z-value	Coef	z-value
SWBt_1	0.463***	21.13	0.478***	23.04
NRCMS	0.072	1.38	−0.006	−0.12
Married	0.013	0.09	0.104	0.84
Disease number	0.074	1.31	0.098	1.62
Inpatient	0.038	0.90	0.022	0.53
IADL	0.010	0.72	−0.022	−1.88
BADL	−0.001	−0.12	−0.008	−0.75
Income (1st quintile)				
Second quintile	−0.089**	−2.47	−0.020	−0.52
Third quintile	−0.008	−0.21	−0.025	−0.58
Fourth quintile	−0.031	−0.68	0.036	0.78
Fifth quintile	−0.073	−1.18	0.010	0.16
Relative income	0.009	0.74	0.005	0.36
Retire	−0.147***	−3.09	0.010	0.25
Social participation	0.046	1.55	−0.010	−0.35
Number of family members	0.017	1.60	0.012	1.12
Living arrangement				
Housing near child	−0.006	−0.12	0.103	1.93
Co-residence with child	0.035	0.91	−0.062	−1.59
NRSPI	0.050	1.55	0.035	1.05
Regions	Yes		Yes	
Year	Yes		Yes	
Constant	0.516	0.29	1.699	0.96
Observations	5,850		6,684	
Groups	4,033		4,671	
R-sq. within	0.309		0.284	
between	0.128		0.129	
overall	0.035		0.051	
F-test that all u_i = 0	F (4032, 1796) = 2.00 Prob > F = 0.000		F (4670, 1992) = 2.05 Prob > F = 0.000	
Hausman test	1404.81(Prob > chibar2 = 0.000)		1607.86(Prob > chibar2 = 0.000)	

Source Calculated based on the data from CHARLS2011, 2013, and 2015

Note

(1) ***$p < 0.01$, **$p < 0.05$.

(2) Dynamic fixed-effects model is used

Table 10.3 Summaries of the results by age group

	(1) Age45–59		(2) Age60–69		(3) Age70–79	
	Coef	z-value	Coef	z-value	Coef	z-value
SWBt_1	0.420***	18.83	0.470***	17.54	0.573***	10.08
NRCMS	−0.013	−0.23	0.061	0.89	0.243*	2.01
Married	−0.252	−1.25	0.152	1.08	0.039	0.17
Disease number	0.124	2.15	0.019	0.24	0.164	0.96
Inpatient	0.028	0.59	0.003	0.06	−0.002	−0.02
IADL	−0.019	−1.21	0.004	0.25	−0.089**	−2.27
BADL	−0.005	−0.38	−0.007	−0.51	−0.022	−0.81
Income (1st quintile)						
Second quintile	−0.044	−0.98	−0.064	−1.43	0.065	0.69
Third quintile	−0.029	−0.69	−0.009	−0.17	0.132	1.06
Fourth quintile	0.000	0.00	−0.010	−0.16	0.229	1.36
Fifth quintile	0.002	0.03	−0.103	−1.15	0.266	0.97
Relative income	0.010	0.80	0.010	0.83	−0.055	−0.75
Retire	−0.002	−0.05	−0.011	−0.21	−0.174	−1.79
Social participation	0.000	−0.02	0.051	1.32	0.009	0.12
Number of family members	0.021	1.81	−0.010	−0.80	0.030	0.98
Living arrangement						
Housing near child	0.092	1.87	0.000	0.01	−0.423	−1.94
Co-residence with child	−0.065	−1.58	0.038	0.80	0.146	1.37
NRSPI	−0.010	−0.30	0.110***	2.62	0.023	0.25
Regions	Yes		Yes		Yes	
Year	Yes		Yes		Yes	
Constant	−1.020	−0.28	1.699	0.96	−12.717	−1.02
Observations	6,203		4,447		1,591	
Groups	4,393		3,354		1,264	
R-sq. within	0.280		0.309		0.339	
between	0.087		0.115		0.029	
overall	0.031		0.049		0.010	

(continued)

Table 10.3 (continued)

	(1) Age45–59		(2) Age60–69		(3) Age70–79	
	Coef	z-value	Coef	z-value	Coef	z-value
F-test that all u_i = 0	F (4392, 1789) = 1.94 Prob > F = 0.000		F (3353, 1072) = 2.09 Prob > F = 0.000		F (1263, 306) = 1.71 Prob > F = 0.000	
Hausman test	1257.97(Prob > chibar2 = 0.000)		881.99(Prob > chibar2 = 0.000)		234.45(Prob > chibar2 = 0.000)	

Source Calculated based on the data from CHARLS2011, 2013, and 2015
Note
***$p < 0.01$, **$p < 0.05$, *$p < 0.1$
Dynamic fixed-effects model is used

income level is lowest in the west rural regions and the reimbursement of medical expenses is lower, there may maintain the severe poverty problem when ill, thus the NRCMS effect is not significant for individuals in the West region.

10.5 Conclusions

How does the NRCMS affect the SWB of middle-aged adults and the elderly in rural China? Does the influence differ by groups, such as gender, age, migration status, income, and region groups? This study conducts an empirical study to answer these questions using three-wave longitudinal data from the CHARLS of 2011, 2013, and 2015. The dynamic FE model and lagged variables of time t_1 model (LV model) was used to address the heterogeneity problems. The main findings are as follows.

First, the cross-section data analysis method results suggest a positive correlation between the NRCMS and SWB; these results are consistent with most previous studies. However, the results using the dynamic FE model show that the NRCMS did not contribute to improve SWB among middle-aged adults and the elderly rural residents. This suggests that heterogeneity problems may be maintained.

Second, the positive effects of NRCMS differ by various groups. Concretely, (1) the positive effect on the SWB is greater for the group aged 70–79 than for other age groups (age 45–59, age 60–69) (Table 10.3); (2) the NRCMS only positively affects the SWB of the high-income group (Table 10.5); (3) the positive effects of the NRCMS is greater for the Central region than for the East and West region (Table 10.6). (4) The differences of influences of the NRCMS on SWB are small between women and men, local rural resident and migrant groups (Tables 10.2 and 10.4).

The policy implications can be considered as follows: The results indicated that the NRCMS positively affects the SWB of the elderly aged 70 and over, and high-income groups. Except for the differences in medical knowledge and health awareness between the different groups, the results are also related to institutional problems. First, although the proportion of OOP expenses is regulated as 30% in both the NRCMS and the UEBMI, the coverage kinds of diseases differ by these two

Table 10.4 Summaries of the results by migrants and local rural residents

	(1) Migrant		(2) Rural residents	
	Coef	z-value	Coef	z-value
SWBt_1	0.453	15.24	0.476***	27.33
NRCMS	0.041	0.60	0.034	0.78
Married	0.120	0.62	0.067	0.63
Disease number	0.128	1.64	0.072	1.49
Inpatient	−0.033	−0.57	0.048	1.41
IADL	−0.069***	−3.33	0.003	0.26
BADL	0.023	1.40	−0.013	−1.37
Income (1st quintile)				
Second quintile	−0.105	−1.67	−0.050	−1.72
Third quintile	−0.038	−0.60	−0.018	−0.52
Fourth quintile	−0.105	−1.50	0.033	0.90
Fifth quintile	−0.006	−0.07	−0.040	−0.76
Relative incomc	−0.013	−0.68	0.012	1.20
Retire	−0.074	−1.29	−048	−1.36
Social participation	0.048	1.16	0.002	0.07
Number of family members	0.060***	3.96	0.001	0.14
Living arrangement				
Housing near child	0.015	0.18	0.060	1.44
Co-residence with child	−0.028	−0.49	−0.013	−0.43
NRSPI	−0.034	−0.77	0.057*	2.11
Regions	Yes		Yes	
Year	Yes		Yes	
Constant	1.186	0.47	1.699	0.96
Observations	3,050		9,484	
Groups	2,156		6,548	
R-sq. within	0.328		0.288	
between	0.096		0.141	
overall	0.029		0.049	
F-test that all u_i = 0	F (2155, 873) = 2.12 Prob > F = 0.000		F (6547, 2915) = 2.02 Prob > F = 0.000	
Hausman test	722.16(Prob > chibar2 = 0.000)		2332.87(Prob > chibar2 = 0.000)	

Source Calculated based on the data from CHARLS2011, 2013, and 2015
Note
(1) ***$p < 0.01$, *$p < 0.1$
(2) Dynamic fixed-effects model is used

Table 10.5 Summaries of the results by income group

	(1) Low		(2) Medium		(3) H igh	
	Coef	z-value	Coef	z-value	Coef	z-value
SWBt_1	0.463***	13.64	0.512***	11.90	0.440***	12.26
NRCMS	−0.049	−0.57	0.035	0.26	0.163*	2.22
Married	−0.019	−0.10	−0.010	−0.03	−0.481	−1.85
Disease number	0.122	1.21	0.251	1.92	0.028	0.37
Inpatient	0.111	1.58	−0.058	−0.78	−0.163*	−2.33
IADL	0.013	0.70	−0.005	−0.19	0.003	0.12
BADL	−0.017	−0.91	0.015	0.68	−0.007	−0.40
Relative income	−0.013	−0.17	−0.053	−0.50	−0.014	−0.90
Retire	−0.031	−0.46	−0.166	−1.91	−0.078	−1.21
Social participation	−0.003	−0.06	0.031	0.51	0.017	0.37
Number of family members	0.018	0.97	0.013	0.55	0.031	1.75
Living arrangement						
Housing near child	0.052	0.61	0.207	1.71	0.113	1.33
Co-residence with child	−0.072	−1.09	−0.003	−0.03	−0.069	−1.09
NRSPI	0.136**	2.46	-0.078	−1.02	−0.021	−0.43
Regions	Yes		Yes		Yes	
Year	Yes		Yes		Yes	
Constant	1.716	0.63	4.192	0.99	3.646	1.29
Observations	4,659		3,731		4,144	
Groups	3,859		3,293		3,404	
R-sq. within	0.290		0.355		0.272	
between	0.087		0.051		0.050	
overall	0.049		0.039		0.031	
F-test that all u_i = 0	F (3858, 782) = 1.72 Prob > F = 0.000		F (3292, 421) = 1.89 Prob > F = 0.000		F (3403, 723) = 2.02 Prob > F = 0.000	
Hausman test	583.97(Prob > chibar2 = 0.000)		388.15(Prob > chibar2 = 0.000)		420.76(Prob > chibar2 = 0.000)	

Source Calculated based on the data from CHARLS2011, 2013, and 2015

Note

(1) ***$p < 0.01$, **$p < 0.05$, *$p < 0.1$

(2) Dynamic fixed-effects model is used

Table 10.6 Summaries of the results by region

	(1) East		(2) Central		(3) West	
	Coef	z-value	Coef	z-value	Coef	z-value
SWBt_1	0.518	13.59	0.402***	10.47	0.470***	22.08
NRCMS	0.048	0.65	0.216*	2.21	0.007	0.13
Married	0.088	0.43	0.162	0.75	0.009	0.07
Disease number	−0.104	−1.10	0.152	1.44	0.091	1.54
Inpatient	−0.017	−0.24	0.138*	2.07	0.022	0.51
IADL	−0.061***	−3.02	0.011	0.55	−0.014	−0.97
BADL	0.024	1.30	−0.038*	−2.04	0.002	0.17
Income (1st quintile)						
Second quintile	−0.152**	−2.55	−0.108	−1.69	−0.010	−0.26
Third quintile	−0.121	−1.76	−0.186***	−2.64	0.108*	2.48
Fourth quintile	−0.002	−0.02	0.013	0.16	0.035	0.69
Fifth quintile	−0.002	−0.01	0.038	0.29	−0.005	−0.07
Relative income	−0.034	−0.75	−0.015	−0.47	−0.008	−0.57
Retire	−0.125	−1.81	−0.069	−0.94	−0.029	−0.65
Social participation	0.123**	2.56	−0.056	−1.15	−0.007	−0.23
Number of family members	0.046**	2.38	0.025	1.33	−0.005	−0.50
Living arrangement						
Housing near child	0.016	0.17	0.027	0.30	0.005	0.10
Co-residence with child	−0.032	−0.51	0.028	0.44	−0.012	−0.29
NRSPI	0.075	1.42	−0.083	−1.35	0.063*	1.96
Year	Yes		Yes		Yes	
Constant	1.250	0.42	−2.650	−0.78	1.595	0.92
Observations	2,146		2,235		6,028	
Groups	1,491		1,557		4,205	
R-sq. within	0.349		0.294		0.295	
between	0.094		0.070		0.130	
overall	0.025		0.020		0.042	

(continued)

Table 10.6 (continued)

	(1) East		(2) Central		(3) West	
	Coef	z-value	Coef	z-value	Coef	z-value
F-test that all u_i = 0	F (1490, 634) = 2.03 Prob > F = 0.000		F (1556, 657) = 2.04 Prob > F = 0.000		F (4204, 1802) = 2.05 Prob > F = 0.000	
Hausman test	552.97(Prob > chibar2 = 0.000)		394.05(Prob > chibar2 = 0.000)		1492.94(Prob > chibar2 = 0.000)	

Source Calculated based on the data from CHARLS2011, 2013, and 2015
Note
(1) ***$p < 0.01$, **$p < 0.05$, *$p < 0.1$
(2) Dynamic fixed-effects model is used

types of medical insurance and the reimbursements of medical care expenses are also different. For example, based on the 2008 Health Care Service Survey by the Ministry of Health China, the proportion of OOP expenses is 56.0% for participants of the NRCMS, whereas it is 31.8% for participants of the UEBMI; the proportion of being reimbursed is 44.0% for participants of the NRCMS, whereas it is 68.2% for participants of the UEBMI. Thus, medical care inequality occurs through the enrollments of different public medical insurances based on the *hukou* system in China (Ma, 2015). Therefore, the results show that the NRCMS did not contribute to improve SWB of rural residents.

Second, the NRCMS is not convenient for migrant workers (Ma, 2015; Shu, 2018). For example, according to the NRCMS, only expenses for health care service paid in medical care facilities (e.g., clinics or hospitals) in rural areas can be reimbursed. However, most migrants live and work in urban areas; when they are inpatient or outpatient in urban areas, the medical care expenditures may not be reimbursed, or they have to return to their hometown to take the application for the reimbursement. Moreover, majority of rural-urban migrant workers have not joined the UEBMI, and the proportion of OOP expenses is higher for the NRCMS participants than the UEBMI participants. To reduce the system disparities between UEBPI and NRCMS and reform the NRCMS to make it more convenient for migrants should be considered in the future.

Finally, this study had the following limitations. Although we used the dynamic FE model and LV model to address the heterogeneity and endogeneity problems, estimating the causality relationship will become an issue in our future research. Next, based on CHARLS, this study focuses on individuals aged 45 and older, and the sample must include the youth in future research. A comparative study between youth, middle-aged, and the elderly based on appropriate survey data may provide more information for this issue.

Notes

1. We also use the logistic regression model and the ordered logit regression model based on a binary variable and an ordered category variable as the dependent variable to perform robustness checks. These results are consistent with the results of this study.
2. For household income function, the dependent variable is household equivalent income, and the independent variables are head of households' age, age squared, sex, education attainment, work status, province, and year dummy variables.
3. Here, the square root of the number of family members is utilized as the equivalent coefficient.
4. The social participation dummy variable is constructed as follows: CHARLS asked respondents, "Have you done any of these activities in the last month?," listing seven types of social activities: (a) interacting with friends, (b) playing Mahjong, chess, cards, or going to a community club; (c) providing help to families, friends, or neighbors who do not live with you and do not pay for your help, (d) going for sport, social, or other club activity; (e) participating in a community-related organization; (f) doing volunteer or charity work; and (g) caring for a sick or disabled adult who does not live with you and does not pay for your help. Seven binary variables of each social participation activity were constructed by allocating "1" to the answer yes and "0" otherwise. A binary variable of overall social participation was constructed by allocating "1" to those participating in at least one type of social participation activity and "0" to others.
5. According to the classifications of the National Bureau of Statistics, China's East region includes Beijing, Tianjin, Hebei, Shanghai, Jiangsu, Zhejiang, Fujian, Shandong, Guangdong, and Hainan; the Central region includes Shanxi, Anhui, Jiangxi, Hernan, Hubei, and Hunan; West region includes Inner Mongolia, Guangxi, Chongqing, Sichuan, Guizhou, Yunnan, Tibet, Shaanxi, Gansu, Qinghai, Ningxia, and Xinjiang; and Northeast region includes Liaoning, Jilin, and Heilongjiang.
6. The migrants are defined as those who own the rural *hukou* and live or work in the urban areas during the survey period.

Appendix

See Table 10.7.

Table 10.7 Descriptive statistics of variables

	Total	Very	somewhat	Not	t-test	
		(a)	(b)	(c)	(a)–(c)	*p*-value
SWB	3.190	4.091	3.000	1.740	2.351***	0.000
NRCMS	0.884	0.746	0.893	0.863	−0.117	0.114
Age	59.538	60.156	58.881	57.648	2.508***	0.000
Female	0.525	0.527	0.505	0.600	−0.073***	0.000
Education						
Junior and lower	0.938	0.898	0.930	0.945	−0.047	0.166
Senior high	0.058	0.083	0.066	0.052	0.031	0.500
College and higher	0.004	0.019	0.004	0.003	0.017***	0.005
Married	0.863	0.873	0.887	0.835	0.038***	0.000
Disease number	0.713	0.577	0.720	0.715	−0.138	0.400
Inpatient	0.120	0.113	0.119	0.150	−0.037***	0.000
IADL	0.841	0.578	0.655	1.338	−0.760***	1.000
BADL	1.922	1.608	1.808	2.642	−1.034***	0.000
Per capita income	7184	10,139	7235	5703	4436***	0.000
Relative income	0.000	0.116	0.001	−0.156	0.272***	0.000
Retire(non-work)	0.262	0.309	0.232	0.258	0.051	0.917
Social participation	0.466	0.501	0.480	0.425	0.076***	0.000
Number of family members	3.511	3.326	3.540	3.556	−0.230***	1.000
Living arrangement						
Housing near child	0.890	0.884	0.886	0.887	−0.003	0.795
Co-residence with child	0.581	0.555	0.577	0.603	−0.048***	0.000
NRSPI	0.489	0.485	0.492	0.435	0.050***	0.000
Regions						
East	0.191	0.171	0.199	0.156	0.015***	0.002
Central	0.212	0.213	0.209	0.263	−0.050***	0.000
West	0.568	0.587	0.560	0.560	0.027***	0.000
Northeast	0.029	0.029	0.032	0.021	0.008	0.109
Survey year						
2011	0.317	0.208	0.318	0.361	−0.153***	0.000
2013	0.331	0.267	0.362	0.378	−0.111***	0.000
2015	0.352	0.525	0.320	0.261	0.264	0.000
Observation	23,649					

Source Calculated based on the data from CHARLS2011, 2013, and 2015

Note

(1) ***$p < 0.01$

(2) Very: Completely satisfied and very satisfied; Somewhat: somewhat satisfied; Not: not very satisfied and not at all satisfied

(3) Sample is limited at age 45 and older

References

Abruquah, L. A., Yin, X. X., & Ding, Y. (2019). Old age support in urban China: The role pension schemes, self-support ability and intergenerational assistance. *International Journal of Environmental Research and Public Health, 16*(11). https://doi.org/10.3390/ijerph16111918.

Akerlof, G. A., & Yellen, J. K. (1990). The fair wage-effort hypothesis and unemployment. *Quarterly Journal of Economics, 105*(2), 255–284.

Appleton, A., & Song, L. (2008). Life satisfaction in urban China: Components and determinant. *World Development, 36*(11), 2325–2340.

Boskin, M., & Sheshinski, E. (1978). Optimal redistributive taxation when individual welfare depends upon relative income. *Quarterly Journal of Economics, 92*(4), 589–601.

Brockmann, H., Delhey, J., Welzel, C., & Yuan, H. (2009). The China puzzle: Falling happiness in a rising economy. *Journal of Happiness Studies, 10*(4), 387–405.

Cheng, L., Liu, H., Zhang, Y., Shen, K., & Zeng, Y. (2015). The impact of health insurance of health outcomes and spending of the elderly: Evidence from China's New Cooperative Medical Sch. *Health Economics, 24*(6), 672–691.

Contoyannis, P., Jones, A., & Rice, N. (2004). The dynamics of health in the British household panel survey. *Journal of Applied Econometrics, 19*(4), 473–503.

Easterlin, R. A. (1974). Does economic growth improve the human lot? In P. A. David & W. B. Melvin (Eds.), *Nations and households in economic growth*. New York: Stanford University Press.

Easterlin, R. A. (2001). Income and happiness: Toward a unified theory. *The Economic Journal, 111*, 465–484.

Fang, Z., & Sakellariou, C. (2016). Social insurance, income and subjective well-being of rural migrants in China—An application of unconditional quantile regression. *Journal of Happiness Studies, 17*(4), 1635–1657.

Ferrer-i-Carbonell, A. (2005). Income and well-being: An empirical analysis of the comparison income effect. *Journal of Public Economics, 89*(5–6), 997–1019.

Frank, R. H. (1985). *Choosing the right pond: Human behavior and the quest for status*. Oxford University Press.

Jiang, S., Lu, M., & Sato, H. (2011). Identity, inequality, and happiness: Evidence from urban China. *World Development, 40*(6), 1190–1200.

Grossman, M. (1972). On the concept of health capital and the demand for health. *Journal of Political Economy, 80*(2), 223–255.

Gu, L. B., Feng, H. H., & Jin, J. (2017). Effects of medical insurance on the health status and life satisfaction of the elderly. *Iranian Journal of Public Health, 46*(9), 1193–1203.

Haller, M., & Hanler, M. (2006). How social relations and structures can produce happiness and unhappiness: An international comparative analysis. *Social Indicators Research, 75*(2), 169–216.

Han, S., Kim, H., Lee, E. S., & Lee, H. S. (2013). The contextual and compositional associations of social capital and subjective happiness: A multilevel analysis from Seoul, South Korea. *Journal of Happiness Studies, 14*(4), 1183–1200.

Han, S. (2015). Social capital and subjective happiness: Which contexts matter? *Journal of Happiness Studies, 16*(1), 241–255.

Helliwell, J. F., Huang, H., & Wang, S. (2014). Social capital and well-being in times of crisis. *Journal of Happiness Studies, 15*(1), 145–162.

Keng, S. H., & Wu, S. Y. (2014). Living happily ever after? The effect of Taiwan's National Health Insurance on the happiness of the elderly. *Journal of Happiness Studies, 15*(4), 783–808.

Hommerich, C., & Tiefenbach, T. (2018). Analyzing the relation between social capital and subjective well-being: The mediating role of social affiliation. *Journal of Happiness Studies, 19*(4), 1091–1114.

Kollamparambil, U., & Etinzock, M. N. (2019). Subjective well-being impact of old age pension in South Africa: A difference in difference analysis across the gender divide. *South African Journal of Economic and Management Sciences, 22*(1), a2996. https://doi.org/10.4102/sajems.v22i1.2996

Layard, R. (1980). Human satisfactions and public policy. *Economic Journal, 90*, 737–750.

Leibenstein, H. (1950). Bandwagon, snob, and vebren effects in the theory of consumer's demand. *Quarterly Journal of Economics, 64*(2), 183–207.
Leung, A., Kier, C., Fung, T., & Fung, L. (2011). Searching for happiness: The importance of social capital. *Journal of Happiness Studies, 12*(3), 443–462.
Luo, C. (2006). Urban-rural divide, employment, and subjective well-being. *China Economic Quarterly, 5*(3), 817–840. (in Chinese).
Luo, C. (2009). Absolute income, relative income and subjective well-being: Empirical test based on the sample data of urban and rural households in China. *Journal of Finance and Economics, 35*(11), 79–91. (in Chinese).
Ma, X. (2015). *Public health insurance reform in China.* Kyoto University Press. (in Japanese).
Ma, X., & Piao, X. (2019a). The impact of intra-household bargaining power on happiness of married women: Evidence from Japan. *Journal of Happiness Studies, 20*(6), 1775–1806.
Ma, X., & Piao, X. (2019b). Income, intra-household bargaining power and the happiness of Japanese married women. In M. C. Tsai & N. Iwai (Eds.), *Quality of life in Japan, quality of life in Asia 13.* Singapore: Springer Nature.
National Bureau of Statistics (NBS). (2020). *China statistic yearbook 2020.* China Statistic Press.
National Bureau of Statistics (NBS). (2021). http://www.xinhuanet.com/politics/2021-05/11/c_1 12743398.htm. Accessed 8 Sep 2021.
Neria, I., Bruna, F., Portela, M., & Garcia-Aracil, A. (2018). Individual well-being: Geographic heterogeneity and social capital. *Journal of Happiness Studies, 19*(4), 1067–1090.
Park, S. M. (2018). Social policy and late-life happiness: The impact of the basic old-age pension on the happiness of older people in South Korea. *Quality in Ageing and Older Adults, 19*(1), 3–13.
Song, X. (2009). Retrospect and prospect of China's medical insurance system in the 60 Years since the founding of the People's Republic of China. *Chinese Journal of Health Policy, 2*(19), 6–14. (in Chinese).
Qin, X., Pan, J., & Liu, G. G. (2014). Does participating in health insurance benefit the migrant workers in China? An empirical investigation. *China Economic Review, 30*, 263–278.
Sasaki, I, Kondo, K., Kondo, N., Aida, J., Ichikawa, H., Kusumi, T., Sueishi, N., & Imanaka, Y. (2018). Are pension types associated with happiness in Japanese older people? JAGES cross sectional study. *PLOS ONE, 13*(5), e0197423.
Schatz, E., Gomez-Olove, X., Ralston, M., Menken, J., & Tollman, S. (2012). The impact of pensions on health and wellbeing in rural South Africa: Does gender matter? *Social Science & Medicine, 75*(10), 1864–1873.
Shu, L. (2018). The effects of the New Rural Social Pension Insurance Program on the retirement and labor supply decision in China. *The Journal of the Economics of Ageing, 12*, 125–150.
Smyth, R., Nielsen, I., & Zhai, Q. (2010). Personal well-being in urban China. *Social Indicators Research, 95*(2), 231–251.
Tran, N. L. T., Wassmer, R. W., & Lascher, E. L., Jr. (2017). The health insurance and life satisfaction connection. *Journal of Happiness Studies, 18*(2), 409–426.
Vendrik, M. C. M., & Woltjer, G. B. (2007). Happiness and loss aversion: Is utility concave or convex in relative Income? *Journal of Public Economics, 91*(7–8), 1423–1448.
Wagstaff, A., Lindelow, M., Gao, J., Xu, L., & Qian, J. (2009). Extending health insurance to the rural population: An impact evaluation of China's New Cooperative Medical Scheme. *Journal of Health Economics, 28*(1), 1–19.
Wang, P., & VanderWeele, T. J. (2011). Empirical research on factors related to the subjective well-being of Chinese urban residents. *Social Indicators Research, 101*(3), 447–459.
Wooldridge, J. (2002). *Econometric analysis of cross section and panel data.* The MIT Press.
Wooldridge, J. (2005). Simple solutions to the initial conditions problem in dynamic, nonlinear panel data models with unobserved heterogeneity. *Journal of Applied Econometrics, 20*(1), 39–54.
Xiao, W., & Su, Z. F. (2017). Does social insurance in China enhance people's well-being? *Journal of Interdisciplinary Mathematics, 20*(3), 821–835.

Yin, X. X., Abruquah, L. A., & Ding, Y. (2019). Dynamics of life satisfaction among rural elderly in China: The role of health insurance policies and intergenerational relationships. *Sustainability, 11*(3). https://doi.org/10.3390/su11030701.

Zhang, C., Giles, J., & Zhao, Y. (2014). Policy evaluation of China' New Rural Pension Program: Income, poverty, expenditure, subjective wellbeing and labor supply. *China Economics Quarterly, 14*(1), 203–230. (in Chinese).

Zhang, Q., & Churchill, S. A. (2020). Income inequality and subjective wellbeing: Panel data evidence from China. *China Economics Review, 60*, 101392.

Index

X. Ma, *Public Medical Insurance Reforms in China*,
https://doi.org/10.1007/978-981-16-7790-8

The manufacturer's authorised representative in the EU is Springer Nature Customer Service Centre GmbH, Europaplatz 3, 69115 Heidelberg, Germany. If you have any concerns regarding our products, please contact ProductSafety@springernature.com

Printed and bound by CPI Group (UK) Ltd, Croydon, CR0 4YY
30/09/2026
02225291-0006